Fine WoodWorking
on Finishing and Refinishing

Fine WoodWorking on Finishing and Refinishing

34 articles selected by
the editors of
Fine Woodworking
magazine

The Taunton Press

Cover photo by Alan Braus

First printing: January 1986
Second printing: October 1986
Third printing: October 1987
Fourth printing: June 1989
Fifth printing: January 1992
International Standard Book Number: 0-918804-46-9
Library of Congress Catalog Card Number: 85-51877
Printed in the United States of America

A FINE WOODWORKING Book

FINE WOODWORKING® is a trademark of The Taunton Press, Inc.,
registered in the U.S. Patent and Trademark Office.

The Taunton Press
63 South Main Street
Box 5506
Newtown, Connecticut 06470-5506

Contents

Introduction

Old-time woodfinishers say there are only two reasons for their art: to protect the wood, and to beautify it. Thus they searched for the glassiest film finish, and each artisan was likely to have his own secret formula for getting it.

These days, in a world of lacquered metal and shining glass, wood that wears a plasticky coat of armor is liable to be considered too artificial, not beautiful. This gives the woodfinisher a pretty problem: he can pour (or spray) from a can a gleaming urethane varnish that will protect the wood almost completely, but contemporary tastes are not likely to enjoy it. We may prefer colored paint, or a light coat of tung oil, or even no finish at all.

In 34 articles reprinted from the first decade of *Fine Woodworking* magazine, this volume presents many finishing formulas and techniques, ancient as well as modern. In addition, authors who are also craftsmen explore the aesthetic problems of finishing, and discuss their reasons for the choices they make. And among these detailed articles, you'll find dozens of finishing questions asked by the magazine's readers, with answers by woodfinishing experts.

John Kelsey, editor

Finishing Materials
What you always wanted to know…

by Don Newell

Choosing a correct finish for your woodworking project is really quite simple, despite the confusing array of types and brands on the market. The key to selection is compatibility—the finish must be chosen with the physical requirements of the particular piece in mind. For example, where the surface will be subjected to wear or abrasion, the finish must be as tough and flexible as possible, with maximum adhesion to the wood substrate or the sealer coat. Where the surface will be exposed to liquids, moisture resistance is important. Where the piece is decorative, clarity and appearance are the deciding factors.

All finishing materials can be categorized as one of two basic types: solvent-release or chemically reactive. In simplest terms, solvent-release finishes (shellac, lacquer) form a solid film upon evaporation of the solvent or thinner. Chemically, the film is not changed. Reactive finishes, however, such as tung oil, linseed oil and varnish, harden by means of a complex chemical reaction. The wet film first absorbs oxygen from the air. This starts a reaction that proceeds through the film, changing it from liquid to solid. Solvent-release finishes can be reliquefied simply by applying the correct solvent or thinner to the surface. Reactive materials usually cannot be brought back to their original fluidity. This is one reason why shellac and lacquer are easier than varnish to spot-repair.

Solvent-release materials

Shellac — Shellac is a natural resin made from the secretion of the *Laccifer lacca* insect. It is available in flakes or buttons ready to be dissolved in alcohol by the user, or in ready-to-use alcoholic solution as either orange or white shellac. As the name implies, orange shellac is colored and will impart some color to the wood. White shellac has no color. If the shellac is fresh, there is little difference in performance between them. However, orange shellac will keep longer in the can without losing its ability to dry. Another difference is that orange shellac is substantially more moisture resistant. For interior use, shellac of either color is much more moisture resistant than lacquer and many varnishes.

By itself, shellac is extremely brittle. But when applied either as a penetrating sealer coat or as a finish *in* the surface of properly sanded wood, it can take abuse and wear without chipping. Because shellac is an alcohol-based, solvent-release material, the dry surface is easily softened by alcohol. Thus, additional coats of shellac bond strongly to shellac undercoats, as does lacquer (because of its solvent content). However, finishes such as drying oils and varnishes, neither of which contain alcohol, won't adhere to shellac films. For good adhesion of these over shellac, the surface must first be sanded thoroughly with medium-grit paper, permitting a mechanical bond between the films.

Shellac has excellent moisture and wear resistance, dries quickly and can be rubbed or French polished to almost any degree of gloss or sheen. However, it can be easily softened or disfigured by alcohol or alcoholic liquids. It also has limited shelf life (about six months) when dissolved, and almost no exterior durability.

Lacquer — Despite certain variations, clear lacquer for wood finishing is generally composed of nitrocellulose dissolved in solvents, plus a small amount of a plasticizing ingredient that helps reduce the brittleness of the film upon drying. Spraying and brushing lacquers are essentially the same. In spraying lacquer, however, the solvent/thinner mixture evaporates quickly, giving the wet film only enough time to flow out evenly before it begins to harden. In brushing lacquer, a different solvent/thinner mix evaporates more slowly so that brush marks can level out before the surface hardens.

Brushing lacquer is seldom thinned before use, but spraying lacquer always is. If you're fortunate enough to have a spray outfit, the type of thinner you use to reduce the lacquer for spraying can make the difference between good and bad results. When lacquer dries, heat is carried away from the surface as the thinners evaporate. If the humidity in your shop is high and you use "fast" thinners to cut drying time, moisture in the air will often condense onto the surface, producing a cloudiness called "blushing." Other things being equal, you're better off using a slower, richer thinner. Among other things, you'll get better flow and gloss.

Lacquer dries faster than oils or varnish, often permitting the application of three or more coats in the same period of time. It produces a good, durable film resistant to wear and abrasion, and can be rubbed out or polished to almost any degree of gloss or sheen. However, it requires many more coats than varnish to produce the same film build, because lacquer has a lower percentage of solids. It is more susceptible than varnish to retaining brush marks in the dried film, and is not as moisture resistant as shellac or some varnishes. Nonetheless, it is quick-drying and produces an attractive, good-quality finish with good interior durability.

Sanding sealers — These are fast-drying, solvent-release materials used on bare wood to fill the pores and level the surface prior to applying the final finish. As the name implies, a sanding sealer is designed to be sanded down to a smooth, even surface. It usually sands so easily that the surface comes away in a cloud of white powder.

Most sanding sealers are based on either nitrocellulose or vinyl, to which is added a large quantity of stearates. The stearates act as a lubricant to make sanding easy, but because they are literally a kind of soap, shellac, varnish and drying oils should never be used over a sanding sealer. Sooner or later, the top coat will simply strip away in sheets. Only lacquer should be used over a sanding sealer, because the solvents in lacquer will bond well to the lacquer base of the

From *Fine Woodworking* magazine (July 1979) 17:72-75

A graphic example of the degree to which a reactive material absorbs oxygen from the air. This can contains a popular brand of rubbing oil (a thin solution of drying oil and varnish). It was stored half-full, but capped. For several months the varnish absorbed oxygen from the air in the top of the can, thus creating a vacuum that sucked the can's sides inward. The reaction also jellied the contents. Conclusion: Varnish remaining from a job should be poured into a smaller container, filling it completely, to keep it usable for any length of time.

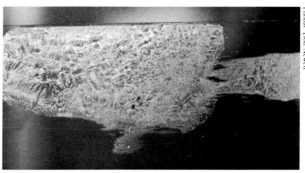

Closeup of a dried film of pure tung oil, rubbed out on glass. The thicker the coat, the more evident the wrinkling. Very thin coats, well rubbed into the wood, will not wrinkle to this extent, but will produce a definite matte or flat appearance.

sealer. Sanding sealer is a good base on small-pored woods, but is not designed to replace filler on coarse-grained wood such as oak.

Reactive materials

Drying oils — Linseed oil is available raw and boiled. Raw linseed oil has nothing to offer the finisher except trouble. Among other things, it contains substantial amounts of what are called "foots," nondrying portions of oil which no amount of heating or aging will harden. Foots are removed during refining by filtering and refrigerating the raw oil, prior to producing boiled oil, but the home brewer cannot make raw oil into boiled oil simply by boiling it.

Boiled linseed oil has the foots refined out, then it is steam-heated and held at a high temperature with the addition of metallic drier compounds. It is a true drying oil and reacts with oxygen to become a solid film. However, solid doesn't necessarily mean hard. Even aged linseed-oil films remain comparatively soft, though thin films will solidify to a

dry-feeling surface. Because boiled linseed is usually applied in thin coats and rubbed in well by hand, the finisher may think he has a good, durable finish. However, because oil that has penetrated down into the wood structure will remain semisoft, linseed films should never be overcoated with lacquer or shellac. The top coat will adhere badly or not at all.

Linseed oil was a favorite old-time finish because it was readily available, easy to apply and repair, and looked good if not subjected to wear. Linseed films have poor moisture resistance, which is one reason old-time paint made from linseed oil seldom blistered or peeled. Moisture in the wood beneath the paint simply passed out through the paint without hindrance. Compared to tung-oil films, boiled linseed oil will pass about twice the amount of moisture.

Tung oil — This is more properly called China wood oil, and is much more reactive than boiled linseed. Tung dries to a harder film and is twice as moisture resistant. It dries through more quickly and completely than boiled linseed. In

---

How to read the label

Except on the smallest of containers, the label on the can usually tells the amount of oil/resin solids in the mix and the nature of the materials in the finish.

Satin-type finishes invariably contain a certain amount of silica and/or silicates, which make the film dry to a low luster. Since these contribute nothing to the film properties, ignore them. You'll not find such flattening agents in a gloss-finish formulation.

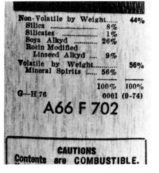

What you should look for are the amounts or percents of oils and resins in the formulation. These will generally be referred to as the nonvolatile part of the finish. Because the nonvolatile materials are what will be left after the thinner evaporates, they are what constitute the ultimate finish on or in the wood. In the example shown in the photo above, under nonvolatiles by weight, you'll see soya alkyd and rosin-modified linseed alkyd, totaling 35%. This means that whatever the amount of wet material you brush onto the surface, about a third of it will be left as a film when it dries. This particular finish happens to be a varnish.

A typical lacquer would list its nonvolatiles as nitrocellulose, and,

possibly, an oil or oil alkyd (used as a plasticizer). In the case of a satin or flat lacquer you may find figures for stearates. If the stearate figure is listed separately, ignore it.

The nonvolatile percentage figure is most helpful in comparing one finish with another. The formulation with the highest percentage of solids will leave the thickest film. A few percentage points mean nothing for practical purposes. But if one formulation indicates 50% solids and another 35% solids, the former will leave a film half again as thick as the latter. Which means that it will require three coats of the second to give you the same finish thickness as two coats of the first.

Where the label lists the nonvolatiles by name, you can determine whether you have a tung or other type of oil base, and what resins are present. This is sometimes helpful where the product name is ambiguous. For example, one popular finish carries a name that strongly implies it is a polyurethane varnish. Yet, on reading the ingredients on the label, it is obvious that the varnish is really an oil-modified phenolic type. If you want a polyurethane varnish, you will not use this one by mistake. Or, if you don't want a poly varnish, you could conclude that this material is just what you have been searching for.

The other most helpful information on the label is in the instructions panel. For example, polyurethanes generally have a sensitive period within which recoating must occur, assuming you intend to use a second coat. If you exceed this time period before recoating, adhesion will suffer. *Always read the instructions.* If you don't follow them, at least you'll know what it is you've done wrong.

my view at least, tung oil has a major shortcoming when used as a final finish. It tends to dry nonglossy, even in thin coats. In heavy coats it wrinkles badly. According to one manufacturer, thinning the oil by half with mineral spirits, followed by steel-wooling after it dries, will reduce the flatness. To me tung oil seems more suitable as a utility finish than as a beauty treatment. If you must have tung oil's moisture resistance while insisting on a decent degree of luster, select a good varnish made from tung oil.

Varnish — The old-time spirit varnishes made from natural resins dissolved in alcohol have largely disappeared. Today's varnishes are reactive materials composed of synthetic resins and oils combined together under heat and pressure, with driers added to speed the hardening process. Thinners are then added, making the varnish fluid enough to brush out.

Alkyd resin varnish — An alkyd resin is a synthetic resin made by reacting a type of alcohol, such as glycerol, with an acidic ingredient, such as phthalic acid. The resulting resin is then combined with or modified by unsaturated oil such as tung, linseed or soya, and driers and thinners are added.

A large percentage of today's varnishes are based on soya or linseed-oil alkyd resin. These produce workable, durable finishes, which generally are not as hard as polyurethane varnish. As a class, alkyd resin varnish is comparatively flexible and can accommodate expansion and contraction of wood in normal interior service. It can also be recoated easily without encountering problems of poor adhesion.

Alkyd varnish produces an easily applied, attractive finish that is highly durable on interior surfaces. Generally, it can be rubbed to the desired degree of luster. For maximum moisture resistance, select an alkyd varnish whose label lists tung oil as an ingredient.

Rosin/ester gum alkyd varnish — The label on some cans lists such ingredients as "rosin-modified" or "ester-gum modified" alkyd. Generally, this type of varnish will dry to a harder film than regular alkyds, and consequently may rub out and withstand wear better. In fact, some gym-floor varnishes are ester-gum formulations.

Phenolic-resin varnish — This varnish is made from a special synthetic resin that dries to a tougher, more moisture-resistant film than alkyd varnish. The phenolic varnishes are primarily for exterior use because of their weather resistance and their ability to withstand the dimensional changes in wood without splitting or cracking. These varnishes are usually labeled spar varnish, super-spar varnish or the like. They're softer than most polyurethane varnishes, which makes the phenolics more flexible and permits recoating without adhesion problems.

Phenolics are notorious for darkening or yellowing, sometimes even when kept in the dark. Some modern phenolic varnishes contain an ultraviolet-absorbing element to help reduce this tendency.

Phenolic resin varnish is not the ideal choice for interior furniture work, but it is a superb utility finish for exterior wood furniture and trim exposed to weather and sunlight.

Polyurethane varnish — "Polyurethane" really refers to a class of material closer to a true plastic than an alkyd resin,

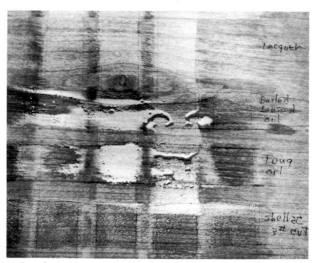

Taken during preparation of the adhesion test panel (p. 5), this photo is proof that neither tung oil nor boiled linseed oil should ever be used over a base or sealer coat of polyurethane varnish. Both of these drying oils refuse to "wet out" the polyurethane surface, actually crawling together rather than spreading out over the surface. While their dried films might hold mechanically on a well-sanded polyurethane surface, almost no chemical bond will be established.

rather than a specific formulation. Consequently, a pure polyurethane varnish will be hard, tough and comparatively brittle. To recoat, sanding down to bare wood and starting over is required.

However, the usual polyurethane varnish you find on the shelf of your hardware store will most likely be modified with a drying oil or alkyd resin. This supposedly makes the varnish less brittle and more recoatable, but your only chance for good adhesion is to follow label instructions to the letter when applying a second or third coat. Actual adhesion tests using a typical brand-name polyurethane varnish sold for furniture indicated some problems, whether in applying it over other types of finishes, under other types of finishes or even over itself. This is not my preferred choice as a finish for my better work for interior use, but some people may like it.

Rubbing oils — This is more a description of a class of finishing formulations than a specific material. The name on the label may imply that it is used by Danes or Swedes or will produce an antique finish (whatever that may be), but it is usually just a dilute varnish containing a substantial amount of oil. Nevertheless, brand-name rubbing oils are excellent products. They penetrate well, dry hard and produce attractive finishes if you work with them enough to really learn how to make them perform. Because they are comparatively thin-bodied, don't expect a great deal of surface buildup. But then, that isn't necessarily a major criterion for a fine finish.

Finishing materials compatibility

When two different materials are used in finishing, they must be able to bond together permanently. Wear, handling, accidental impacts and normal expansion and contraction of the wood substrate place great stress on any finish, and the better the bond the longer the finish will last without chipping, peeling or crazing.

Generally, maximum compatibility is achieved by using a single type of finish. For example, in finishing with a varnish, the first coat may be thinned down for greater penetration as

The Adhesion Test

I used seven different materials to test the adhesion and flaking potential of various finishes over and under themselves as well as other finishes. First, each was applied in vertical strips on bare cherry veneer, using three good, wet coats with 24 hours of drying time between. Then, the same materials were applied in horizontal strips over the first set. Once again, three good coats were applied with 24 hours of drying time between.

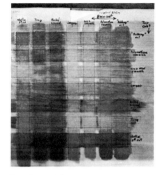

After allowing a week's drying time for the composite panel, each finish-on-finish square was lightly punched through from the back with a roundnosed, ¼-in. punch. By examining the torn edges of each punched hole, it was easy to determine how well the top coats adhered to the undercoats.

Where the top-coat finish broke away from the undercoat cleanly, adhesion obviously was at a maximum, and these samples were rated good or better, depending on the degree. Where some peeling was found, the sample was rated fair. Where the top coat appeared to be stripping away in sheets, it was rated poor. Very poor means almost no adhesion.

Any undercoat/top coat combination rated good or better in such a test will probably have sufficient adhesion and durability to be used with confidence on furniture or cabinet work to be subjected to wear or handling abuse.

If nothing else, this test illustrates two points. One, that nothing adheres as well to a base material (used as a sealer coat) as the same material itself—except for polyurethane. And two, that to the degree that the particular brand of polyurethane used represents all polyurethanes (and there's no guarantee that it does), a poly varnish must be recoated within its sensitive period or it shouldn't be recoated at all.

The same seven finishes used in the adhesion test were also tested for flexibility and film integrity. The seven were painted heavily on a sheet of Teflon as shown in the photo, and allowed to dry thoroughly. The dried films were then carefully stripped off the Teflon and bent, twisted and torn to determine film strength. Here are the results:

Shellac: glass-like, brittle, no film strength.

Tung oil: tough, coherent, fair film strength, but it dried cloudy and wrinkled.

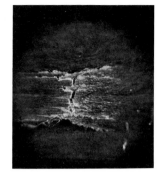

This section of a typical punched hole from the adhesion test shows some minor flaking or stripping off of the top coat from the undercoat at the edge of the break, and would be classified as fair adhesion. The materials are rubbing-oil film over alkyd-varnish film base. Photo was taken through a low-power microscope.

MATERIALS APPLIED AS TOP COAT (FINAL FINISH)	MATERIALS APPLIED AS BASE COAT ON CHERRY VENEER						
	Shellac 3 lb. cut	Tung oil (unthinned)	Boiled linseed oil	Lacquer (satin)	Alkyd (soya) varnish	Polyurethane gloss varnish	Rubbing oil
Rubbing oil finish *Over*	Poor	Fair	Good	Fair	Fair	Fair	Good
Polyurethane gloss varnish *Over*	Very poor	Poor	Poor	Very poor	Very poor	Very poor	Very poor
Alkyd (soya) varnish *Over*	Poor	Fair	Good	Poor	Good	Poor	Fair
Lacquer (satin) *Over*	Excellent	Good	Good	Excellent	Good	Very poor	Good
Boiled linseed oil *Over*	Fair	Excellent	Excellent	Fair	Fair	Fair	Good
Tung oil (unthinned) *Over*	Poor	Good	Good	Poor	Poor	Poor	Good
Shellac, 3 lb. cut, *Over*	Very good	Very poor	Poor	Fair	Fair	Poor	Good

Boiled linseed: softer than the tung-oil film, but fairly coherent and strong. It can remain semisoft even after a full week of drying.

Polyurethane varnish: very tough, strong and coherent.

Alkyd varnish: somewhat softer but otherwise equal to polyurethane varnish.

Lacquer: similar to shellac in brittleness. Poor film strength.

Rubbing oil: very strong, clear and coherent film.   —D.N.

---

a sealer coat, followed by one or more top coats of the same varnish used for the final finish. Because the sealer coat and top coats are soluble in the same thinner, each coat will bond well with the preceding coat. The one exception is a material such as polyurethane varnish which generally has a so-called sensitive period, after which the surface becomes so hard or inert that following coats will not adhere well. However, if the finisher follows instructions on the label, this should not be a problem.

But compatibility, or the lack thereof, can be a real problem when using one material for the sealer coat and a different material for the finish coat: Varnish top coats over a shellac sealer coat, for example. Because varnish is a reactive material dissolved in a hydrocarbon thinner such as mineral spirits, and shellac is a solvent-release material dissolved in alcohol, the bond between them tends to be weak. The chemical bond, that is. A good mechanical bond can be achieved by sanding the shellac/wood surface with medium-grit paper to give it "tooth."

In addition, because the shellac sealer coat obviously will not have filled the porous wood completely to surface level, a certain degree of porosity will remain. Consequently, even though the wood has been "sealed" by shellac, the varnish can still penetrate the surface somewhat, further enhancing the mechanical bond.

The more chemically compatible two finishing materials are, the greater the probability that the resulting finish will be strong, coherent and resistant to separation or finish failure in the long run. The less compatible, the more the finisher has to depend upon a good mechanical bond. A good rule of thumb is to use reactive materials over reactive undercoats, and solvent-release materials over solvent-release sealers. Drying oils such as boiled linseed can be used over almost anything, since they are generally applied in such thin coats that film strength is not a factor.   □

Don Newell, of Farmington, Mich., is an amateur furniture maker and a paint and varnish chemist.

Q & A

The right light

Before the year is over we will be able to add an extra room to our woodworking shop. We intend to use this room exclusively for woodfinishing. The room is not very big, only 12 ft. by 15 ft., but adequate for our hobby. We have a small spray outfit and an exhaust fan in one corner. Our problem is the lighting. The room has a 9-ft. ceiling but no light whatsoever. What is the best lighting for a finishing room? —Eva Eshleman, Allentown, Pa.

GEORGE FRANK REPLIES: A very pertinent question, congratulations. More finish on wood is ruined by improper lighting than by any other single cause. Yet few people worry about the light in the finishing room, and I've never seen any guidelines in books. My own answer may turn out to be controversial.

You must have as much light as you can possibly create, and it must be as close as possible to natural daylight. Your best bet is the long 6-ft. or 8-ft. fluorescent fixtures, with half the tubes cool white and half daylight-imitating. Install them as high as possible, well sheltered from dust, and clean them frequently.

Right   Wrong

Don't install the lights directly over the working area. The object you are working on should reflect the light to your eyes. Assume you are working on a flat object on top of your bench. If you put a flat mirror on top of your bench, you should be able to see in it the whole light fixture. The lower the angle of reflection, the better it is, the ideal being about 45°. This means that the angle between your eyes, the work and the light should be about 90°.

I would go a step further and install one or two movable lights about 6 ft. off the floor, so you can arrange the light to reflect off the top of a high piece like a chair or chest.

Lights near the work or over the spraying area will have to be inside protective fixtures, and you might have to use incandescents. But all artificial lights distort colors—incandescents add a definite red hue. Never match colors by artificial light. Do it by daylight and in shadow.

A 40-watt fluorescent tube called Vita-Lite, developed for medical examining rooms a few years ago, is as close as possible to daylight with very little glare. The tubes last for 33,000 hours. Any electrical supply house or electric-fixture store can get them. —A.T. Martin

Tack rags

Some years ago I ran across a formula for making tack rags, but now that I am retired and working in my shop, I can't find it. —W. Muir, Bainbridge Island, Wash.

GEORGE FRANK REPLIES: Rosin, or colophony, could be found in every old cabinet shop. We used to break it into powder (in a mortar) and dissolve a teaspoon of this powder in a pint of mineral spirits. We added a few drops of linseed oil and soaked our clean rags (linen is best) in the mixture, then squeezed out as much as possible. A less elaborate method is to soak the rag in mineral spirits and sprinkle a few drops of varnish onto it. With repeated squeezing you can work the ingredients together, then squeeze out all the liquid you can.

Oil/shellac finish

Have you ever heard of mixing white shellac (preferably 3-lb. cut) with an equal amount of boiled linseed oil and using it as a finish? It sounds incompatible—a solvent-release and a chemical-reactive finish. It also seems that you would have drying problems. But this is not so, according to my mother-in-law. A number of years ago, she was told by an old refinisher to use it as a finish on her old piano. —Carmine I. Santarelli, Lorain, Ohio

DON NEWELL REPLIES: I tried mixing shellac and boiled linseed 50/50 and it does not work for me. Mixing the boiled linseed and shellac together, then shaking vigorously, produces a milky suspension of oil in shellac. Upon standing, the oil separates out and rises to the top. I applied the shellac/oil suspension to a previously varnished surface and to new unfinished wood, rubbing it over and in with a cloth pad soaked in the mixture. Upon standing, the oil separated from the shellac and came to the surface in an oily layer that would not dry. I wiped the oil away and was left with an uneven, unacceptable film of shellac on the varnished surface. Over the new-wood surface, the shellac and some of the oil apparently went into the wood, as expected, but an oily layer remained on the surface.

GEORGE FRANK REPLIES: Don't ever argue with your mother-in-law. Let her use the mixture of shellac and oil on her finishing projects, and use the good old proven finishing materials on yours. You will not be sorry. She will.

TAGE FRID REPLIES: Your mother-in-law is partly right. An oil-and-shellac finish gives fast and beautiful results if done right. I first used the finish about 35 years ago to repair the side of a cabinet that had gotten badly scratched as it was being unloaded from a truck. Since it would have taken me about three days to restore the original oil finish, I decided to take a chance on an untried method. Once I had scraped and sanded the damaged side, I applied some oil and followed it with an application of shellac. When the surface had dried thoroughly, I rubbed it down with steel wool, and it came out as beautiful as the rest of the furniture.

When I first demonstrated the method to my students, they named it the "four-F" finish (Frid's fast fine finish). Before trying the finish yourself, make sure to get the right ingredients—raw (not boiled) linseed oil or Watco, and orange (not white) shellac. Don't mix the oil with the shellac, but apply the oil evenly and sparingly to the prepared surface with a rag. Then immediately brush on a 3-lb. cut of orange shellac, leave it until it gets tacky and then rub the surface with a pad of 3/0 steel wool. Next wipe it clean with a clean, dry cloth, taking care to remove all of the oil and shellac from the surface. If any excess remains, the finish will turn grey. If necessary, another coat can be applied a short while later, but this time using less oil.

This finish is best for small pieces and things like chairs and table bases, because it is not waterproof. If water is left on it for a while and it spots, you can repair it easily. Put oil on the spot, steel-wool or sand until the spot disappears and wipe off all the excess.

Mineral oil vs. linseed oil

I'd like your opinion on using mineral oil instead of linseed oil to treat and protect wood. I don't know anything about mineral oil except it is highly refined (edible) petroleum, it doesn't stink, and it's available in three weights. Thus, mineral oil could be a terrific treatment for salad bowls and tabletops. On the other hand, if it's so terrific, how come no one uses it? When my furniture gets its seasonal linseed oiling, the house plain stinks.

—*William Marsano, Toronto, Canada*

R. BRUCE HOADLEY REPLIES: I do not consider mineral oil a wood finish. It would seem to offer little to "treat and protect wood," since it does not polymerize and would therefore be neither physically stable nor a barrier to moisture. If applied to raw wood, it would enter the cell structure, but changes in temperature and atmospheric pressure could result in its bleeding out on the surface.

I have used mineral oil as a vehicle for pumice and rottenstone in rubbing down varnish finishes. Unlike water, it will not swell the wood if the wood is incompletely protected by finish. It could also be used as furniture polish, to occasionally revitalize surface appearance by temporarily restoring light-reflectiveness and serving as a lubricant, but for this, I prefer lemon oil.

GEORGE FRANK REPLIES: Boiled linseed oil to which you add about 5% Japan drier will offer far greater protection to wood than mineral oil. The correct manner to use linseed oil has much to do with the final result. The oil-drier mixture should be applied generously and left 15 to 30 minutes on the wood, so it can penetrate well. Then, as much oil should be taken off as possible by rubbing the wood with rags, hard. The oiled surface should be given ample time (a week at least) to dry. The microscopic film of oil that remains on the wood will go through a chemical change and will become hard, solid, like a fine coat of varnish. You repeat this five, six times and you build up a fine protective shield on your wood, which, because of the repeated rubbing, also becomes pleasantly smooth. True, linseed oil does not compete with Chanel No. 5 for pleasant smell, but the smell goes away with proper drying and hardening. Mineral, or paraffin, oil will not harden and I never use it as a protective coating. However, when French polishing I would never use anything else.

MICHAEL MCCANN REPLIES: William Marsano asked about using mineral oil instead of linseed oil to treat and protect wood, especially salad bowls. George Frank suggested using boiled linseed oil with about 5% Japan drier added in for a good, protective finish, but neglected to caution against using this treatment on wooden utensils for food.

Woodworkers should be aware that any item they sell to contain food or drink is subject to the regulations of the Food and Drug Administration, which restricts what coatings can be used in contact with food (Code of Federal Regulations, Title 21, Part 175.300). According to Ralph Mayer's *Artist's Handbook of Materials and Techniques,* most boiled linseed oil is not actually boiled, but is heated with driers; lead, though no longer allowed by the FDA, was one of the most common driers used. Likewise, lead has also been used in Japan driers, and even if the drier does not contain lead, there's a good chance it might contain toxic impurities.

Problem with tung oil

I am having a problem with a pure tung-oil finish. A tall stool/plant stand in solid cherry developed a rough surface similar to water-raised grain after the tung-oil finish had dried for several weeks, though the surface was satin-smooth immediately after application. The roughness comes out on the turned legs as well as on the top. However, the very center of the top, the 6-in.-diameter portion that was under a plant pot, has fared better. The stool certainly has received no obvious abuse that would cause such a problem, so I speculate that exposure to direct sunlight is the cause. I also have this same finish on a white oak plant table and a small walnut stool, neither of which is suffering any ill effects. I currently have only two coats of tung on the stool, and I hesitate to build up additional coats for fear of compounding this problem.

—*William C. Pellouchoud, Boulder, Colo.*

DON NEWELL REPLIES: You do have a problem, and I don't think it's caused by sunlight or that it's raised grain caused by moisture. That other items with the same finish do not exhibit the same symptoms though in the same environment would seem to bear this out. Moreover, grain-raising is seldom uniform over the surface of a piece of furniture; it is usually much more pronounced where end grain comes to the surface, and much less pronounced where the grain runs parallel to the surface. However, the turned legs on your stool are rough all over. Try this experiment. Take some of the tung oil from your container and rub it out to a moderate thickness on a clean piece of window glass (not so thick that it runs). Let it dry for a few weeks. If a roughness develops in the film, you know the problem is with the tung, since glass is not notorious for grain-raising.

I suspect your problem is with dirty tung, and that as the surface film dries and shrinks, particles of tung that have polymerized to hard specks right in the can will emerge. Tung oil is highly reactive, and chances are that if you used the same tung for the oak table and walnut stool as for the cherry stool, enough oxygen was admitted to the container to cause the formation of hardened particles. The spot under the pot is smoother than the rest probably because handling and moving the pot abraded the graininess in that area.

Polymerized tung oil

What is the formula for making polymerized tung oil from plain tung oil? From what source can polymerized tung be purchased? —*John Chapman, Lexington, N.C.*

Tung oil is polymerized by heating to about 500°F, a tricky procedure that requires very sensitive temperature controls and timing to produce predictable results. You can buy polymerized tung oil (as well as tungseed oil) from Sutherland Welles, 113 W. Main St., Carrboro, N.C. 27570, or Vartung Coatings, Box 1042, Picayune, Miss. 39466. McCloskey Tungseal is tung oil polymerized with added resins.

Finish for redwood

How shall I finish my redwood picnic table and benches? The store advised a redwood stain, which turned out to be mostly paint and flaked off. We've sanded it down to the bare wood. —*Jonathan Wagman, Ulster Park, N.Y.*

GEORGE FRANK REPLIES: Redwood is so beautiful it doesn't need any stain to enhance it. It also resists fungus and weather quite well. Mix equal amounts of boiled linseed oil and any good brand of varnish. Spread this mixture generously on the furniture, but before it dries—about 15 to 30 minutes later—wipe off all that you possibly can. Use a burlap-type rag and plenty of elbow grease. The very thin coating that remains in the wood will offer surprisingly good protection and it can be still improved by repetition. Give each application a week to dry and put the emphasis on the rubbing—that is what makes it beautiful.

Q & A

Using lacquer

My questions revolve around lacquers and I have been unable to find answers in the literature. Where does lacquer fall in the scheme of hardness? How appropriate is lacquer for tables and surfaces that are subjected to hard use? Is it a popular finish? What techniques are common?
—*R.C. Legge, Jr., Rochester, N.Y.*

GEORGE FRANK REPLIES: As of today lacquer finishes are the best. They offer excellent protection to the wood and, if they are properly applied, enhance its natural beauty. Moreover lacquers are versatile and there is a special kind for nearly every need.

The difficulty is that lacquers must be sprayed. To work with them one needs compressed air and a spray gun. Spraying lacquer creates a fire hazard and charges the air with noxious fumes, which is why for the home craftsman lacquering is almost out of reach. There are some brands on the market that can be applied by brush; Ace is one of them. If you can get some, experiment with it.

There also are the so-called "padding lacquers," which are to be applied somewhat like French polish. The best is Qualasole, manufactured by H. Behlen and Bros., Rt. 30N, Amsterdam, N.Y. 12010 (write them for the location of your local distributor).

Flat or glossy lacquers, which is harder?

I've been using lacquers of various gloss levels in my shop and some of my customers say that the flat finishes are softer and scratch more easily. Is this true?
—*R.J. Burke, Belmont, Calif.*

HERB YATOVITZ REPLIES: Technically yes, practically no. Straight lacquers are high gloss and are made flatter by adding flatting agents such as silica gel or magnesium silicate. These chemicals crystallize in the lacquer film when it dries, and break up light as it strikes the surface, thus reducing the reflectivity or gloss. As more flatting agents are added, the crystals slightly reduce the lacquer film cohesion, and this does make it a bit softer. But the practical difference in hardness is so slight that it is generally not noticeable.

Wood sealer for dip coating

Is there a clear thin wood sealer (for dip coating) that will not raise the grain? I make wooden hair-combs, and it is not practical to resand and repolish between the teeth. I have tried many finishes but am not satisfied.
—*H. Warren Beach, Edgartown, Mass.*

GEORGE FRANK REPLIES: I would dip the combs either in a half-and-half mixture of clear lacquer and clear lacquer thinner, or into tung oil cut slightly with mineral spirits (about 80% tung oil to 20% mineral spirits). After thorough drying, I would rub in between the teeth with a nylon thread twisted into a strand, something like a horse's tail. Dip the horse tail in some fine garnet abrasive powder (you can buy it from Universal Shellac and Supply Co., 495 W. John St., Hicksville, N.Y. 11801) and hang it from the ceiling. Put a flat container underneath to recover the powder that comes loose. Then comb the horse tail until the comb is perfectly smooth between the teeth. With 4/0 steel wool I would make the outside as smooth as a good sales pitch, and my combs would be ready for market.

DON NEWELL REPLIES: Most good sealers or thin finishes should not raise the grain. Is it possible that what you thought was raised grain was simply dust or dirt particles present in the finish, which became apparent when the finish dried down hard? To eliminate this possibility, strain your thinned finish through fine, clean cloth before dipping. Waterlox Clear Transparent Seal should work well. Deft (clear lacquer) should also serve your purpose, and will dry faster than the Waterlox varnish sealer. Thin down any finish you use to almost water consistency before dipping to prevent the narrow spaces between the teeth from clogging.

Water-based finishes

Do water-based finishes offer a practical means of avoiding the toxic solvents in conventional finishes? What are the performance characteristics of the water-based products?
—*Bruce Jacobson, Makanda, Ill.*

DON NEWELL REPLIES: Yes, it's true that water-based (so-called latex) finishes do not contain the organic solvents found in conventional finishes. They perform very differently from conventional finishes, but not better, in my view. I've run comparative tests on wood using Valspar Water-Based Varnish, Sears Latex Varnish, Deft Acrylic Wood Armor, and Flecto Varathane Ultra Plastic Finish. Some of these are clear liquids and others are milky, but all dry to a clear film. The solids content varies from about 21% to 34%, compared with a solids content of up to 45% in conventional varnish, so it takes about two coats of latex varnish to equal the film thickness of one coat of conventional varnish. Compared to lacquer, the latex gives about the same film thickness, coat for coat.

The one major disadvantage I found was that, because of their water content, they all raised the grain of the wood. Frankly, they didn't handle or work as well for me as the conventional varnishes or lacquers, nor did they produce what I feel is a "good" finish. They seemed compatible with most types of stains, but they were all hard to rub out. The Valspar and Deft latexes were very runny for brushing, while the Sears and Flecto felt more like genuine varnish. But all flowed out well, leaving few, if any, brush marks. All had excellent adhesion when dry and did not show marks when tested with water or alcohol, with the exception of the Deft, which was severely affected by alcohol.

Non-allergenic floor finish

Is there a non-allergenic finish with no petroleum distillates suitable for refinishing an oak floor? Would pure tung oil be durable enough?
—*Evan Fales, West Branch, Iowa*

DON NEWELL REPLIES: Shellac contains no petroleum distillates and would be a durable floor finish.

Apply two thin coats, scuff-sanding between coats to remove whiskers. You'll get maximum durability if the shellac penetrates the wood rather than builds up on top of it.

In my view, tung oil would not be suitable. While it is extremely durable and resistant to liquids, it is probably not as wear-resistant as you need. Also, pure tung oil dries flat—another reason I wouldn't choose it for finishing a floor.

Avoiding wood cracks

I made a modified Parsons-style dining-room table of supposedly dry oak. I sealed the underside with wood sealer and used liquid grain filler, then finished with many coats of Watco satin oil. The problem is that after a year the oak is developing longitudinal cracks. What type of treatment and finish can I use to keep the wood from developing cracks?
—*Robert Schneider, De Ridder, La.*

GEORGE FRANK REPLIES: There is no finish that can seal moisture permanently in the wood. You are paying the penalty for not using properly dried wood. I am sorry, but I cannot help you.

Sanding
The basic tools and techniques

by Ben Green

Sanding equipment includes (left to right) a Merit Sand-O-Flex, a belt sander, a drum sander, an orbital sander and a sanding block.

Many woodworkers don't have a clear understanding of the role of sanding in finishing and refinishing. Commonly asked questions include: Does this need sanding? How much? What paper and what sander should I use? What is coarse grit? Should the final sanding always be done by hand? Almost everyone agrees that some sanding must be done, grabs the sandpaper and gives it a shot. If sanding is incorrectly or hastily done, however, the finish will never be as fine as it could be. Sanding is work and takes time, but the many recent improvements in equipment and abrasive papers make it possible for today's finisher or refinisher to surpass even the most meticulous craftsman of yesteryear.

Equipment needs depend on the job being done and the kind of shop being outfitted. A well-equipped shop would have a belt sander, an orbital (pad) sander, a Sand-O-Flex, drum sanders (attached to an electric drill), a sanding block and various pieces of stationary bench equipment. For those just starting out, however, about $20 (all 1978 prices) will buy an orbital sander that will do an excellent job.

The belt sander, designed for fast sanding of large, flat surfaces, is ideally a part of the cabinet shop, though optional for the refinishing shop. It effectively sands new wood before it is assembled and sands down large surfaces that have been glued up from narrower stock. In the refinishing shop the belt sander is useful for sanding down tops that have been reglued, warped areas or pieces that were particularly rough to start with. Belt sanders should have a low center of gravity and a 4-in. belt. Vacuum pickup is a must. Belt sanders are heavy, powerful and quick-cutting. It is important to keep them flat to the work, which is why the 4-in. width and the low center of gravity are important. Make sure the belt size is standard, such as 4 in. by 24 in., or 4 in. by 36 in. Standard belts are more readily available and competitively priced.

The orbital sander removes stock quickly and smoothly by the circular motion of its sanding pad. In a typical shop, it probably does about 90% of the sanding. There are two popular sizes. The size that takes ⅓ of a sheet of sandpaper is best in a refinishing shop. If a cabinet shop has a belt sander, then the ⅓-sheet size is a good companion to it, otherwise the ½-sheet size is better, because it is large enough and heavy enough to cut down new wood before it is assembled. There are two popular orbit speeds, 4,000 and 10,000 rpm. The 10,000 speed doesn't work faster, but is somewhat easier to handle. Some pad sanders can be shifted from orbital to in-line motion, and while this appears to be desirable, I do not find it very useful. Orbital motion cuts faster than inline motion, and in the 120 to 320-grit range will not leave swirl marks, as commonly thought. The price range of ⅓-sheet orbital sanders is from about $20 to $100. If you have extra

Ben Green works at Sears in Chicago, Ill. He has been teaching furniture refinishing for several years.

money to spend on equipment, this is the place to spend it. Top-of-the-line sanders last longer and can be worked harder, accomplishing more in a given period of time.

The Sand-O-Flex (manufactured by Merit Abrasive Company) is useful in a refinishing shop but would be optional in a cabinet shop. It has six sanding surfaces backed by bristle brushes that contour the sandpaper to the surface being sanded. It can be attached to a ¼-in. or ⅜-in. electric drill or to a flexible shaft on an electric motor. It is one of the few methods of effectively sanding turned, carved or irregular surfaces. The Sand-O-Flex sells for less than $20, and sandpaper refills cost about $2. The sandpaper comes in coarse, medium and fine (fine is 150 grit). It is either scored or unscored, but scored is the best for irregular surfaces. The Sand-O-Flex should not be confused with tools called "flap sanders." Flap sanders are less expensive but cannot be refilled with sandpaper. I find they do not do as good a job as the Sand-O-Flex.

Small drum sanders attached to an electric drill are useful for irregular edges, such as those cut with a band saw or jigsaw. Several sizes are available. Something in the 1½-in. to 2½-in. diameter range is a useful size to have. A sanding block is a must for hand-sanding. It gives the hand something large to hold on to and apply pressure to, and it ensures that the abrasive paper is applied flat to the surface, avoiding the uneven pressure that would be applied by three or four fingers. A good sanding block uses ¼ of a sheet of sandpaper and has a rubber surface between the paper and its metal parts. Don't buy a block that must use special paper—the paper will be more expensive than cutting your own from regular sandpaper sheets.

Stationary bench sanding equipment includes belt sanders, disc sanders and drum sanders. Their usefulness is so limited in the small shop that the expense of owning them is usually not justified. The common disc sander that is attached to an electric drill can be used for fast cutting if nothing else is available, but use it with extreme care, with about 100-grit paper, and only as a preliminary step.

Modern abrasive papers allow the refinisher a quality that was not available even as recently as 50 years ago. They are somewhat confusing in their generic names and in the different methods of grading.

Silicon-carbide paper, either black or white in color, is the best available. Its features are hardness (resistance to wear), adhesion of the grit to the backing, and resistance to loading (filling up the grit with the abraded surface). Black silicon carbide is generally waterproof, for wet sanding with water or finishing liquids. There is no difference between the two when comparing equal grits of both. Silicon carbide is difficult to find but worth the effort and the price.

Aluminum-oxide paper, grey in color, is a good abrasive, readily available and close in quality to silicon carbide. Garnet paper, the most widely used good-quality abrasive paper, is the choice of many refinishers and cabinetmakers. Its popularity is probably due to the fact that it has been on the market longer than the other good abrasive papers. Flint, the original "sandpaper," is a waste of money and should be used only when absolutely nothing else is available.

Select an abrasive paper according to personal preference, price and availability. Papers can be purchased in large packages of 50 to 100 sheets at a considerable saving. Abrasive paper can be kept indefinitely if it is stored flat and wrapped in plastic to protect it from moisture.

Paper for orbital sanders and sanding blocks can be cut from regular sheets—cheaper than buying precut paper. A

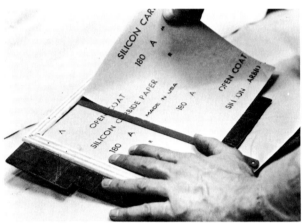

A simple jig for cutting standard sandpaper to fit an orbital sander is made by mitering and gluing two strips of wood to a base of Masonite or plywood. The hacksaw blade is glued only under the top strip. To use, slide the paper under the blade and against the side strip. Then rip, with the thumb holding the blade down.

Sandpaper grading

The most common gradings on sandpaper package labels are "fine," "medium," and "coarse," and degrees of these, such as "very fine." These terms are practically useless to the serious finisher, because their meaning is variable. Two accurate methods of describing sandpaper grading are the use of aughts and grit numbers. High grit numbers, such as 400, and many aughts, such as 10/0, represent very fine abrasive paper. Low grit numbers, such as 80, and few aughts, such as 2/0, represent coarse abrasive paper. At least one of these grading methods will be printed on the backing of most abrasive paper, although it may be necessary to open the package to find the grade.

Grit #		Aughts
400	Very fine	10/0
320		9/0
280	Fine	8/0
240		7/0
220		6/0
180	Medium	5/0
150		4/0
120		3/0
100	Coarse	2/0
80		1/0
60	Very coarse	1/2
50		1

cutting jig can be constructed from a piece of Masonite or plywood, a hacksaw blade and two strips of wood.

Sanding is a critical step in the total finishing/refinishing process. When refinishing, the proper application of paint and varnish remover may leave the work so clean and smooth that it is tempting to proceed directly to the final finish. Don't. When building a new piece, the wood may look so nice that the maker is tempted to skip sanding. Again, don't. Every piece of furniture that is being refinished or finished for the first time can be vastly improved by a good sanding.

The first rule is to sand with the grain. You must resist the natural tendency of the arm to work in an arc. Position the piece so that the grain of the wood runs with the body and not opposite it. On most jobs, sanding should start with 120-grit (3/0) abrasive paper. If the piece is already quite smooth, start with a finer grit, such as 150. On the other hand, if the piece is especially rough, begin with a coarser grit, such as 100. Coarse grit papers should always be used sparingly and carefully because the scratches they make are too deep and hard to remove at later stages.

All areas of the piece that are to be finished should receive the same amount of sanding. The initial sanding should correct any bad spots, such as burns or gouges that can't be filled, and when it is done all areas of the piece should be the same color and smoothness. Any crack filler that has been used in repairs should have been smoothed out. This step accomplishes most of the work and the next two steps will only lighten the color and smooth out the surface slightly.

Certain areas, such as depressions, warped boards and tool burns, will require the application of more pressure. In effect, these areas will become "dished out," but only slightly, and will not be noticeable unless closely inspected.

After initial sanding, the piece must be sanded twice more with finer paper. The second sanding should use 180-grit paper. Final sanding should use 280-grit paper or finer. These are suggested grits—use what is available. Don't skip the intermediate sanding; in particular, don't go from coarse paper to very fine without an intermediate paper. Sanding removes imperfections but if an intermediate grit is skipped, then the big scratches left by initial sanding will not be removed and will show through the finish. This is true for sanding by hand or with an orbital sander.

When trying to judge if a piece has been sanded enough, feel it as well as look at it. Stain and finish don't cover up a poor sanding job. In fact, they tend to amplify imperfections such as swirls left by an orbital sander.

Ideally, the final sanding with the finest paper should be done just before applying the first coat of finish or stain. In any case, the time between the final sanding and the first coat of finish or stain should not exceed 24 hours. It is too easy to soil or damage a project, and raw, unsealed wood can pick up moisture from the air. It may appear perfect after standing a week after the final sanding, but stain or finish will often show up dark areas, or an edge that might have been slightly bruised will show up dark. If some time has passed since the final sanding, a quick touch-up with the final paper will prevent a serious problem later.

Wet-sanding, feathering the grain after the final sanding and then sanding again, is an old but commonly used technique. Many people think this is the best way to get a smooth finish, but I think that modern abrasive papers and a good orbital sander have eliminated the need for it. To wet-sand, the wood should be slightly dampened with a rag or sponge after the final sanding. After the wood has dried, the grain will be slightly raised; these "feathers" are then cut off with fine paper. This step is necessary if the wood is going to be stained with a water-based stain, but not if you use modern penetrating oil or non-grain-raising stains.

Power equipment can speed up the sanding of any piece and make it a great deal easier. Most of the principles that apply to hand-sanding also apply to power sanding, but always remember that power-sanding cuts away more material than hand-sanding does. The use of coarse papers should therefore be restricted with power sanders. Never sand cross-grain with a power sander, and take care to avoid rounding off an edge, corner or the raised part of a carving.

Many pieces can be completely sanded with an orbital sander. As with hand-sanding, the starting grit should be 120, the intermediate 180 and the finish 280 or finer. There is no reason to hand-sand over an area that has been properly sanded with an orbital sander. Always move the orbital sander with the grain of the wood, in a natural swirling motion, allowing its weight and its motion to do the work. The sander can be held on areas that are particularly rough or discolored because it will cut even when standing still.

Belt sanding does not eliminate any hand or orbital sanding steps, but is only preliminary to initial sanding. Use nothing coarser than an 80 or 100-grit belt. If the belt sander has both a low and high speed, use the low speed.

Sanding new wood before assembly is advantageous because the parts can be worked on flat before they are connected. They are easier to get to and there are no inside corners. Plywood is generally smooth enough not to need any sanding before assembly. Regular mill stock should be sanded with a belt sander and a 100-grit belt, followed by an orbital sander with 120 or 150-grit paper. At this point paper finer than 150 should not be used, because assembling, handling and storing will soil or mar the piece to the point where the final sanding would only have to be repeated.

Turnings should be sanded to 280-grit or finer while still chucked in the lathe. Even though some sanding may have to be repeated after the piece is assembled, these pieces can be sanded effectively only while they are rotating in the lathe.

After the project is completely assembled, touch-up sanding with the initial paper will have to be done. Glue joints should be carefully sanded with coarse paper, followed by intermediate and fine sanding.

Irregular surfaces are difficult to sand because most power sanding equipment conforms only to a flat surface. This is a problem for the refinisher, because old pieces usually have intricate carving, spindles or applied decoration. Many times these irregular areas will stand out after the piece is finished, because they were not sanded as well as the flat surfaces. Start with an extra good job of cleaning with paint and varnish remover. After the top coats of paint or varnish have been removed, the paint remover should be applied again and carefully worked into corners and crevices with a pointed stick. After the last coat of paint remover has been removed with a coarse rag or fine steel wool, the surface should be scrubbed with a dry scrub brush. If a water-wash paint remover has been used, these areas can be scrubbed with a brush and soap and water. The grain will be raised but getting the wood completely clean is worth it.

Whenever water is used on wood, it should be immediately

Molded edges can be sanded with a wadded-up piece of used sandpaper. Start with 120 grit, follow with 180 grit, and finish with dry 4/0 steel wool.

Sand spindles by twisting some wadded sandpaper around them, or by twisting the paper with one hand and the turning with the other.

Places that are hard to reach can be sanded with a long, narrow strip of sandpaper worked like a shoeshine cloth.

and thoroughly dried, especially in cracks or crevices. Allow the piece to dry overnight before starting to sand.

The sanding of carved surfaces, applied decorations, pressed wood designs or intricately molded edges is best started by wadding up a used piece of 120-grit paper. Use a gentle scrubbing motion to work the wadded sandpaper into the intricacies of the design, but take care not to rub off the sharp corners that give the design its character. If deep or delicate areas of the design cannot be reached with the wadded sandpaper, they should be gently scraped with a small knife blade. Then follow with a wadded, used piece of 180-grit paper. The final step should be a gentle scrubbing with dry 4/0 steel wool.

Turnings can also be sanded with a wadded piece of sandpaper that is wrapped around the spindle. Either twist the paper around the turning, or if the piece is apart, twist the paper with one hand and the turning with the other. Follow with 180-grit paper and finish with dry 4/0 steel wool. Closely spaced spindles can be sanded with a long, narrow strip of sandpaper that is wrapped around the turning and worked like a shoeshine cloth. These narrow strips can be cut from paper-backed abrasive paper, but emery cloth or used sander belts are much stronger. The edges of the narrow strips are very sharp and can make a mark in the turning if they are not moved carefully. It may be necessary to cut strips of varying widths to reach all surfaces of the turning. This will be cross-grain sanding but it compares to the way such pieces were sanded while still on the lathe. The final sanding should be with a wadded piece of 280-grit paper, going with the grain.

No matter how good a building project or how fine an antique, a poor job of finishing results in only mediocre projects and so-so antiques. The proper equipment, good abrasive paper and a consistent approach to sanding will provide the basis for a fine finish. □

Getting rid of glue

I built a cabinet out of cherry wood and glued with Elmer's Carpenter's Glue. Some glue got in the corners. I wiped it clean immediately and later sanded the best I could. I stained it, but where the glue oozed out is a bland white. How can I get that glue off?
—Alton R. Stephenson, Manassas, Va.

ANDY MARLOW REPLIES: You have not sanded deeply enough. Sand till the glue spot is invisible and sand again as much.

When glue squeezes out of a joint, do not wipe it, as this pushes it into the pores of the wood. Let it harden, then cut it away with knife or chisel. This will leave the wood clean. —William Quinn, N. Fond du Lac, Wis.

Combining reactive and solvent-release finishes

I've worked in shops that use shellac as a sealer under alkyd varnish. It seems to work well, but all my research suggests that reactive finishes like varnish shouldn't be used over solvent-release finishes, and vice versa. What's the deal? —Jon Brandon, Amissville, Va.

DON NEWELL REPLIES: Shellac is a solvent-release finish, which means that when its alcohol solvent evaporates, it leaves behind a glossy, solid film that remains resoluble in alcohol. A second coat partially dissolves the first, resulting in a strong bond between consecutive coats.

A reactive or polymerizing finish like varnish reacts with oxygen and forms a strong cross-linked chain of molecules that, once dry, is no longer soluble in the original solvent. With reactive finishes, the second coat doesn't dissolve the first coat but adheres via a mechanical bond. Also, because there's no alcohol or other strong solvent, reactive finishes won't soften a base coat of solvent-release finish.

Varnish works well over a thin sealer coat of shellac or lacquer because the wood surface still has enough irregularities for the varnish to develop a mechanical bond. It won't adhere to a slick, heavy coating of shellac unless the surface is first roughened with sandpaper. Don't, however, apply lacquer over a varnish, because lacquer solvents will soften most varnish finishes.

Hot wax recipe

My uncle recently told me of a recipe for a finish that my grandfather used on oak cabinets. It calls for one part melted beeswax, one part boiled linseed oil and one part turpentine. These three ingredients are heated together until liquid, then applied while hot. After a few minutes any excess finish is buffed off. Is anybody there familiar with this finishing method? What are the merits of this type of finish when applied to oak? —Jim Smith, St. Louis, Mo.

IAN J. KIRBY REPLIES: The recipe for hot wax you describe is not uncommon. Like many earlier finishing recipes it is extremely imprecise, though it produces an excellent finish nonetheless. The recipe calls for one part melted beeswax, one part boiled linseed oil and one part turpentine. Does this mean one part of each ingredient by volume or by weight? There is an enormous amount of room for variation, and an excess of one or the other of the ingredients will alter the result, but mildly. For instance, excess beeswax will increase drying time, though not as much as excess linseed oil. Excess turpentine will increase the speed of drying. The merit of this finish is that once warmed, it will go into the surface of the wood, and into the open grain of oak particularly well. The coldness of the wood will soon harden the mixture so it can be polished. This was frequently done with a soft brush, especially where there was any form of carving or molding.

Notes on Finishing
Avoid the unseemly rush to glue up

by Ian Kirby

Compared to the paucity of attention given to the preparation stages of woodworking, a plethora of technical data is available about various wood finishes. Despite this, many otherwise fine pieces of work are spoiled at this final stage. Finishing problems seem to create as many problems at the end of a job as bad preparation of wood creates at the start.

Everybody seems to understand the need for extreme care and discipline when cutting joints and fitting pieces together. Yet when it comes to the finishing work, the time needed is usually underestimated. Then the urge to get the piece put together for the last time often overrides the need to assemble and finish in a considered sequence and under careful conditions. Ironically, an undignified rush to glue up before everything is absolutely ready inevitably requires substantially more time for finishing than would otherwise have been the case, and the result can only be less than acceptable.

This is not another article about wood finishes as such. It is an attempt to make a few points, which in my experience seem often to be forgotten at the finishing stage.

Cleaning up, applying a finish and assembly are all related parts of the finishing stage. The most common error is not to see them as such, especially where assembly is concerned. People glue together full or part assemblies and forget that it is far easier to clean up a piece of wood when it is separate from any other than to clean it up when it is glued into an assembly. Where two or more pieces come together at right angles to each other as in, say, a frame, it is virtually impossible to plane the inside surfaces or even to sand them properly without considerable frustration and sometimes taking the skin off the knuckles. Even when one is prepared to make this sacrifice, it remains impossible to reach right into the corners and a good crisp result simply cannot be achieved. It is also difficult to apply finish, at least by hand methods, to inside surfaces.

In general, it is best to prepare the surface for finishing with a minimum amount of sanding. The best finish comes from wood that is carefully smooth-planed, then sanded lightly (if at all) with 220-grit paper. This is particularly true when working ring-porous hardwoods, which may have considerable variation in density between earlywood and latewood. Excessive sanding cuts down the harder tissues in each growth ring, and depresses the soft tissues. As soon as the finish hits the wood, the compressed soft tissue springs back and the surface may become quite rough.

Once the piece is ready to go together, a sequence has to be worked out for each particular job, along the following lines: All inside and subsequently inaccessible surfaces should be planed with a very sharp smoothing plane and sanded lightly with fine garnet paper. Then they need to be dusted and given their full, final finish. Great care must be taken not to contaminate the surfaces to be glued during assembly, since the finish would prevent adhesion. Nevertheless it is neces-

From *Fine Woodworking* magazine (Summer 1978) 11:64-67

sary to apply the finish right up to the part to be glued.

Doing it this way saves time and energy and ensures high quality. Other benefits also accrue. During assembly glue inevitably will squeeze out from the joints, leaving beads and dribbles on the work. If the surface of the wood is polished these can be, indeed should be, left strictly alone to cure. Resist the strong temptation to wash or scrape them off immediately. Once they have cured they will simply fly off when the edge of a chisel is eased gently under them, leaving no trace or mark. Had the work not been polished, the glue would have penetrated the wood. Even if an attempt had been made to wash it off immediately, some would have still entered the surface tissue of the wood, since washing only dilutes the glue and increases its rate of absorption. If the wood is cleaned up before assembly but not polished, the squeezed-out glue will have to be chiseled off. This can only result in damage to the surfaces, in precisely those places inaccessible to cleaning-up tools. Further, the residual glue on the surface of the wood forms a barrier to polish applied over it, and shows up as an unsightly mark about which little can be done.

These considerations don't matter with surfaces on the outside or accessible to planing after assembly, because they won't yet have been cleaned up. Indeed, it would be unwise to smooth-plane such surfaces before assembly, as they are often scuffed and dirtied while the piece is being put together.

Why finish?

Wood finishes have to cater to at least five requirements: 1) to keep dirt out of the wood; 2) to prevent degrade of the wood surface as a result of abrasion and heat; 3) to produce visual and tactile qualities; 4) to bring out the colors in the wood, and 5) to slow down moisture exchange with the air.

I don't intend to go into great detail about all the different finishes available nor to describe the merits or debilities of each, relative to these five requirements. Indeed, a full accounting would require a lengthy excursion into exotic chemical technology. The point I do want to emphasize is that no one finish can be regarded as best, separate from the specific requirements of the job at hand.

In all but the most stringently clean conditions, wood will be degraded through discoloration from dirt, unless the finish provides a barrier. If it were not for the fact that wood absorbs debris from the atmosphere and through direct contact, it would need no finish at all.

The second requirement, to prevent degrade of the surface, is related to the first. But here I have in mind potentially more harmful agents such as physical and chemical abrasion and wet and dry heat. The degree to which such degrade can be repaired is a factor to weigh against the longevity of any finish that is not easy to repair.

The available choices of visual and tactile qualities are determined primarily by whether the finish resides in the wood, such as waxes and oils, or on top of its surface, such as lacquers and varnishes. This is a decision about texture. Once this decision has been made, the maker must choose the degree of gloss the surface is to have. The range from gloss to matte is narrow with waxes and oils, but very broad with varnishes and lacquers, from totally matte to mirror glossy. However, the choice is determined by the manufacturer—there is little a maker can do to transform a glossy varnish into a matte finish, and vice versa.

It has to be stressed that in touching a piece that has been

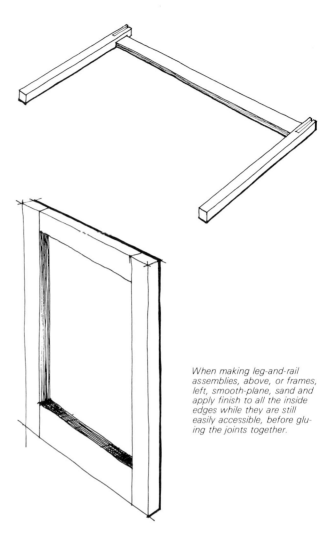

When making leg-and-rail assemblies, above, or frames, left, smooth-plane, sand and apply finish to all the inside edges while they are still easily accessible, before gluing the joints together.

lacquered or varnished, one is not in contact with the wood at all, but with the film lying over it. The number of coats of varnish or lacquer also affects visual and tactile qualities. Two light coats of varnish put directly onto the natural wood leave an open finish, in contrast to the full finish achieved by first filling the grain and then creating a build with a number of coats, each one being cut back before the next is applied, and the final one polished.

The fourth requirement, that of bringing out the colors in the wood, is often regarded more from an emotional point of view than from a practical one. For while some finishes do accentuate the visual characteristics, usually by differentiating light and dark features, others can discolor the wood far more than one might wish. Staining is a complete topic in itself, but it ought to be said that in the main it kills the visual qualities of wood, making it bland and lifeless. So much of the furniture one sees is adulterated in this way, and it's sad that so much beauty is stained away for spurious reasons.

The principal spurious reason for this state of affairs is usually given as economy. Manufacturers take wood randomly from the pile and cut whole sets of furniture "en suite," in whatever manner wastes the least, and then employ men to stain it all to uniformity. The public has come to expect walnut or maple always to have the same color it does in the furniture store. It probably would cost the industry less to employ a man to select the lumber at the start, as does a maker working alone, according to subtle variations in color and figure. The saving in finishing materials would offset any additional waste in cutting. And despite industry's perception of the public's expectations, most people—once they are given the chance—quickly come to relish the juxtaposition of heartwood and sapwood on a surface, and the beauty of the wood in all its color and variety. Indeed, this is a part of what gives custom furniture its quality. I never use stains, except when matching new parts to old in repair work.

Generally speaking, the visual qualities and certainly the tactile qualities of the wood are best brought out by the finishes that reside in the surface. However, some light woods such as maple and sycamore tend to turn yellow, and lacquer or varnish inhibits this better than wax does. It is always a question of weighing one factor against the other.

Finally, no finish will prevent wood from taking up or losing moisture as the humidity of the atmosphere varies with the seasons, nor as a consequence from shrinking and expanding. Finishes do, however, provide an effective barrier against sudden changes in relative humidity and in this respect varnish or lacquer offers the most protection. This is also why all wood surfaces, both visible and invisible, should be finished in top-quality work.

Varnish and lacquer

Most people are aware of the advantages of varnish or lacquer over oils and waxes when it comes to protecting horizontal surfaces against wet and dry heat, and chemical abrasion. The tendency is, however, to think of on-the-surface finishes as entirely appropriate in all other situations, irrespective of whether the work is likely ever to meet harsh conditions, and in spite of the fact that varnish and lacquer have disadvantages in other directions, when compared to wax and oil. Also, there is no reason that one must apply the same type of finish to every part of a piece. For instance, a vertical surface rarely needs to be highly resistant to the wet and dry heat or chemical abrasion that a horizontal surface is liable to encounter. The tabletop clearly needs protection, while the apron and legs usually do not. Also, because of the way light and shadow work, we rarely see the same effect from a horizontal surface as from a vertical surface. There is no reason why they shouldn't be finished differently, to capitalize on the combined advantages of a variety of finishes.

I have used the terms varnish and lacquer together to refer to on-the-surface films. This is because there is tremendous confusion about just what each word means, aggravated by advances in chemical technology over the last 50 years. A century ago, each town or locality had its own paint maker who mixed varnish according to his own secret recipe. Usually the base was boiled linseed oil, with the addition of various gums, resins and dryers. The same preparation became paint with the addition of whitening and pigment. Such preparations were soluble in oil, turpentine and mineral spirits. The original lacquer, on the other hand, was shellac, prepared from the resinous deposits of the lac insect and soluble in alcohol. But things changed soon after the turn of the century with the development of nitro-cellulose lacquer, and since then with the creation of a veritable flood of synthetic resins.

Manufacturers first introduced these synthetic resins into existing varnish and lacquer mixtures. But chemists quickly developed more sophisticated, and more highly reactive, preparations that required new formulations. Most began as two-can products which the user had to mix, but people are notorious about experimenting with directions and the resulting disastrous finishes forced the chemists to devise single-can preparations that polymerized upon contact with oxygen or moisture in the atmosphere or by internal catalysis. The result today is a profusion of clear wood finishes, marketed under the familiar old names of varnish and lacquer, but containing few of the original ingredients of these materials.

This is a case where big is better, since the research that goes into a modern finish is extraordinarily expensive, and so is the factory required to produce it. Indeed, most synthetic resins are made by a few large firms and sold in bulk to smaller producers of paint and varnish. These resins are vastly better than the products they have replaced, but they ought to be applied according to the directions on the can. Many furniture makers begin with commercial varnishes and mix their own oil-varnish preparations, according to experiment and intuition. It's possible to achieve good results this way (see article on pages 46-47), but I never do it. I don't think I can match the research facilities of DuPont or Farben, especially when the label usually doesn't even tell precisely what is inside the can.

Most lacquers and varnishes may be sprayed on, but they can be applied with a brush or rag. If they are being applied to a veneered surface where the veneer has been bonded with white or yellow glue, it is always best to apply the first coat sparingly with a rag to form a seal, because an excess of lacquer may seep through the veneer and attack the glue line, resulting in blisters. I don't mean to dilute the preparation, but to rub a little of it over a large area. Once the grain has been sealed by the first coat, which must be abraded to de-nib the surface, subsequent coats should be applied sparingly and quickly without too much brushing in. Each coat should be allowed to flow out and left to cure.

One hazard to a glossy lacquer or varnish finish is floating dust from the air. The best way to avoid the problem is to work in a dust-free finishing room. Without such a room, one can guard against dust fall-out only by scrupulous cleanliness. Clear all the tools and debris from your bench, sweep well, and cover the bench top with a piece of clean plywood. Have nothing on the bench but the tools and materials you need for finishing. Apply finish to the furniture parts and lay them out flat on the plywood, then block up another piece of plywood over the work, as an umbrella against falling dust. If despite these precautions you do get dust in the finish, then you will have to sand out the offending spots with fine, worn paper and refinish.

Many makers attempt to turn a gloss finish into a matte finish by sanding or rubbing with steel wool. This scatters the incident light by abrading the top surface of the finish. The scratches are large at first, but the more rubbing the finer the scratches and the glossier the surface becomes. A glossy finish dulled with steel wool or pumice and oil will soon become shiny again under the normal abrasion of routine household cleaning. If you want a matte finish, buy a matte varnish or lacquer. These products contain stearates in suspension, which scatter the incident light by their presence throughout the film.

Wax and shellac

A wax finish gives, in the main, excellent visual and tactile results. It protects well against knocks and physical abrasion and is very easy and fast to apply and repair. It is entirely suitable for vertical surfaces in most situations. The quickest and easiest way to achieve a good finish is with a coat of shellac to seal the wood, followed by wax, for polish. An equally good method is to finish with oil, or with oil followed by wax, although the speed of drying and ultimate curing is considerably longer than with wax and shellac.

While lacquers and varnishes are bought as prepared products with full data sheets and instructions, the best furniture wax is made up in the workshop from beeswax. Beeswax is the basis of most commercial furniture waxes, although it is often adulterated with paraffin wax and other substances. I use the word "adulterated" advisedly, for often the proportion of beeswax to other substances is very small in name brands. A good mix can be made quite easily from a block of pure beeswax grated with an ordinary household grater or pared with a wide chisel. Put the chips into a wide-necked container, that is, wide enough to get your hands in, such as a large mayonnaise or peanut-butter jar. Pack them loosely and add pure turpentine to half the depth taken up by the chips and set aside to dissolve. This will take about 24 hours. The final consistency should be that of soft butter just before it melts into oil. If it is too thin add more wax, or if too thick, more turpentine. When stirring, take care not to splash because, while it won't damage the skin, it can be very painful in the eyes.

Store the mix in the same wide-necked vessel with a lid, to prevent evaporation of the turpentine and hardening of the wax (although if it does harden, it can always be softened again by the addition of a little more turpentine).

Additives can be used with this sort of preparation, but it is questionable whether it is worth it in the long run. Carnauba wax, which is added while heating the mix, results in a wax that finishes out harder than beeswax but becomes more difficult to use. Drying can be speeded by the addition of up to 25% gasoline, but the easiest and safest way is to use pure beeswax and pure turpentine. Incidentally, if you heat this wax up, you should use a hot water bath or double boiler.

Before waxing, apply an initial sealing coat of dilute shellac with a large, soft brush called a "mop" or with a "mouse" rubber. A mop is a round, squirrel-hair brush about 1½ in. in diameter, and it is best to keep it right in the shellac, suspended through a hole in the lid. The diagram shows how to make a mouse. Its advantage is that while it has a substantial reservoir of liquid, it allows fine flow control according to the amount of pressure exerted by the fingers. You can obtain a more even coat than with the brush. Only one application of shellac is necessary, to act as a barrier to inhibit the wax from penetrating the wood so deeply that it eventually disappears. If the ground of shellac were not there, it would take very much longer, and more wax, to finish the surface. The best is pure shellac dissolved in wood alcohol, rather than a commercial preparation that also contains polymerizing agents, rapid drying agents or gums. Shellac dries rapidly anyway, and you don't want to achieve a build.

Apply the wax with either a rag or brushes. The brushing method, all too infrequently used, is very similar to shining shoes or horse tack, in that two brushes are used, both of which need fairly soft bristles. Whether the brush or rag is used, apply the wax across the grain in circles to get an even, light spread, then make the final strokes with the grain.

A common mistake is to apply too much wax, leaving a deposit on the surface, on the false assumption that it will harden and disappear into the wood. The result is a sticky, uneven surface that is very difficult to level. Two or three light coats of wax are much better than one heavy one.

Oil finishes

Oil is also a sound finish in itself or as a base for subsequent waxing. Oils for furniture are usually based either on linseed oil to which polymerizing agents have been added, or on synthetic resins with hardeners added. These latter oils are often referred to as "teak" oils or "Danish" oils but this should not be taken to mean that they are used only on teak or by Danes. They can be used on any wood where the main concern is to protect and enhance the visual and tactile qualities.

Oils do, however, present more problems at the pre-gluing stages because they are highly fugitive—it is easy to contaminate gluing surfaces with oily fingers or with a touch or drip from the rag. Great care must be taken to avoid the risk of poor adhesion due to oil contamination. Also, because of its volatile nature, oil tends to creep along the grain, which makes working up to joint lines more of a risk.

It is the maker's responsibility to advise customers about the finish, its expected performance and daily care. For your own protection and reputation, this should not be merely verbal. A printed sheet giving all the information necessary should accompany the delivered furniture. ☐

Left, a squirrel-hair 'mop' kept in a shellac bottle. Below, how to make a 'mouse.'

A square of cotton cloth is wrapped around a wad of cotton batting a little smaller than a tennis ball. Finishing material is poured in, and the cloth is folded and twisted around. Hand pressure controls the flow onto the wood.

Ian Kirby is a designer, cabinetmaker and educator at his studio in Cumming, Ga.

Glue size with stain

I'm using water/aniline dyes and I sand the wood before applying them, then after drying I use water to raise the grain and sand again. Following this the water stain still raises the grain like crazy. I've heard that a glue sizing may be used before the water stain. Is this right? How do you do it? It sounds like any sizing would prevent or retard dye penetration. —J.A. Osborn, Severna Park, Md.

GEORGE FRANK REPLIES: You have the right answer. Before using a water dye, you should wet the wood first with water to raise its grain, let it dry and sand it. However, you need a little finesse. First, you must use new, fine sandpaper that is sharp and will cut; second, your sanding strokes must not go in the direction of the grain, but on a slight bias, so as not to push the fibers back into their original cradles, but to cut them off permanently. After staining, sand the wood again, with even finer paper.

A glue size is always a good thing and stain will penetrate it. You can use fairly thin hide glue, but the best is rabbit-skin glue, which is used by gilders and can be bought wherever gold leaf is sold. You must sand after every step.

Stain before filling

I recently used a paste wood-filler on walnut. I stained the filler and finally applied Watco oil. The filler seemed to leave a surface finish that prevented the oil from penetrating. Should the stain be applied before the filler? —Kenneth A. Sovereign, Aurora, Ill.

OTTO H. HEUER REPLIES: If you're going to use stain, apply it before the filler. First, sand the wood with fine sandpaper, remove the dust and wipe the surface clean. Then apply the stain with a rag and wipe off the excess. I prefer an oil-based, pigmented wiping stain somewhat lighter in color than the wood filler. You can use either walnut-colored filler or a natural paste wood-filler colored to the desired shade with oil or oil-and-japan colors, available from paint stores in small tubes.

Reduce the filler following the instructions on the label, or mix equal volumes of paste filler and mineral spirits. Apply the filler with a brush, then follow up by padding the filler into the pores with a rag. When you see the solvent flash, scrub off the excess filler with a piece of burlap, wiping across the grain. You may need several coats to fill all of the large pores in the wood.

Finally, wipe with the grain using a clean cloth and very light strokes. Allow to dry in a warm room for 24 hours, then rub lightly with very fine steel wool. You may now apply a light coat of Watco or some other oil finish, but the oil won't penetrate the same as on unfilled wood. You may want to use only the oil wiping stain and omit the filler. If you do, let the stain dry for 24 hours and rub lightly with fine steel wool, then apply the final oil finish.

Homemade wood filler

I've heard of cabinetmakers' using sanding dust for filler. I've tried mixing my dust with glue and water, but the filler always turns darker than the wood. A friend suggested that I mix my sanding dust with lacquer, fill, sand and then finish, but my filler still turns darker than the wood. Any suggestions? —Tom Caudill, Louisville, Ky.

GEORGE FRANK REPLIES: There are several fillers on the market, the main ingredient of which is wood dust. These fillers are sold in various shades, and though you can try to mix them together to get the color you want, it's almost impossible to get them to match the wood 100%. Hence the need for homemade wood fillers.

We old-timers made filler by spreading hide glue on the end grain of a piece of wood of the species to be filled. Scraping the end grain with a sharp chisel made a paste thick enough to fill gaps in the wood. Talcum powder, chalk, scrapings of a lighter wood, or some powdered earth color can be added as needed to vary the color and texture. In this filler the hide glue is the binder, but you can experiment by using clear or even tinted lacquer, or liquid shellac as a binder. Or just mix your sawdust with hide glue or white cabinet glue, liquid shellac, or clear lacquer (which is known by the trade name Plastic Wood). The quality of your sawdust is important—the finer it is, the better your chances of success. Above all, though, you must experiment.

Commercial fillers

All of the experts I've read maintain that wood filler should be made of silex and get hard overnight. But the fillers on the market today are made of gypsum and do not get hard. Where can I buy a good filler? —Ed Spinks, St. Louis, Mo.

DON NEWELL REPLIES: Fillers should dry hard, but the hardness comes from the set-up characteristics of the liquid (vehicle) portion of the filler, not from the hardness of the inert particles it carries. Silex, or silica, is preferred, if you have a choice. But I would guess that gypsum or calcium carbonate would work too. In the 18th and 19th centuries, common fillers included such diverse substances as pulverized brick dust and plaster of Paris.

The key is the vehicle, which should be a varnish-type material rather than a drying oil. One larger chain retailer carries a wood filler that lists on the label linseed oil as the vehicle. I would guess that other commercial fillers also use the same basic formula.

Frankly, I don't know of a good, hard-drying filler on the market, and because of this I've given up using fillers. The work of applying soft fillers isn't worth the results produced.

Graying wood filler

I am having trouble with wood filler turning gray under a lacquer top coat. I am using a brown mahogany filler thinned with naphtha, allowing drying time according to the directions on the can. I use a lacquer sealer over the filler before I spray on the top coat. Thanks for any help you can give me. —Ralph R. Fox, Grafton, Va.

OTTO HEUER REPLIES: The graying of your wood filler may be due to the slow evaporation rate of the naphtha. If the naphtha hasn't escaped through drying, it will cause the nitrocellulose in the sealer and the lacquer to come out of solution, forming a precipitate that clouds the finish. Usually naphtha is used as a wood filler solvent during the cooler winter months. During the summer, you can use a less volatile solvent such as mineral spirits.

Letting the filler dry longer may help; fillers can go stale, however, and lose their drying properties. To check, reduce a small amount of filler with the recommended solvent, then rub it on a clean piece of glass to a film about as thick as it would be on the wood. This film should dry hard in 24 to 48 hours at room temperature and should be hard enough to resist scratching with a fingernail.

You could also try a lacquer washcoat consisting of one part lacquer to three parts thinner. Spray on a mist coat before you rub in the filler. The washcoat keeps the naphtha from penetrating most small pores and crevices in the wood. The addition of 10% by volume of a retarder (butyl cellusolve) to the lacquer top coat will reduce graying of the lacquer in the pores that may still harbor naphtha.

Stain won't take

I use white glue on all of my woodwork, but no matter how well I sand, white areas appear after I've applied stain. What causes this and what can I do to prevent it?
—*S.M. Gurtan, Norcross, Ga.*

R. Bruce Hoadley Replies: Your problem is familiar. Excess glue can easily contaminate wood surfaces and prevent uniform absorption of stain. There is no single cure-all, but the following hints, alone or in combination, should reduce the problem.

First, avoid excessive squeeze-out by not using too much glue. Franklin makes a product called Shop and Craft Glue that is the consistency of toothpaste and won't run at all. Clean up squeeze-out as soon as you can with a cloth dampened with hot water. Use a stiff brush to get into hard-to-reach places.

Careful sanding and scraping will usually remove adhesives that have already dried and will also smooth grain raised by the damp-cloth cleanup. Sometimes you can prefinish troublesome areas, such as up to tenon shoulders and miter joints.

Finally, if all else fails, color the glue before you apply it, with a water-soluble stain that matches the finished color of your wood.

Colored-wax filler

I used to buy colored wax to fill up small holes like countersunk nails and such, but I can't find any in this area. Can you tell me how to make it, or where I can buy it readymade? —*Jim Smith, Vancouver, Canada*

George Frank Replies: Melt equal quantities of beeswax and paraffin wax in a double boiler, add dry powdered colors, then for every ounce of wax add a drop of linseed oil. You can make small paper tubes with one end closed and pour the well-stirred liquid into them. The oil will cause the wax to remain malleable.

You can buy prepared burn-in sticks in a wide variety of colors, wax-like stain pencils, and dry pigments from Mohawk Finishing Products, Rt. 30N, Amsterdam, N.Y. 12010.

Sand walnut, don't fill it

Walnut has a tendency to pick up when run through a molding mill. What material and method of application do you suggest for filing this surface roughness that will not affect subsequent finishing and final appearance?
—*R. Henderson, Albuquerque, N.M.*

Lelon Traylor Replies: Sharp shaper knives cutting good-quality walnut leave a beautiful, smooth finish on the molding. Knives that are dull, cutting walnut that is of poor quality, i.e., soft and spongy, will pick up or rough up the surface. If you are forced to use poor-quality walnut, get a smooth surface by using 150- to 280-grit garnet paper and a liberal amount of elbow grease. Leave the filler in the can.

Filling open-grain wood

One of the things I just can't learn to do is to apply filler to open-grain wood. All the books make it sound easy, but I never can get the surface flat. I don't understand how you can avoid getting a slight concavity when you wipe the stuff off with a piece of burlap.
—*H.N. Capen, Granada Hills, Calif.*

George Frank Replies: With the exception of a special and hard-to-use water-based filler also involving a great deal of sanding, no filler will fill the pores of the wood entirely. The subsequent coatings with finishing material are supposed to do that.

Before the Finish
Whiskering, patching and staining

by Don Newell

Taking a wood surface to its final state, ready to receive the finish, appears to be straightforward. The professional and the long-experienced amateur woodworker may well have put all their cut-and-try mistakes behind them, during the early years of learning what worked best for them. But for the amateur whose only woodworking time is a few weekend hours, many mistakes are yet to be learned from.

The phrase "what worked best for them" expresses a truth about the art of finishing wood that every serious devotee must come to recognize. In most cases, one's specific materials or tools are probably less important to fine results than one's technique in using them. The successful artisan works *with* his materials, rather than trying to force them to act as he thinks they should. Nevertheless, in learning what to expect from your materials, and what they demand from you, the crucial word is "work." If the finish is to do justice to the cabinetwork and the wood, you need to get the feel of the finishing materials before you apply them. And the essential tools for learning the feel are scraps or ends or extra boards of the same wood from which you've built the piece.

Try out the finishing system you've selected, so as to know beforehand what will happen. Does the stain hide the figuring, rather than enhance it? Experiment by thinning the stain. What does the finish material do to the stain? Does it go muddy, or does it clarify? If you plan on rubbing out lacquer or varnish to a desired sheen, how well does it rub out? How much rubbing does it take to cut through the finish coat to the wood itself? Does the finish really dry, if it's a varnish/drying oil concoction you've thrown together on your own? Or does it merely surface-dry, with the base remaining soft and susceptible to easy fingerprinting and marring? Trial-run your entire finishing system on sacrificial scrap before you entrust your cabinetwork to it: What you're going to get in the end is what you see now.

Sanding — The beginning of a fine finish is the physical condition of the top few thousandths of an inch of wood, which is all the viewer sees, and which is going to have to withstand the continuing presence of dirt, dust, moisture, glass-rings and human handling. The finish must protect the wood but the condition of the wood, in turn, must help the finish achieve maximum effectiveness.

The two commandments of sanding are Thou Shalt Not Use Flint Sandpaper, and Thou Shalt Not Sand Across The Grain. Flint paper is cheaper per sheet than production-type aluminum oxide or silicon carbide paper, but flint costs much more to use in the end. It can lose its grit particles, which will roll under the sanding pressure and gouge the surface.

As to grit size for finish sanding, 240 grit is coarse enough to eliminate the last cross-grain scratches. Follow it with 360 grit for final sanding, as the sanding marks are fine enough to be made invisible by whatever finish you use. Purists will be

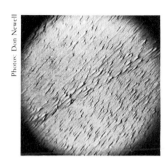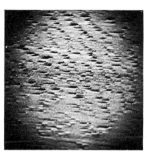

Photos: Don Newell

Left, walnut board is lit from the side to emphasize the raised grain, which is the ends of wood fibers meeting the surface at an angle. Photo was taken through a low-powered microscope. The board was wetted with water, then dried with the flame of a propane torch. The faint band through the center of the microscope field is a pencil line, right. Above the line, the wood was whiskered with a ball of steel wool; below, it was whiskered with sandpaper. Then the wood was wetted and dried again. The section that was steel-wooled remains smooth, while in the sandpapered section a number of fiber ends have popped up.

permitted one more run with 400 paper.

There is one essential step after final sanding: Play the light from a reflector floodlight, spotlight or even a flashlight across the surface of the wood at a very low angle. Scratches, indentations and other imperfections that were invisible under normal overhead worklights will instantly pop into view. It's much simpler to correct them at this stage than to attempt it after the finish is complete.

Grain raising is a common, vexing problem. The one-time solution is an established practice among professional gunstock makers, though I've seldom seen the technique mentioned in books dealing with furniture. Grain raising is simply the expansion of wood fiber ends above the surface, due to moisture absorption. It probably occurs continuously during the building process, but because the wood is being sawed, chiseled, planed, carved, filed or sanded, the minute roughness is never noticed. Only at the end, when you've finally filed and sanded and scraped the surface to baby-cheek smoothness, then left your little beauty in the humid basement or garage workshop overnight, does the grain ob-

viously raise. If you're lucky. When you're not lucky, you proceed to finish the workpiece, spending long hours brushing or hand-rubbing or whatever, only to have those whiskers come right through the finish some muggy August day.

The usual solution is to sand the surface lightly, at a slight angle to the grain, to cut off the raised tips of the fibers. Some finishers apply a dilute glue or shellac size coating, to freeze the whiskers in place for sanding, but I prefer not to.

The gunstocker's answer to grain raising is steel wool, used to pull the fiber ends up and out of the wood. Once you've removed the fiber ends, none are left to raise through the finish, regardless of moisture changes. Whiskering, as the process is called, is simple. First, deliberately raise the grain by wetting the surface well with a wet, not dripping, sponge or rag. Let the water sink in, then come back over the wetted area with the flame from a propane torch. Play the flame over the wood, keeping it moving so as not to char or darken any spot, until the surface is completely dry. Be careful at edges and corners since the flame will char the wood if allowed to stop there even momentarily. In this water/flame technique, water is taken into any susceptible fiber.ends, which expand almost immediately. The subsequent heat evaporates the water, some of it turning into steam which further contributes to the wood's expansion.

Now you have a veritable forest of whiskery fiber ends standing up, ready for removal. Form some medium-grade steel wool into a loose ball and firmly whisk it against the protruding ends of the fibers, always in line with the grain, never across the grain. The loose ends and loops of steel wool hook under the raised fibers and pull them out of the wood. Keep in mind that you're trying to rip the whiskers off the surface.

Two or three whisks of the loosely balled steel wool will eliminate the raised grain for good. One treatment of the water/heat/whisk process is usually sufficient, though two won't hurt. Of course, grain raising occurs only where the wood fibers run out of the surface. If your wood has the fiber structure running truly parallel to the surface, you'll not get grain raising.

The quick stick repair —Even the most experienced woodworkers occasionally gouge or nick the surface. Or small checks may open when wood is taken down to its final dimension. Repair recommendations often range from filling the imperfections or damage with a sawdust/glue mixture, to using a rub-in putty-type stick or crayon, to the ultimate repair of inlaying a matching-grain wood patch.

The method that works well for me is far quicker and easier. It's stick shellac, which is simply everyday shellac molded into stick form and available in a goodly range of colors and shades, including transparent. To use it, clean the gouge of all dust and debris. Where possible, especially with shallow depressions, rough up the surface. Then melt the stick shellac, as much or as little as needed, into the hole and let it cool. In less than a minute the shellac hardens all the way through, ready to file or sand level. And your repair is ready for the stain/finish coating.

A soldering gun is best for melting stick shellac. Its small tip makes it easy to melt just enough shellac, which can be flowed onto the wood where needed. Hold the shellac stick directly over the damage and trigger the soldering gun until the shellac begins to flow down into the hole. Trigger the gun off and on so the shellac stays hot enough to flow easily, but

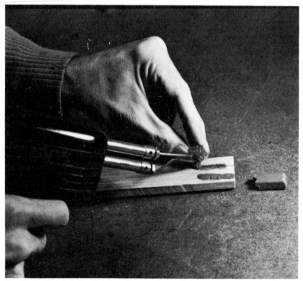

Stick shellac, melted into place with a soldering gun, is a quick, permanent and hard repair for nicks, gouges and cracks. Shellac can be applied in minutes and filed smooth, ready to finish, in seconds.

From *Fine Woodworking* magazine (May 1979) 16:69-71

not so hot that it begins to blacken and burn. Let the flowing shellac build up a little above the surface, since it shrinks slightly upon cooling. If the hole is a deep crack or seam, keep the hot tip of the gun in the pool of molten shellac for a few moments to help the shellac penetrate as deeply as possible. A little practice will give you the feel of the gun and the amount of heat needed to let the shellac flow well.

Color matching to the final stain/finish should be done with a piece of scrap wood. Because the shellac will not accept color from a subsequent stain, the problem is to stain the scrap the way you plan to stain the workpiece, then select the shade of shellac that most closely matches the color of the stained scrap upon drying. If you select a shade of shellac to match the color of the wood when it is finished, you can generally create a repair indistinguishable from the adjacent surface. It will also take almost any finish you wish to put over it without danger of losing adhesion, since the area of such a repair is generally very small.

Stains — When should you consider using a stain or dye, and when should you leave well enough alone? The only reason to use a stain is when you want to enhance the beauty of the wood. Plain or weakly figured wood benefits greatly from the judicious application of a colorant. By brushing or ragging a stain selectively into a barely discernible figure, you bring out the wood's character. Strengthening the figure without changing the color of the adjacent areas is sometimes the only way to achieve the beauty your joinery deserves— particularly with the plain-figured wood many amateurs obtain via mail order.

Staining (dyeing) doesn't have to be an overall color bath. But when the entire piece cries out for a little more color or a little deeper darkening, the stain material *must* be chosen in relationship to the finish coating you plan to use. The critical factor is *compatibility within your finishing system.* Anytime you use more than one kind of material on the wood, you create a system made up of two materials that either will work together or will not work together. If they are compatible with each other, a bond is formed where one interfaces with the other. If the two materials are compatible, the bond will be strong and the two will effectively harden into a single structure. If they are not compatible, you have two hardened layers without much to hold them together. The result too often is that the top layer flakes or peels off under the slightest stress. The simple expansion or contraction of wood under changing humidity is often enough to loosen the top coat. When this happens, the only recourse is to sand to bare wood and begin again.

But back to the stain. Water-based, alcohol-based and oil or solvent-based stains (see George Frank's article, "Stains, Dyes and Pigments," pages 40-41) generally are compatible with almost any varnish, assuming that the stain coat is thoroughly dried all the way through. Occasionally, oil/solvent stains, commonly called pigment stains, have linseed oil as their main ingredient. Never use a linseed oil-based stain under any finish coat containing lacquer. Read the labels. If the finishing material label lists such things as nitrocellulose and aromatic hydrocarbons, that's lacquer. You are building in trouble if you put it over linseed oil, no matter how thoroughly you may think it has dried.

You are also asking for trouble by putting shellac over a linseed oil base. The reason is the same, incompatibility. If

Left, test beads of shellac, transparent (top) and tan-colored (bottom), were melted into saw cuts in oak to determine the proper shade for filling a crack in an oak table. Both beads were filed to a level surface, then the scrap was stained and varnished to match the table itself. Although the saw cuts are apparent since they are straight and quite long, both patches blend well, right. But the tan-colored shellac on the bottom is the better match.

Oak tabletop was cut from the best part of an old, larger table and mounted on a new pedestal. An open butt joint where the old glue had given way was mended almost invisibly with shellac (close-up). Before applying the shellac, the two boards were clamped tight and dowel pins were glued into holes drilled at an angle from below to cross the crack line.

the two materials (stain and finishing coat) can be dissolved by a common solvent or thinner, you have a compatible system. If they cannot be dissolved by a common thinner, they should not be used together. As an example, most oil/solvent (pigment) stains have as a main ingredient an aliphatic solvent, usually mineral spirits or something very much like it. Most varnishes also use aliphatic solvents to make them brushable and flowable on the wood. Thus, pigment stains and varnishes are almost universally compatible and they will bond well to each other upon drying.

As an example of a potentially incompatible system, take the same oil/solvent (pigment) stain and lay a coat of brushing lacquer (or even spraying lacquer) over it. Chances are, the powerful solvents and thinners in the lacquer will attack the oil base of the stain, no matter how well it has dried. The lacquer will generally cause the surface of the stain material to swell, wrinkle and attempt to lift off the surface. Even if it doesn't, the adhesion of the dry coat of lacquer to the oil in the surface of the wood will, at best, be minimal.

The potential incompatibility of a finishing system can be anticipated by reading the labels. If there is no major, single ingredient common to both formulations, the finisher should expect trouble. The chemical-reaction type of water-based stains are compatible with any finishing material. So are alcohol-based stains. Only the oil-based pigment types occasionally cause compatibility problems, and then only under shellac or lacquer. □

Don Newell, of Farmington, Mich., is a gunstock maker, paint and varnish chemist, amateur furniture maker and author of an industrial finishing textbook.

Repairing Finishes: Two Ways

1. Burn-in resins hide deep scratches

by Rick Bütz

It's frustrating to discover a deep scratch in a nicely finished piece of furniture. A scratch rarely goes unnoticed and it may be unfairly interpreted as a glaring defect in the furniture itself. With any luck—and light damage—a surface scratch may be easily rubbed out with steel wool, but usually not.

Over the years, furniture makers have developed lots of tricks for touching up damaged finishes. A favorite method for repairing deep scratches is called "burning-in." The repairer fills the scratch with melted shellac resin, matches the color and grain of the surrounding wood with stains and a small brush and, finally, touches-in the appropriate finish. Damage to oil, varnish, shellac and lacquer finishes can be burned-in; polyurethane and other plastic finishes sometimes blister.

For burn-in work, you'll need shellac sticks of various colors, a special knife, a heat source, padding lacquer and powdered blending stains. Burn-in sticks are sold in hundreds of colors, but I keep only a dozen on hand in the colors of woods I usually repair. Clear or translucent sticks are available and they can be color-matched using the blending stains. Burn-in or shellac sticks are made of various pigments and resins and have a consistency similar to the wax used for sealing letters. My burn-in knife is like a palette knife with a curved, flexible blade. A small alcohol lamp is a good heat source. Use the lamp carefully; never leave it burning unattended. Although electrically-heated knives can be used, I prefer the alcohol lamp for its more delicate heat control.

To repair a scratch heat the knife tip with the concave side toward the flame. This keeps any soot that forms from contaminating the resin. Judging the proper temperature takes practice. If the resin bubbles and smokes when it touches the knife, it's too hot. If it forms drops that quickly resolidify, it's too cool. When it's right, it's almost watery. Once you've found the correct temperature, hold the knife like a pencil and carefully flow the hot resin into the scratch. The knife can touch the wood surface, but you must keep it moving to get an even flow. Fill the scratch, clean the knife by heating it and wiping it with a rag, then level the resin by heating the knife once more and moving the convex face quickly over the surface. Keep the knife moving whenever it's hot enough to soften the resin, or you will damage the surrounding finish. Aged shellac and varnishes can be particularly sensitive to heat. If the resin from the burn-in stick bubbles up and sticks like chewing gum instead of flowing smoothly when heated, the stick is probably stale and should be replaced. The sticks have a shelf-life of six months to two years and if cracked and checked are probably stale.

When the scratch is completely filled and the surface is smooth, the final leveling is done with a piece of 600-grit wet/dry sandpaper wrapped around a small felt block. With water as a lubricant, gently remove any excess resin. Be careful not to sand through the finish surrounding your repair.

There's another method using a different burn-in stick—called a Nolift-stick—which was developed several years ago by Mohawk and Behlen. It uses a resin stick that dissolves in a solvent that won't affect the surrounding finish. During sanding the solvent is used as a lubricant and can be applied directly with a felt block. The solvent is called Brasive by Mohawk; Behlen sells it as Abrosol.

Regardless of which stick is used, once the surface of the repair is level with the finish around it, color and grain differences can be matched. The traditional method of applying color over a small area is to use a French polishing technique with padding lacquer and finely powdered blending stains. These dry stains come in many different shades and can be mixed to create an infinite range of colors. You can match the most delicate shades with surprising control. Padding lacquer is compatible with many finishes, but you should experiment with it before trying to repair a valuable piece. If the lacquer's gloss is higher than the surrounding finish, you can rub it out with fine steel wool. An alternative to commercially made padding lacquer is a traditional French polish solution of equal parts of boiled linseed oil, 5-lb. cut shellac and alcohol. Experiment with the proportions to get a quick-drying mixture.

To use the padding lacquer or French polish, make a cloth rubbing pad out of lint-free, absorbent cloth. Fold the cloth upon itself to make a ball about the size of an egg. Apply a small amount of padding lacquer to the cloth and tap the palm of your hand against it to evenly disperse the liquid. Don't saturate the cloth. Then apply the lacquer over the scratch by stroking lightly in the direction of the grain, with the pad barely touching the wood. You want to build up a thin layer of lacquer, to which the stain will adhere.

Next, select the desired color of blending stain and apply a thin layer with your index finger. Again, pad lacquer several times over the filled area and wipe a thin layer of the stain from your fingertip onto the surface. Once the stain has been applied, lightly pad lacquer over it. The powder will dissolve when it comes in contact with the liquid, and create a stained finish. Repeat this process until the desired shade has been gradually built up over the burned-in area. If the color should go too dark or doesn't match, clean away the stain with alcohol or padding lacquer solvent. Let the finish dry for a few minutes before starting over. Padding technique requires a little practice, but in time, you will be able to match the most subtle color variations. The real secret is to apply the padding lacquer with as light a padding stroke as possible. This will prevent the stain from "shifting" or washing away. It's better to apply too little stain than too much, as it is easy to darken an area but impossible to lighten it without starting over. Experimenting on scrap pieces will give you a taste of controlling color. Use as little stain as possible to achieve the desired effect.

With the wood color matched, the grain lines can be touched in. If the original wood finish shows porous grain texture, as in oiled walnut, teak or oak, it's a good idea to duplicate this texture in the repair. Use a needle or razor blade to carefully scratch the grain texture

From *Fine Woodworking* magazine (May 1982) 34:92-94

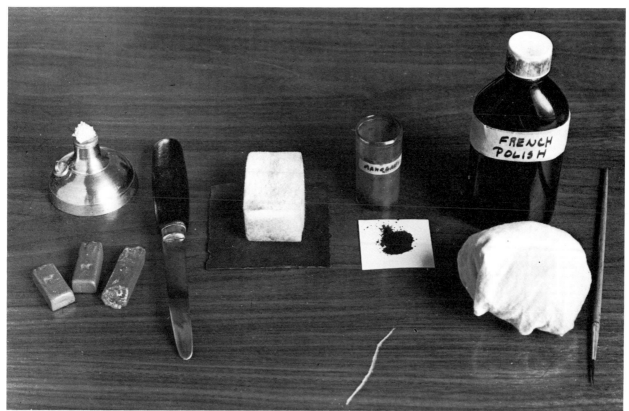

For repairing finishes you'll need (from left to right) an alcohol lamp, resin sticks, a burn-in knife, and a felt sanding block. To match colors, blending stain, French polish or padding lacquer, a cloth pad and a fine brush are used.

With the heated burn-in knife, concave side down, fill in the scratch by flowing hot resin into it (above, left). Be careful not to get the knife too hot. When the scratch is filled, reheat the knife and wipe it clean with a rag before leveling the built up resin (above, center). Keep the knife just hot enough to make the resin flow as you work it. After the repair has been leveled and sanded with 600-grit wet/dry sandpaper, apply padding lacquer or French polish to act as a base for the powdered blending stain (above, right). The stain evens out color differences. Use a fine sable brush to touch-in grain detail over the repair (left). Then pad over a couple of coats of padding lacquer and when that has dried overnight, gently rub out the repair with steel wool and blend it into the surrounding finish.

into the resin. Then mix a few drops of padding lacquer and dark powder stain on a small piece of glass. Carefully paint in the grain lines over the repair, using a fine sable brush. Blend these lines and carry them into the natural grain on either side of the repair. After letting the repair dry for 30 minutes, lightly pad several layers of padding lacquer over the patch to seal and protect it.

You can let the padding lacquer serve as a final finish but it's better to apply a coat of the finish used on the rest of the piece. Once dry, the entire repair can be rubbed with steel wool or pumice to match the gloss. The result will be an invisible repair permanently bonded to the wood and indetectable under the closest scrutiny. □

Rick Bütz is a professional woodcarver and he repairs furniture in Blue Mountain Lake, N.Y. Photos by Ellen Bütz. Materials for burning-in can be purchased from H. Behlen and Bros., Inc. (write to ask for local distributors) and from Mohawk Finishing Products, both at Rt. 30N, Amsterdam, N.Y. 12010, and by mail from Constantine, 2065 Eastchester Rd., Bronx, N.Y. 10461, or Garrett Wade Co., 161 Ave. of the Americas, New York, N.Y. 10013.

2. Knife technique makes the difference

by John Revelle

You can fill scratches by burning-in on new furniture and in refinishing, repair or restoration work. In the first two, knife technique isn't important since the repair will be finished over. In repair and restoration work, however, a hot knife in a clumsy hand can damage as much as it can fix.

When burning-in already finished work, I like to run the resin into the scratch and smooth it completely with my knife, skipping padding lacquer and stains and all but a cursory sanding. I prefer the Nu-Glo sticks made by the Star Chemical Co. Inc. These sticks were developed for marble repair and have an indefinite shelf life. They don't crack and go stale as do other types. Mohawk sells an equivalent product called MF or marble-fill stick. There's an assortment

of colors so it's not hard to match whatever wood you happen to be working on. Since I don't use stains, I pick a stick that exactly matches the background color of the wood I'm repairing.

I've found that Star's Opal #750 knife works best for me. The tool has a ¾-in. wide flexible steel blade with a shallow bevel ground on one side of its skewed working end. It's sometimes sold as a cement finisher's knife. I use the electric knife-oven sold for the Opal knife. If you use two knives, one can be heating while you work with the other. It takes about a minute to bring a knife to the right temperature. To make a repair I heat the blade and touch the bevel side of the knife's heel (its obtuse point) to a resin stick so it melts just a small bead. I quickly push the resin-coated heel into the scratch at a point farthest away from me. Rocking the knife gently back and forth flows the resin evenly into the scratch. I repeat the process until there is just enough to fill the scratch level with the surrounding surface. Then I wipe the hot knife clean with a rag or a paper towel and reheat it. To level the patch, I drag the heated knife along the scratch, bevel-side down, in light rapid strokes, lifting the knife off the surface between strokes. Moving the knife continuously is critical. You can light a cigarette with a hot knife, so stopping it even for an instant will char the finish around the repair.

Small repairs can be done with just a bead or two of resin, larger ones take more. Take care not to mound the resin above the level of the surface around it, or the repair will be conspicuous. If you do get too much resin in the repair, hold the knife firmly, bevel down, and with short, chevron-shaped strokes work the excess resin back and down into the scratch. If air bubbles turn up, pierce them with the heel of a hot knife and rework the resin. The temperature of the knife can be varied to help control resin flow. As the knife gets cooler, the material gets harder to spread. With practice, you should be able to smooth the resin without sanding. But if you can't get a perfect surface with the knife alone, complete the smoothing with 400-grit or 600-grit wet/dry paper.

With the scratch filled and leveled, you can grain the wood with a hot knife and a resin stick that matches the color of the grain lines in the wood. Draw a hot knife's sharp edge through the darker stick to coat it from heel to toe,

To fill a scratch, apply a bead of resin to the heel of the hot knife. Then push the resin-coated heel into the scratch and rock it gently to distribute the resin.

Clean and reheat the knife and drag it bevel-side down to smooth the resin to the surrounding surface.

then press the sharp edge straight into the repair in the same direction as the grain you are simulating. Some of the darker color will transfer to the patch. Continue the process until the grain lines match the surrounding wood. You can smooth the patch by dragging it with a hot knife as before. If you're repairing an open-grained wood, skip the smoothing step and sand with 400-grit wet/dry paper using mineral spirits or sanding oil as a lubricant.

Finally, I match the repair to the sheen of the existing finish by rubbing with fine steel wool or a soft cloth and rottenstone. I usually don't put any finish over the repair since I'm never sure what the original is. Overlaying with the wrong finish will often cause more problems than it will cure. □

John Revelle is a professional furniture restorer in Rohnert Park, Calif. Photos by the author. The materials he describes can be purchased from Star Chemical Co., Inc., 360 Shore Drive, Hinsdale, Ill. 60521.

Old Finishes

What put the shine on furniture's Golden Age

by Robert D. Mussey

Finishing is the least studied and most inaccessible aspect of our antique furniture heritage. The proportions and workmanship of a Philadelphia highboy are direct and observable manifestations of the skills of its maker. But what of its finish? Is the mellow patina, much admired today, anything like the finish that left the workshop 200 years ago?

We can't learn much from the pieces themselves. Most museum conservators agree that perhaps only one percent of our antique furniture bears indisputable remnants of its original finish. Scientific tests may inadvertently detect later refinishings or modern materials indistinguishable from the originals: there's no way to tell new beeswax from old.

When we turn to historical documents, much obscure, ambiguous or mysterious material conceals the pearls of hard information. The old craft guilds guarded their trade secrets as closely as the independent finishers who proudly, and loudly, announced the discovery of the "perfect" finishing potion. Formularies, cabinetmakers' and varnishers' account books, bills, histories and dictionaries of the period are difficult to interpret. Account books, for example, so rich in information about woods used and prices charged, say little about finishes. When materials are mentioned, the names vary from region to region: 25 different words may describe just one material. And more than 200 different resins, oils, fillers, waxes and pigments were used in 18th- and early-19th-century furniture finishes.

It is equally difficult to say who did the finishing in 18th-century American workshops. I haven't found a single reference to finishers in any of the hundreds of account books I have examined. Finishing was not a specialized trade in the U.S. as it was in Britain, though there were one or two well-known specialists in large cities, like Thomas Johnson in Boston, who did Japanning, graining, marbleizing and gilding. Fancy painting, as on the Baltimore chair, was done by fine-art painters. It seems probable that cabinetmakers, particularly in small shops, did their own finishing, aided by various guide books and formularies.

I have spent the past five years negotiating these obstacles, comparing and analyzing some 5,000 documents, reformulating many of the recipes for stains, dyes and finishes, and applying them using original methods to see how they work and to watch how they age. I have placed more emphasis in my research on books that were frequently reprinted. An often-reprinted book was probably a popular one with working craftsmen. The first furniture-finishing guidebook known to have been printed in America, *The Cabinetmaker's Guide*, (Greenfield, Mass., 1825), was reprinted numerous times, and parts were pirated for other books throughout the 19th century. The *Guide* was pocket-sized, easy to use. I have two copies, from 1827 and 1837; both are dog-eared, paint-splattered and muddied—signs of a well-used book.

I have formed some broad conclusions from my research; several of these have surprised me. I started out wanting to prove that shellac and French polishing were widely used during the 18th century. Instead, I discovered that French polish was not invented until about 1810, and that oil and wax were the predominant finishes of the period, favored even on many high-style pieces. And I found that the finish that left the shop was not mellow and glowing, but probably brilliantly colored, bright and shiny.

Stains, dyes, oils and waxes will be discussed here, limited to the period 1700 to 1830. Before that time, references are too scattered to be of use and, after 1830, mass production, chemical advances and burgeoning world trade profoundly changed furniture finishing. (I discuss the varnishes of the 18th and 19th centuries on pages 28-31).

Surface preparation—The quality of the piece determined how much surface preparation it received. No elaborate smoothing practices were used on common pieces, and many table tops clearly display the corrugations left by hand planes. Finer furniture required more careful preparation. Andre Jacques Roubo's three-volume treatise, *The Art of the Woodworker* (Paris: 1769-74) suggests this elaborate sequence for veneered and marquetry pieces: smoothing planes followed by a variety of hooked cabinet scrapers, a hard rub with bundles of rushes (shave- or saw-grass), abrasion with solid pumice-stone blocks lubricated with water, further abrasion with sealskin, and finally, burnishing with slightly rounded blocks of hardwood.

The Cabinetmaker's Guide recommends glass-papering the surface after careful scraping. The author complains that glass-paper was being cheapened by adding sand, then gives his own instructions: pulverize broken window glass in an iron mortar, put it through sieves of appropriate fineness, and sift onto the glue-covered surface of heavy cartridge-paper.

Early in the 19th century, many recipes appeared using plaster of Paris, "hartshorn," and other natural clay-like materials to fill open grain before finishing. These could be dyed or stained and were mixed with a binder such as linseed oil or honey. Such fillers were previously used only on Japanned and gilded pieces where intensely pigmented varnish-paints were laid over a thick filler-ground. If clear finishes were applied over plaster-type fillers, the stain would eventually fade, and the filler would appear as unsightly white speckles.

In an earlier grain-filling method, the surface was covered with a thin coating of linseed oil and then abraded with a flat block of solid pumice stone. With enough pressure the resulting paste of oil and fine wood dust would at least partially fill the grain. After dyeing, the excess was wiped or scraped off.

Coloring—Craftsmen of the 18th century experimented with a vast range of materials for coloring wood and wood finishes. Documents of the period complain that colors "flee with the light," and the search for permanent natural pigments and dyes, not only for wood but also for fabrics and paints, spawned an entire industry and vast "scientific" research. The American colonies were a major source of colorants, such as logwood, indigo, oak bark and walnut bark, all of which were exported in quantities of hundreds of tons.

Craftsmen then used the terms "stain" and "dye" as imprecisely as craftsmen today. We define "stain" as a thin layer of colored pigment lightly penetrating the surface of the wood. "Dye" is any substance producing color changes by chemical reaction with the wood fiber or by diffusion of the colored dye-stuff deep into the cellular structure of the wood. Most 18th-century stains and dyes would have colored the wood in several ways at once. Stains with strongly acidic vehicles, like uric acid, or stains containing material like iron filings, would have colored by chemical reaction as well as by pigments contained in the stain. Likewise, many dyes contained pigments, which lodged in the wood fibers.

The Cabinetmaker's Guide distinguishes stain from dye by degrees of penetration: "Staining differs from the process of dyeing, inasmuch as it merely penetrates just below the surface of the wood, instead of coloring its substance throughout, as it does in dyeing; and the one is used for beautifying the face after the work is finished, while the other is employed on the wood before it is manufactured, in the state of veneers, to be cut into strings or bands...for inlaying borders...and which has of late years got much out of use, principally owing to the fault so much complained of, of the colors flying...."

Nearly all the stains and dyes of the period were extremely fugitive by modern standards. Some would not have lasted more than a few years. Often a museum piece displays only the faded glory of the finisher's art. Red and yellow colorants, frequently used, faded quickly. Brown stains, mixed with reds, greens and blacks, soon faded to the faint green tint we see today on some antiques. I have found bright red areas preserved beneath the brasses of mahogany pieces, a far cry from the brown, red-brown or yellow-brown stains used for period reproductions. Some of my reformulations of original mahogany stain recipes come close to this brisk hue.

There is strong documentary evidence that staining of furniture before finishing was much less common in the 18th century than we assume. Thomas Sheraton, in his 1803 *Cabinet Dictionary*, wrote, "The art of staining wood was more in use at the time when inlaying was in fashion;...at present red and black stains are those in general use." It is also possible that staining was more common in America than in England, but the documents I've examined from throughout the colonies infrequently mention staining and staining materials. Rural cabinetmakers may have used stains more often than their city cousins. Rural clients couldn't afford the finely figured woods or expensive mahogany favored in high-style Boston or Philadelphia work. So cabinetmakers imitated exotic woods by graining, mahoganizing and staining, or emphasized the wild grain of a favorite wood, like tiger maple.

Nearly all colorant formulas were based on water or alcohol. These have great clarity and penetration, and deeply accentuate the structure and figure of wood. The rather muddy oil-based-pigment stains common in today's hardware stores were unknown in the 18th-century finishing shop. Likewise, only a very few period stains resemble the modern class of chemical stains, in which colorants or acids in the wood react with chemical counterparts in the staining solution.

More than one hundred different materials were used in the 18th century in the making of stains and dyes. These range from the exotic to the mundane—like old files or walnut husks in solutions containing vinegar, urine or wine. *The Cabinetmaker's Guide* calls for chipped logwood, a source of a valuable red-black dye, verdigris (copper acetate), copperas (iron sulphate), and barberry root among other ingredients for dyes. Stains might require archil, a Canary Island lichen, or dragon's blood, a resin from the fruit of the East Asian rattan palm. A red stain was made from brazilwood extract soaked in quicklime slaked in urine and painted hot onto the wood. If the customer only knew!

Attempting to give more brilliant lightfast colors, many of the recipes used such strong vehicles as sulphuric, muriatic or uric acids. Unfortunately these acids contributed to the decomposition of varnishes applied over the stains. The resins and oils used in the 18th-century varnishes were very sensitive to acids and alkalies, and may be rapidly degraded in reaction with these. This helps account for the survival of so few original varnish finishes.

Besides staining and dyeing the wood directly, finishers also colored the spirit varnishes they applied to the wood. Used to match the colors of diverse woods or to improve drab wood, they were called "changeing varnish," and were colored with various unusual substances as well as with wood chips and bark of oak, chestnut, walnut or sumac. Similar mixtures applied to tinware, brassware or furniture brasses were called "lackers." Shellac was the dominant resin in these "lackers," its reddish or golden color heightening the golden effect desired from brass. Shellac is a spirit-soluble resin that polymerizes significantly, the process speeded by heat. Shellac-based "lackers" were often baked onto metals, giving a very hard, lustrous surface, resistant to oxidation, discoloration, and the formation of copper acetates. Original furniture brasses were probably bright and "brassy," not at all tarnished like those favored on today's reproductions.

Finishes—Once the wood surfaces were leveled, smoothed, filled and stained, one of several types of coatings was applied. These fall within four broad categories: oil finishes, wax finishes, varnishes, and combinations of these.

Eighteenth-century writers on finishes list a whole array of criteria for the ideal finish: preservation of the wood from decay and insects, preservation of the color of the wood, and exclusion of atmospheric moisture. It should also be hard, shining, transparent and flexible, should not yellow or crack with age or turn white with spills, and it should hold up to hard use. The same qualities are sought by coatings manufacturers today, and no finish, then or now, fills the whole bill. Finishers experimented with an amazing range of materials in the 18th century, and some of their solutions were excellent. Indeed, some are still used today.

Since ancient times, craftsmen have known that various animal, vegetable and seed oils help to preserve wood. A wide selection of these was offered for sale by American merchants and manufacturers in the 18th century. Linseed (flaxseed) oil, the vehicle for most housepaints, was by far the most frequently used furniture-finishing material. Poppyseed and walnut oils were preferred for their light color and transparency, but they were expensive. Since the men who finished furniture were also gilding picture frames, Japanning tea waiters and painting houses and carriages, it is not surprising that, where possible, they used the same materials throughout their work.

Linseed oil finishes were widely used—despite their disadvantages: they were not durable, waterproof or alcoholproof, and they darkened with age, though they were repaired easily with fresh oil and some rubbing. Free from tariffs imposed by the English, both boiled and raw linseed oil were cheap and widely available. In lists of hundreds of furniture types, several influential English and American trade price-books quote prices only for oil finishing and polishing.

Pressed cold, linseed oil has a very light color; pressed hot, it is more plentiful, but considerably darker. To bleach out this color, fresh-drawn linseed oil was placed in shallow pans or bottles in the sunlight. Alternatively, the solid impurities were precipitated by adding fuller's earth (a naturally occurring aluminum silicate) which absorbed the brownish coloring matter. Egg-white was sometimes added as a purifier.

Linseed oil dries very slowly on its own. Coatings of raw oil may remain tacky for years. Over centuries, many methods had been tried to make it more siccative, or fast drying. In the late Middle Ages, the oil was merely boiled. Later, burnt horn and bone, garlic, powdered lead-crystal glass, or alum were added to the boiling oil to try to enhance its drying properties. Most recipes of the 18th century employed lead com-

French polishing with wax

Andre Jacques Roubo's *The Art of the Woodworker* was published in Paris between 1769 and 1774. Although it's out of print this excellent book is available in French at major libraries. Roubo, a master craftsman, set down detailed accounts of carpentry, carriagemaking and furnituremaking, illustrated with hundreds of engravings. This plate shows the methods, materials and tools used in finishing the finest veneered furniture, called *ébénisterie*.

Figures 1 and 2: Preparing the surface. A finely set toothing plane worked diagonally across the grain as indicated by the lines would not disturb the veneer fibers or joints. Planing as in *figure 2* is cautioned against because it will probably break the joint.

Figures 3, 4 and 5: Scrapers, shown here, followed the planes, worked in the same fashion or as indicated in *figures 14 and 15*.

Figure 6: Sharkskin, or "dogfish" skin, was used as an abrasive. For fine veneered work, the fins or "ears of dogfish skin" were recommended, also worked across the grain.

Figure 7: After planing and scraping, abrading with sharkskin or *prêle* (horsetail, a species of rush with corrugated stems) polished away the remaining fine scratches on the veneer.

Figures 8 and 9: The polisher, a bundle of ordinary rush, was bound tightly, dipped in hot wax which rose into the stems, allowed to cool and rubbed over the veneer.

Figures 10, 11 and 12: Polishing sticks, small strips of walnut or other finely grained wood, were shaped to various sizes and used to push wax into areas too small for the polisher or on moldings with delicate arrises.

Figure 13: A finisher forces wax into the grain of a veneered panel with the rush polisher. —R.D.M.

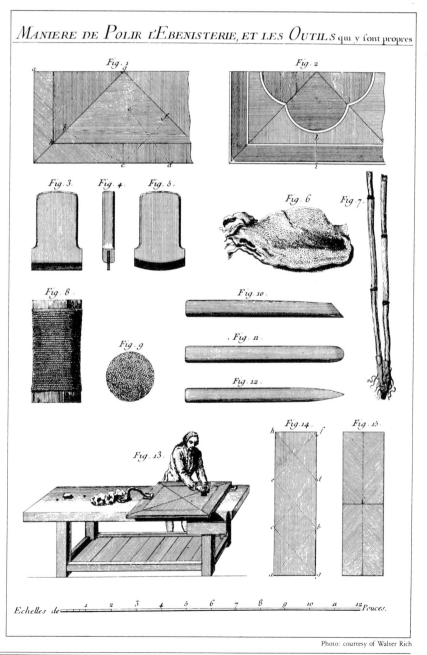

MANIERE DE POLIR L'EBENISTERIE, ET LES OUTILS qui y font propres

pounds as siccatives: litharge, massicot or minium, all lead oxides long used as artists' pigments. Once boiled, filtered, cooled and bleached, the oil was ready for use. The boiling and purification of linseed oil provided considerable income for many painters and varnishers in New England, but the occupation carried with it the danger of fire. Fire and lead poisoning were the bane of the finisher.

Oil finishing was as simple then as it is today. The oil was applied with a rag or brush, full strength or thinned with turpentine, and allowed to soak into the wood. The excess was wiped off with a coarse rag. After a day's drying time, another coat was applied, and ideally this was repeated until the wood would accept no more oil. In practice, a few superficial coats were probably all that were used. Total oil-finishing time for a desk may have amounted to only two to four hours. Prices for oil polishing formed a small proportion of the total costs recorded for making a piece.

Basic oiling practices varied. Sheraton, in his *Cabinet Dictionary*, outlines a method using brick dust and linseed oil, plain or stained red with alkanet root. Brick dust and oil formed a slightly abrasive paste which was rubbed on the surface until the wood warmed, then cleared off with wheat bran, leaving a bright surface. For off-color mahogany, or better grade mahogany that "wants briskness of color," Sheraton recommends a reddish polishing oil including alkanet root, dragon's blood, and rose pink, a pigment made with brazilwood dye.

I was surprised to find that wax finishes were also among those commonly used by 18th-century cabinetmakers. Wax, like oil, was cheap, available and easy to use. It was frequently listed in account books and mentioned in the literature of the period.

Other natural waxes were known, but beeswax had been favored for centuries as a finish on wood, a medium for paint, a waterproof stopping for boats, an embalming resin, and a flatting agent and final moisture barrier for varnishes. It is probably the natural organic finish most resistant to destructive oxidation. A modern analysis of beeswax used on a Punic warship showed that the wax remained chemically unchanged after 2,000 years. This extreme longevity was noted repeatedly by 18th-century writers on finishes. Beeswax was produced in large quantities in New England, where bee culture was a highly developed art. Samuel Grant, a prominent Boston upholsterer and merchant, bought up to 450 lb. at a time for use in his own shop, for sale to other cabinetmakers and for export to England.

The purification of wax by extraction of the honey impurities with water was cheap and simple, and two forms of purified wax, yellow and white, were known. The yellow still contained some impurities and was less expensive. The white, or clear beeswax, carefully filtered and bleached in the sun, was preferred for the finest work.

Thomas Sheraton describes two methods of wax polishing he says are typical. "Sometimes they polish with bees wax and a cork for inside work. . . . The cork is rubbed hard on the wax to spread it over the wood, and then they take fine brick-dust and sift it through a stocking on the wood, and with a cloth the dust is rubbed till it clears away all the clammings. . . . At other times they polish with soft wax, which is a mixture of turpentine and beeswax, which renders it soft, . . . a cloth of itself, will be sufficient to rub it off with."

For chair polish, Sheraton mixed wax with a small quantity

of turpentine, heated this in a varnish pan (a double boiler), added Oxford ochre for color and a little copal varnish. The cooled mixture was worked into a ball and applied with a stiff brush, forced into the grain, and then rubbed off.

Wax finishes were widely used on high-style 18th-century French furniture. The only complete description of this process that I have found is in Roubo's *The Art of the Woodworker.* For veneered cabinetwork, finest quality wax was melted into a polisher, which was a bundle of rags bound tightly with wire, and with which the whole surface was then rubbed. The heat generated melted the wax, and the rubbing forced it into the pores. Roubo cautions against using cork polishers, which can get too warm and loosen the veneer.

When the wax was evenly spread, the excess was scraped off. Roubo's wax scraper was similar to a cabinet scraper, but with a slightly rounded edge instead of a burr. Cleaned and polished with a rag, the work was "extremely even, and glossy as a mirror." For porous or reddish woods like rosewood or amaranth, powdered shellac was spread over the wax and rubbed in vigorously with the polisher to fill the open grain and heighten the color. Colophony (rosin) was used to stop up open grain in black woods like ebony.

A high-gloss finish was typical of nearly all high-style furniture finishes of the 18th century. Experimenting with Roubo's wax finish, I found that it gives a much higher gloss than we associate with wax finishes today. Roubo built up a wax finish in the same way as a varnish finish, and the wax became a fairly thick coherent body on top of the wood. And he used only 100% pure beeswax, which has better refracting qualities than today's wax emulsions.

Roubo prescribes a different process for common furniture: the wax was mixed with one-third tallow and rubbed off with a serge cloth. "In order to spread the wax better and drive it deeper into the open pores, one uses sometimes a sheet-metal pan in which glowing coals have been put, and this is held as close as possible to the work in order to warm the wax. In place of the pan one can also use a glowing red-hot piece of iron, which is even better, because it makes the wax liquid which flows into the open pores more easily."

Though it was possible to get a high gloss finish with wax, most finishers probably found the required method too time-consuming. Wax also has many of the same disadvantages as oil finishes. An 18th-century writer summarized the advantages and disadvantages of the common wax finish, noting: "Waxing stands shock; but it does not possess, in the same degree as varnish, the property of giving lustre. . . and of heightening their tints. The lustre it communicates is dull, but this inconvenience is compensated by the facility with which any accident that may have altered its polish can be repaired, by rubbing it with a piece of fine cork."

Easy to obtain, fast and easy to use and repair, oil and wax finishes were ideally suited for 18th-century finishing needs. Though pure beeswax finishes are rarely used today, the many virtues of oil finishes, particularly their low sheen, are once again appreciated and have made them a finish of choice, as they were 250 years ago. □

Robert Mussey, of Milton, Mass., trained as a cabinetmaker and wood finisher then served an internship in furniture conservation at the Henry Ford Museum. He is head of the furniture conservation workshop at the Society for Preservation of New England Antiquities in Boston, Mass.

Stains and dyes from *The Cabinetmaker's Guide*

I reformulate original stain and dye recipes to determine what the original colors were like. But I use alcohol soluble anilines for restoration or conservation work because they dry quickly, don't penetrate as deeply or rapidly as water soluble anilines, and because they are reasonably lightfast—I want my conservation to last more than ten years.

One of the first principles of conservation is to make any repair reversible, so it can be redone if a better technique is discovered. Original colors are dramatic, and not yet completely accepted for conservation, so when I color a piece I put down a barrier coat first, then color the finish that goes over it. The stain has not soaked into the wood so the coloring is reversible. On new work, the choice of color is my own; furniture makers have much more freedom than conservators. I think original colors will become acceptable for furniture conservation, used where appropriate to show people what the maker saw when he had completed the piece.

These recipes are from *The Cabinetmaker's Guide:*

The Cabinetmaker's Guide, *possibly the first finishing guidebook printed in America, was a workshop standby throughout the 19th century. It hasn't been reprinted recently but may be available in major libraries. Note the worker polishing a tabletop by the fire, which is a good way to keep the wax flowing freely.*

Red dye. Take 2 pounds of genuine brazildust, add four gallons of water, put in as many veneers as the liquid will cover, boil them for 3 hours; then add 2 ounces of alum, and 2 ounces of aquafortis, and keep it lukewarm until it has struck through.

Brazildust; dust of brazilwood, *Caesalpinia echinata,* gives a very bright red dye. It was such an important item of commerce that the country was named after the tree. Aquafortis is nitric acid, reagent grade concentration.

Fine blue. Take a pound of oil of vitriol in a clean glass phial into which put four oz. of indigo, and proceed as before directed in dyeing.

This dye, and others for similarly unusual colors, would have been used for marquetry or by musical-instrument makers. Oil of vitriol is sulphuric acid.

To stain beech a mahogany color take 2 ounces of dragon's blood, break it into pieces and put it into a quart of rectified spirits of wine; let the bottle stand in a warm place, shake it frequently, and when dissolved it is fit for use.

Dragon's blood has been used for centuries. It is a dark red resinous exudation from the fruit of the rattan palm, *Calamus drago.* Spirits of wine is alcohol distilled from wine; rectified means purified. Ethyl alcohol or shellac thinner from a paint store is the same thing. My reformulation of this stain came out a very bright red. Dragon's blood, when compared to other reds, is fairly lightfast. If you stain the wood directly, it is fugitive; but if you dye shellac with it, it is much less so, because the shellac locks the color in.

Another method for black stain. Take one pound of logwood, boil it in two quarts of water, add a double handful of walnut peeling. Boil it up again, take out chips, add a pint of the best vinegar and it will be fit for use; apply it boiling hot. Note—This will be much improved if, after it is dry, we take a solution of green copperas dissolved in water, in the proportion of an ounce to a quart, and apply it hot to the above.

Logwood was an important dyestuff from *Haematoxylum campechianum,* a tree found in Central America and the West Indies. It gives a range of colors from red to purple to black and was used as dust, shavings or chips.

I have obtained materials for these and other recipes from the following firms: H. Behlen and Bros., Rt. 30 N., Amsterdam, N.Y. 12010; Laurence McFadden Co., 7430 State Rd., Philadelphia, Pa. 19136; A.F. Suter and Co. Ltd., Swan Wharf, 60 Dace Road, Bow, London E3, England; James B. Day Co., Day Lane, Carpentersville, Ill. 60110.

For further information: *The Artist's Handbook of Materials and Techniques,* Ralph Mayer, Viking, New York, rev. ed., 1982. *Painting Materials, A short encyclopedia,* Rutherford Gettens and George Stout, Dover, 1966. —*R.D.M.*

Early Varnishes

The 18th century's search for the perfect film finish

by Robert D. Mussey

The 18th-century finisher looking for a durable, high-gloss surface had only a few choices. He could, and usually did, finish with a wax or an oil (see preceding article). Varnish, however, offered greater protection from moisture and wear, and produced a more lustrous shine than all but the most elaborate oil or wax preparations. Today, when we want to use varnish, we can go to any paint store and select from numerous scientifically formulated brands. But in the 18th century, varnishmaking was an imperfect science at best. Achieving a smooth, glossy surface demanded great skill and patience from the finisher.

Varnishes are solvent solutions of resins and gums that dry to form a thin, tough and glossy film on the surface of the wood. In the 18th and early 19th centuries, alcohol and various vegetable oils were the common solvents. Natural gums, which are soft, water-soluble plant fluids, were used only in small quantities as plasticizers. Natural resins, exuded by a vast range of living plants and several kinds of insects, or mined from fossilized vegetable remains, were the most important varnish constituents. They are soluble in oil, alcohol or other organic solvents and vary in hardness. Today most of these natural resins have been replaced in varnishes by chemically synthesized resins or modified natural resins.

Resins, essential to America's growing shipbuilding industry, were readily available to the varnishmaker, more so in urban than in rural areas. When varnishes had a high concentration of hard resin to solvent, they produced a hard, brittle film that could be abraded glass-smooth and polished to a mirror shine. A high proportion of drying oil to certain resins produced an elastic, durable, virtually waterproof film. Each resin had its own advantages. Sandarac was almost perfectly clear and transparent, easy to dissolve. Copal was very tough. Colophony (a type of rosin) gave a high gloss. Tremendous research focused on the varnishmaking industry, hampered by the imperfect understanding of chemical principles and the relatively small number of appropriate resins. During the 150 years prior to 1800, the same 15 or so resins appear in endless combinations in varnish formulas—in the search for a magic elixir that would possess all the advantages, but none of the disadvantages, of the individual resins.

This complex, kitchen-recipe approach to varnishmaking was opposed, however, by a famous Parisian varnishmaker named Watin. He held that, "The real secret of the artist is the simplicity of his procedures.... The art should be like Nature when possible, to do the greatest with the least, without complication, without effort." And so, after 40 years of effort, Watin announced in 1776 that he had developed the "perfect" varnish. Of course, he kept its exact formula secret.

These two approaches, the complex and the simple, and a spectrum in between, can be found in the thousands of varnish recipes of the 18th and 19th centuries. It is difficult to form simple conclusions about these recipes. I have looked at

18th-century varnish resins

Here is a list of common alcohol-soluble resins used in 18th- and 19th-century varnishes. It is possible to buy some of these in small quantities, although resins other than shellac can be expensive. H. Behlen and Bros. (Rt. 30N, Amsterdam, N.Y. 12010; write for local dealer) carries copal and a range of shellacs. A.F. Suter and Co. (Swan Wharf, 60 Dace Rd., Bow, London E3, Eng.) stocks most of these resins.

Benzoin: Often called "benjamin," benzoin is derived from the tree *Styrax benzoin,* of Borneo and Sumatra. Used in many 16th- and 17th-century spirit varnishes, it was later added as a plasticizer, or for its pleasant smell. Today it is used as a final glaze over French polish, to impart gloss.

Turpentine: Called "rosin" in Colonial America, turpentine is the resin obtained from the gum (sap) of fir, balsam, pine, larch, spruce, or other conifers. It was used in inferior spirit varnishes in several forms, including chio turpentine from Mediterranean pines, Strasburgh turpentine from the German fir tree *Abies excelsa,* venice turpentine from the European larch tree, and rosin (also called colophony), the resin of various species of American pine tree.

Sandarac: From the North African conifer *Calitris quadrivalvis,* this brittle resin was often called gum juniper.

Elemi: Also called allemy, any of a large number of resins from the *Burseraceae* family of trees. A softer resin, it was added to varnishes for toughness and flexibility.

Mastic: This soft resin makes a perfectly clear varnish. It is exuded by the Mediterranean tree *Pistacia lentiscus.*

Copal: A tremendous variety of resins, some hard, some soft, are called copal. The hard copals, African, and probably of fossil origin, were highly valued, and insoluble in alcohol. A widely used soft copal, largely soluble in alcohol, was derived from the common American sumac *Rhus copallinum.*

Anime: No one seems to know what resin this actually was. Possibly it was a spirit-soluble soft copal and may have come from the Zanzibar tree *Trachylobium mossambicense.*

Shellac: The best known of the three resins exuded by insects, shellac is deposited on branches and twigs by the insect *Coccus lacca,* which feeds on the sap of the tree. The natural grades are reddish, the finer grades are bleached white and used to produce a hard but flexible spirit varnish.   —R.D.M.

From *Fine Woodworking* magazine (July 1982) 35:54-57

many, in six European languages; each language has its own tangled, inconsistent set of terms and nomenclature. Writers had considerable difficulty differentiating resins. When a recipe called for copal, it could have meant any of 40 different materials, depending on the country of origin, the country of use and the date. Moreover, varnishmaking and finishing practices in Europe and America differed, as did those between urban and rural areas within America. And early varnishmakers may well have deviated from the published recipes. Varnishmakers were competitive and secretive; many of the finest formulas probably never were published. "Almost every varnisher," observed one 18th-century writer, "has at least one or two compositions peculiar to himself, the superior value of which rests chiefly in his own opinion."

Even when the varnishmaker worked his best magic, many obstacles loomed between the finisher and the perfect finish—temperature, dust, moisture, and numerous complicated surface preparations and polishing techniques. The best of the 18th- and 19th-century finishers, driven by necessity and fashion, mastered all these problems. The evidence of their skill remains today in carefully preserved museum pieces.

There are three broad groupings of 18th- and 19th-century varnishes: spirit, essential-oil and fixed-oil. Each is named for the vehicle used to dissolve its resins and gums. Spirit varnishes have alcohol or other volatile vehicles that evaporate, leaving a film of dried resin. Essential-oil varnishes use fluids distilled from one of several natural resins or oils; today we would consider them another type of spirit varnish. Fixed-oil varnishes are solutions of resins and gums in a drying oil, such as linseed, poppyseed or walnut. These varnishes dry by chemical change as well as by solvent evaporation, and they leave a more complex film, a combination of resins and oxidized oils. Resins dissolved partly in a drying oil and partly in alcohol constitute varnishes of a fourth and minor class that was used infrequently and will not be discussed.

Spirit varnishes

The cheapest and easiest varnish to make is the spirit-solvent variety. Because spirit solvents evaporate rapidly, a considerable body of varnish in numerous thin coats could be built up in a short time. And they could have great clarity, or "whiteness," because the dissolution usually did not require heat, and so avoided darkening the resins. On the other hand, spirit varnishes were brittle, cracked easily, were readily spoiled by alcohol or water spills, and were not as easy to polish as drying-oil resin varnishes. They required careful formulation and skillful polishing to get a high gloss.

"Spirits of wine," as alcohol was then called, was the usual solvent for 18th-century spirit varnishes. The production and trading of rum, brandy and other alcohols was an essential part of the New England economy. Cabinetmakers' account books are littered with records of "spirits" purchases, though it is unclear how much of it was used in varnish.

Most 18th-century solvent alcohol was quite impure, as much as half water. It was usually distilled from wine, and frequently from brandy. Some recipes even recommend extremely strong brandy itself as the solvent. Several methods were used to purify these spirits. Repeated distillation in a glass double-boiler called a *bain-marie* was the usual method. This process, also called rectification, could produce a very pure alcohol. Adding potassium carbonate (salts of tartar) or potash to alcohol, a process called tartarization, also absorbed some of the water and strengthened the solvent.

Several tests to "prove the truth" of the spirits were recommended by various guidebooks. One book suggests half-filling a spoon with gunpowder, covering it with the alcohol, then lighting it afire. Pure alcohol would burn off and the powder would ignite; if the powder had absorbed too much water from the alcohol, it would not. The fanciest, and safest, method was the hydrometer—I've found them advertised in several Philadelphia papers of the late 18th century.

Making spirit varnishes

Only the very lightest, clearest, "whitest" resin lumps, free from dross, sticks and impurities,

Hot sand

Varnish pan

From the second edition (1851) of *The Painter, Gilder, and Varnisher's Companion* comes this description of a varnish pan (drawing is speculative) used by finishers throughout the 18th and 19th centuries: "The best vessel for holding your varnish while using it, is a varnish pan....It is made of tin, with a false bottom; the interval between the two bottoms is filled with sand, which, being heated over the fire, keeps the varnish fluid, and makes it flow more readily from the brush....a false bottom comes sloping from one end to the other, which causes the varnish to run to one end."

were recommended. Inferior resin must have been common, and the formularies cite many methods for telling real from false. Of all the resins, sandarac was the most common and most highly regarded. Once the best resin pieces were selected, they were powdered or granulated in a mortar, or pounded in a cloth bag, then submerged in a glass bottle or jar of alcohol. The resins dissolved easily in cold alcohol if the jar was agitated occasionally or placed in sunlight. When the liquid had settled, its top layers were poured off and filtered—this filtrate was the final spirit varnish.

Instead of being filtered, to achieve dissolution the spirit-resin mixture could also be warmed. This was done in a sandbath varnish pan, a sort of tin double-boiler. The sand below the bath's false bottom kept the bottle from direct contact with the fire. It was a dangerous process, and explosion and fire were the varnishmaker's greatest enemies. If the resins were heated too much, the varnish darkened. The lightest, most transparent varnishes were the ultimate goal.

Shellac

Restorers and furniture historians have long assumed that shellac was the main resin used in varnishes of 18th-century America. All the evidence from my research directly contradicts this assumption. For centuries shellac had been the primary source of the valuable red coloring matter called lac dye. It was rarely used in 18th-century America. It was relatively expensive, and the resultant dark varnish obscured all but the darkest woods. The reddish dye could be only partially extracted from the resin, and it was not until the late 18th century that chemical bleaches enabled the production of colorless shellac resin. Modern shellac is actually a spirit varnish consisting of shellac resin dissolved in alcohol.

Until about 1820, spirit varnishes were applied only with a brush, and were usually thinned considerably and warmed to make them flow out and dry rapidly. The method of rubbing on spirit varnishes that is called French polishing was first mentioned, as far as I know, in the 1818 London edition of *The Cabinetmaker's Guide,* where it was compared favorably with beeswax. The *Guide* gives seven formulas for spirit varnishes that may be French polished, none of which calls exclusively for shellac resin. One of them, called "The True French Polish," includes one pint of spirits of wine, a quarter-ounce of gum copal, a quarter-ounce of gum arabic, and one ounce of shellac. This influential recipe is repeated exactly in over 30 formularies dating up to the 1920s, and several museum restorers have recently begun to use a French polish based on it. The method the *Guide* describes for ap-

plying this French polish is nearly identical to that used today (see article, pp. 72-74). Open-grained woods were sized with glue and lightly sanded. The polisher, a wad of coarse flannel wrapped in a fine, soft linen rag, was dampened with the polish and rubbed onto the work with a circular motion, covering about one square-foot at a time. The whole surface was rubbed until the rag appeared dry, then the process was repeated three or four times, producing, the *Guide* says, "a very beautiful and lasting polish." A final polish of half a pint of best rectified spirits of wine, two drams of shellac and two drams of gum benzoin was recommended.

Fixed-oil varnishes—With the English publication in 1776 of the "Genuine Receipt for Making the Famous Vernis Martin," British and, eventually, American workers finally possessed the recipe for the most famous Continental varnish (see box at left). For 150 years Europeans had sought to imitate the finest examples of Oriental lacquerware. Craftsmen of each country touted their "Chinese" or "Japanese" or "Turkish" varnishes, raving about the brilliant colors, high gloss and durability. Although Europeans could not get the actual resin of Oriental lacquer (which was obtained from the shrub *Rhus vernicifera*), that didn't stop them from trying every available alternative. The Martin family of Paris, eight makers of lacquer and varnish spanning two generations, produced varnishes that were said to achieve unparalleled brilliance, clarity and durability, in addition to being waterproof and crack-free. The Martins had overcome, or so it was claimed, all the disadvantages of oil, wax and spirit-varnish finishes. The Martins' ingredients and laborious procedures represented the peak of the varnishmakers' art, but they became typical of most such hard-resin, fixed-oil varnishes of the 18th century.

Fixed-oil varnishes employed a drying oil (linseed, poppyseed or walnut) in which one or more oil-soluble resins were dissolved. Suitable resins included copal, amber, rosin, dammar and anime. Copal and amber, vegetable resins of both fossil and recent origin, were the hardest resins known, and also the most difficult to dissolve. By liquefying, "running," the resins at high temperatures (300°F to 400°F), they would, on cooling, become soluble in hot oil. This process is described in the recipe for the Martin copal varnish. A second method employed tartarization or a similar process. Here, various strong alkalis (tartar salts, lye, potash or ammonia solutions) broke down the resin chemically, by alkaline hydrolysis, then it was dissolved in hot oil. A third method, involving infusions of water, alcohol or ether, extracted some of the resin constituents that were insoluble in oil.

Ironically, both heating and tartarization probably contributed significantly to the rather rapid deterioration of these hard-resin varnishes. Both the extreme heat needed to run the oil and the chemistry of tartarization accelerated destructive oxidation. The widespread use of both processes makes it unlikely that any of these hard-resin amber-copal varnishes remain on antique woodwork today.

Copal and amber varnishes were valued for four reasons. They were extremely clear and colorless when first applied. They far surpassed the spirit varnishes in hardness and durability. They could be rubbed to a very high polish. And they were waterproof—made with a large proportion of drying oil, they would hold up outdoors better than any other varnish then known. Because of the difficulty and expense of making

GENUINE RECEIPT
FOR MAKING THE FAMOUS
VERNIS MARTIN

After the melting pot is warmed, we pour into it four ounces of chio or cyprus turpentine; we let it dissolve till it is fluid, then pour to that eight ounces of amber finely bruised and sifted; mixing it well with the fluid turpentine, and then we set it on the fire for a quarter of an hour. After that time, we take off the pot, and gently pour into it a pound of copal bruised fine, but not to a powder; these we stir well together, and to these we add four ounces more of the chio turpentine just mentioned, and a gill [4 fl. oz.] of warm turpentine oil; set it again on the fire, blowing it rather more briskly.

When it hath stood on the fire about half an hour, we take it off, uncover the pot, and stir the whole well together, adding as we stir, two ounces of the finest and whitest colophony. We then set it again on the fire, blowing more briskly than before, and let it remain till the whole is dissolved and fluid as water. This done we take off the pot, remove it...and let it stand a few minutes....Having now twenty-four ounces of poppy, nut or linseed oil, made drying, ready at hand, we pour it into the dissolved gums, by degrees, boiling hot...and stir the whole well together with a long stick....When we have thoroughly incorporated the fluid gum and oil, we set them over the fire a few minutes till the whole boils once up, then we take it off, carry it to some distance, and pour into it a quart of turpentine made hot over the second fire. All these we stir well together, and give them one boil up, then take it off again, and again pour into it a pint more of turpentine made hot....

If the gums are thoroughly melted, and have incorporated well, the varnish is made.

This recipe, like others of the period, uses the terms gum and resin almost interchangeably. No true gums are used here, and they appear only in small quantities, as plasticizers, in other recipes. It goes almost without saying that the process as described here was extremely dangerous.

such varnishes, even the finest finishers often bought them ready-made. Copal varnish was probably the most common hard-resin, fixed-oil varnish in 18th-century America.

A number of softer resins could be dissolved in drying oils to make a second type of fixed-oil varnish, called "common brown varnish." Boiled linseed oil was the usual vehicle and solvent, and rosin in one of its various forms was the common resin. Colophony, venice turpentine, Strasburgh turpentine or plain turpentine was mixed in the drying oil at a low temperature. Various resins were then combined in the mixture, in an attempt to borrow the best quality of each. It was not durable, did not stand up to water, and had a dark color. But it was cheap, easy to get and simple to make. Despite the widespread use, it is unlikely that many original soft-resin varnish finishes remain.

Essential-oil varnishes—In the 18th century it was believed that oils or fluids derived by distilling resins were the essential volatile oils of those resins. Oil of rosemary and "spirits of turpentine" (derived by distilling conifer sap) were in this category. Today we know that the latter is a complex organic solvent with some resin impurities, and we would classify varnishes made with it as spirit varnishes. These solvents dry strictly by evaporation, not by the complex oxidation reaction of resin and drying oil or by polymerization and cross-linking of resin molecules into molecular networks.

Essential-oil varnishes were soft and not durable, and were recommended only when the varnish had to be periodically removed, as on fine paintings. Inferior furniture might have been finished with these varnishes. I have found a number of references in account books to "turpentining" a table or a wheel. Turpentining probably refers to the application of raw conifer sap as a preservative, but it may also mean a cheap varnish made with spirits of turpentine as the solvent and rosin as the resin. It is unlikely that any of these varnishes remain on surviving furniture.

Varnish polishing—The "Genuine Receipt for Making the Famous Vernis Martin" describes how to apply and polish it. The process is laborious and the explanation takes three full pages. In summary, the procedure starts with the laying on of six coats of varnish, each allowed to dry in a warm room-size chamber heated with stoves. Then the panel is rubbed smooth with a coarse wet rag dipped in pulverized, sifted pumice stone. After the surfaces have been washed, another ten or twelve coats of varnish are laid on, each coat again "stoved." The varnish was probably quite thin, which might explain the many coats required. This built-up finish is then rubbed down with the same pumice-stone process as before. A rubbing with fine emery powder follows, "till our pannel bears a surface smooth and even as glass." The emery is dried and wiped off, and the process continues with fine rotten-stone. The final polish is achieved with a rubbing of "sweet oil" (olive oil), the excess oil cleared with fine powder or flour. Last, the panel is burnished to a high shine with fine flannel dipped in flour, giving it "a lustre as though the [panel] were under a glass . . . ."

This process is fairly typical, although the most extended I have found. Many abrasive materials were used, including sandleathers (soft, wet leather impregnated with sand or tripoli), shave grass, soft rushes, sealskin and sharkskin.

True "English polishes" (spirit varnishes made with copal

Roubo's spirit varnish

Of all spirit-varnish recipes of the 18th century, those using sandarac (from the North African alerce tree *Calitris quadrivalvis*) were the most common and the most highly regarded.

In *The Art of the Woodworker* (Paris: 1769-74), Andre Jacques Roubo offers a recipe for white (clear) varnish to be used on fine woods such as rosewood or holly, to alter their color minimally. The varnish is "composed of a pint or two pounds spirits of wine, five ounces of the palest sandarac possible, two ounces of mastic tears, one ounce of gum elemi, and one ounce oil of aspic [oil of lavender], the whole dissolved in a *bain-marie,* not allowing the alcohol to boil; when the varnish is cooled, one filters it with a width of cotton, so that it is free of any kind of dirt or filth." Roubo recommends building up a surface with up to eight thin coats.

I have reformulated several of the old recipes and found it virtually impossible to get satisfactory results when mixing up only small quantities of the ingredients. Also, making fixed-oil varnishes is dangerous. You can buy ready-made varnishes that use traditional resins from artists' supply stores. Windsor and Newton produce sandarac, elemi, mastic and copal varnishes, and possibly more. These come in small quantities, and are very expensive.   —R.D.M.

and shellac resins) of about 1815 were rubbed to a high polish, after the varnish had dried, with a cotton cloth wrapped around a wool cloth and saturated with pumice powder and linseed oil. Hartshorn (powdered animal horn) removed the oil residue. This polish was said to give the same beauty as the finest rubbed amber and copal varnishes, even if it wasn't as hard or durable.

Until the first quarter of the 19th century and the advent of French polishing, final polishing with a rag or pad moistened only in alcohol or other spirits was never mentioned in the guidebooks. Nor have I seen any reference to backing up polishing leathers, cloths or pads with any sort of flat rubbing block (cork or wood), as is the common practice today. Perhaps the extraordinarily careful preparation and smoothing of wood grounds made this less necessary than it is today.

Despite the variety of varnish-polishing techniques and materials, writers of the period agreed on one thing: the final polished surface should be "brilliant, delightful and shining and glossy as glass." None of the formulations contains anything that could be considered a flatting agent like the metallic soaps (stearates) used today. Flat, semigloss, or rubbed-effect finishes were simply not wanted in the 18th century. They suit today's taste and they can hide manufacturing defects. But, in an age when people were surrounded by rough-hewn, worn surfaces, a perfectly flat, highly lustrous surface was a mark of consummate workmanship, eagerly sought by those patrons who could afford it.   □

Robert D. Mussey is head of the furniture conservation workshop at the Society for the Preservation of New England Antiquities in Boston. For more about period varnishes, consult the published Proceedings of the Furniture and Wooden Object Symposium, *which was held in 1980, available from the Canadian Conservation Institute, 1030 Innes Road, Ottawa, Ont.*

Q & A

Cratered finish

I removed the original finish of a tabletop with Hope's Furniture Refinisher and applied a polyurethane finish, but it cratered in small spots. I removed the polyurethane finish with Formby's Paint Remover, sanded the top down to bare wood, and restained, and I applied Deft. This also cratered. —R. William Furman, Ft. Collins, Colo.

DON NEWELL REPLIES: At some time, silicone must have been applied to the tabletop—perhaps in a polish. Silicone is very tenacious stuff, and solvents and removers tend to spread it around rather than remove it. These craters, called "fisheyes," happen when silicone prevents the finish from adhering.

Wet 400-grit wet-or-dry sandpaper with mineral spirits, and sand down to bare wood. Dry the wood and wipe off all the sanding dust. If you're going to restain, do it now. Next, brush on a very thin coat of shellac, thinned three parts denatured alcohol to one part shellac. Don't build up a thick layer. Let this dry, and apply Deft normally. You should not have cratering this time. To be absolutely sure, I'd add a small amount of fisheye remover (available from Constantine, 2065 Eastchester Rd., Bronx, N.Y. 10461) to the Deft; it's an additive designed to eliminate fisheyes caused by silicone and other impurities.

Removing rings in finishes

I get numerous questions about a method for removing white rings caused by water on furniture finishes. I have listened to many "heard from" methods that I am hesitant to try or pass on. —Arthur B. Sayer, Morrison, Colo.

DON NEWELL REPLIES: Water rings on finished surfaces can be removed using gentle abrasives. Dab a paper towel into cigarette ashes and gently rub or scrub the white areas. It may take several rubbings and frequent renewal of the ashes to eliminate the rings. You could also use rottenstone in place of the ashes. It's available at most hardware stores and is about as gentle an abrasive as can be found.

My wife has a method she has been using for more than 25 years without fail. Apply a liberal coat of Vaseline petroleum jelly over the water ring and let it stand for a day. The water ring will be gone and you merely have to wipe off the Vaseline. It even works on large areas, like the footboards of teenagers' beds after they go and leave wet towels on them. —Robert J. Noeth, Arnold, Md.

Cleaning smoke discoloration

Our cabin recently burned down and, fortunately, we were able to rescue some of our furniture. However, the smoke and heat damage was extensive, and although alcohol easily removed the soot from our furniture, the wood underneath remained discolored. The pieces we are most concerned about were finished with Danish oil and the woods involved are maple, apple, mahogany and sycamore. Could you advise us? —Peg Klouda, Anaconda, Mont.

DON NEWELL REPLIES: Simple surface staining of the woods by smoke and heat is one thing but actual color changes due to finish degradation is something entirely different. I'd start with another cleanup using fine to medium steel wool wetted with mineral spirits. Dip the pad frequently in fresh solvent to rinse out what you have removed from the surface. Mineral spirits is a mild solvent that shouldn't affect what remains of the old finish: its acts as a lubricant and dirt carrier rather than as a stripper of the old Danish oil.

GEORGE FRANK REPLIES: Your real problem may not be removing surface discoloration but dealing with the wood itself being charred or scorched. If such is the case, there is no trick, magic or chemical that can bring the wood back to its original state. All charred particles must be scraped or sandpapered away, and only when a fresh surface appears can you begin your new finishing job.

JIM CUMMINS REPLIES: I've had luck removing the smoke glaze from fire-damaged picture frames only by using ammonia. If all else fails, try non-sudsing ammonia on some hidden spot. Even if it seems to work, resist doing the whole job for a few days. Wait to see how the cleaned wood accepts refinishing.

Dye or stain?

I stripped a heavily carved, late-Victorian, white oak bookcase with a methylene-chloride-based stripper. Then I washed it with water and bleached it with a warm solution of oxalic acid (4 oz. to 1 qt. of water). The wood appears to have been colored with a red stain that resists bleach. I repeated the bleaching process twice more, with no success. I also tried both Clorox bleach and a mixture of potassium permanganate and sodium thiosulfate. How can I remove this stain? —Gerard Ferretti, Brooklyn, N.Y.

GEORGE FRANK REPLIES: Your bookcase was dyed, not stained. Here's how to solve your problem. To a quart of water, add enough lye to make a strong solution. Stir in 2 oz. of wallpaper paste to thicken the solution (don't use an aluminum container, because lye ruins aluminum). Heat this mixture until it's warm, put on rubber gloves, and spread the creamy solution on the wood with a rag. Keep the wood wet for 10 to 15 minutes. Next wash off this lye solution with lots of water and a scrubbing brush, preferably with stainless-steel bristles. Let the wood dry, then bleach it with Clorox. Neutralize the Clorox with vinegar. When dry your bookcase can be dyed any color, and finished any way you wish.

Refinishing mahogany tabletop

Some time ago, I bought a Sheraton dining table that had been made in Scotland about 1800. The finish was cloudy and marred by a couple of ugly burns from hot dishes, so I undertook to strip and refinish it. Unfortunately, I found that the mahogany tabletop was impregnated with wax, which I've spent hours trying to remove with lacquer thinner and steel wool, followed by soap and water, in order to apply an oil and varnish finish. Is there a fast way to remove this wax or can it be neutralized in some way? Incidentally, some English friends examined the table, and told me they would refinish it with button polish. What's that? —C.B. Koester, Ottawa, Ont.

GEORGE FRANK REPLIES: Your method of washing off the wax finish with lacquer thinner and soapy water is excellent, yet you can improve upon it by using a nylon scrub brush (with both solvents) to clean down into the pores of the wood. Another suggestion: When the wood is as clean as you can get it, apply a wash coat of thin shellac prior to the actual refinishing. This will seal the residual impurities in the pores of the wood and keep them from contaminating the finish you apply later. And this thin coat of shellac will not interfere with the finish.

Answering your second question: Shellac is marketed either in dry or liquid form. Dry shellac is sold in three forms—granulate (seedlac; see p. 74), flakes (in several grades, of which superfine is the best) and buttons. These buttons are about 3-in. discs, ⅛-in. thick, mostly broken. Dissolved in alcohol, they make an excellent finishing material. Most probably, "button polish" refers to such a finish, and I agree with those who recommend this finish for your table.

Matching old stains and finishes

Robert Mussey wrote about old finishes and how they were made (see pages 23-27 and 28-31). When I make furniture repairs, I match the old wood in color, grain and texture, but I find it difficult to stain this new wood to match because some of the old finish around the patch gets disturbed. When you are matching stain, how do you confine the stain to the patch?

—*Rick Ludwick, Libertytown, Md.*

ROBERT MUSSEY REPLIES: Touching up stain in repairs is an art, and there can be many solutions to one problem. The biggest trick in stain-matching is starting out with a stain as light as the lightest color present in the original wood. Then use artists' brushes to add the necessary detail and shading to make your repair match the old finish. Frequently, you don't have to disturb the finish around a new patch. Put several coats of wax on the old finish around the patch, let in the patch and trim it flush with a sharp plane or chisel. Sometimes you can even stain or dye the repair before you put it in. After the stain is dry, wet the patch with naphtha or paint thinner to get an idea of how it will look when finish is applied. Play around with samples first before you glue the patch in. Stains and finishes can also be applied with great control using an artists' airbrush. The finish should be thinned, and the tip and nozzle of the brush adjusted very fine. Keep the brush moving so you don't get blotches. When the stain is dry, check your match by wetting it with naphtha.

Sometimes blending the repair into a larger area makes protecting the old finish less critical. Shading lacquers or tinted shellac can be sprayed along a line extending through the patch. Final selective sanding or rubbing with steel wool will help match the sheen of the new finish to that of the old. Easy does it—you don't want to sand through the repaired finish. The flatter the sheen of the overall finish, the easier it is to make a patch blend in.

There are no hard and fast rules; just practice and don't be afraid to try everything under the sun.

Brightening old black walnut

My son's family is using a black-walnut trestle table that is now in its fifth generation in the family. The joints are reasonably tight and the wood is sound. A complete restoration job is possible, but from our standpoint might detract as much as it would add. Brightening up the wood itself will be enough. After many years of farm use and being scoured with lye soap, and more years overhead in the woodshed gathering dust, it is smooth and clean but faded. I'm thinking of an oil treatment, possibly with added stain. Possibly just a good furniture polish. But in a case like this might the resins set up and preclude further recovery of the natural color?

—*Henry Howard, Cambridge, Minn.*

GEORGE FRANK REPLIES: Your table brings a story to memory: I had an old aunt who, although she was close to 90, was bright and alert. Her hair was white, her wrinkled face clean of cosmetics, and her whole person radiated goodness. When she died, I went to the funeral parlor for a last farewell and had a shock. Was this my aunt in the casket? The woman there had bright red cheeks, rouge on her lips, penciled eyebrows, the works. She looked like the bad woman in a Hollywood film, not like the aunt I loved.

Now back to your table. Please don't use any makeup on it. Wash it down once more with lye soap, scrub it hard and scrub it clean. Rinse it clear with water and leave it alone. If you really feel it needs protection, get some beeswax, cut shavings off it with a hand plane, fill a jar with the shavings,

barely cover them with high-octane gasoline and let soak a couple of days, shaking the jar from time to time. The wax will become semi-liquid. With this wax you can coat your table, but be sure to take off all excess before it dries. When dry, bring up the shine with a wool rag and a scrubbing brush.

Don't use any coloring. The beauty of your table is in the fact that it is old, worn and faded . . . keep it that way.

Finish-reviver

I recently found a recipe for a furniture reviver that calls for raw linseed oil, vinegar and terebene. My problem is that nobody has heard of terebene. The chemical dictionary defines it as a "mixture of terpenes, chiefly dipentene and terpenene." Could you tell me who sells it, or if it's called by another name? —*Joe Wolinski, Minneapolis, Minn.*

ROBERT MUSSEY REPLIES: Terebene is a generic name applied to a class of driers that were added to oils and varnishes during the late 19th and early 20th centuries. Combined in formulas containing linseed oil, terebene was supposed to keep the oil from remaining sticky and gummy. One recipe for terebene I found in an early-20th-century formula book is a mixture of medium kauri (a copal varnish resin), boiled linseed oil, flake litharge (a lead oxide), resinate of manganese (another metallic oxide drier) and American turps. All of these are available today except kauri—which may be just as well, since readily available, commercially made driers are easier to use and probably cheaper.

I don't suggest making and using this reviver. Even boiled linseed oil remains tacky for years before it finally polymerizes, and raw linseed is worse. It collects dirt and darkens with age, eventually becoming black if applied repeatedly. Linseed oil revivers finally polymerize so completely that they're nearly impossible to remove without damaging the finish they were meant to restore, tempting the dutiful polisher to add another coat, which makes the mess worse. A good portion of my yearly work involves formulating solvents to remove linseed oil polishes, so I strongly advise against their use. Waxes are my favorite final coating for finish restoration. They are easy to apply and easy to touch up if damaged.

Restoring faded rosewood

I have a Danish rosewood dining table. Its top has faded quite badly and doesn't match the pull-out leaves, which are generally protected. I suspect that the red in rosewood furniture is achieved with a dye. How can I restore the original color of this table?

—*L.M. Foster, Chappaqua, N.Y.*

GEORGE FRANK REPLIES: Whether your tabletop was dyed and the dye faded, or whether the natural pigmentation of the wood yielded to the bleaching action of sunlight, or even if the finish has become hazy with age, there is no simple way to bring back its original color. However, if the fading is in the finishing product and not in the color of the wood, there may be some hope of avoiding a complete refinishing. Dissolve some oil-soluble red aniline dye in mineral spirits. Next mix 50/50 the tinted mineral spirits with mineral oil. Cover the tabletop with this mixture and let it soak in well before wiping off the excess. It may bring back the color and the vigor of the finish.

If the wood itself has faded, your best bet is to wash off all the finish from the top, and also from the extra leaves, and sand everything until you have matching colors. It is hard work, but I am afraid this is the only way out. You may experiment with stains, dyes, or chemicals with very little chance of success.

Notes on Clear Finishes
Why I use Watco, Minwax and Deft

by Oscar MacQuiddy

Oscar MacQuiddy buffs a carved Italian table (c. 1929) he's refinished. The smooth, glossy surface is achieved by rubbing Watco into the wood with fine-grit wet/dry paper. The oil/sawdust slurry fills the grain and protects the wood.

I became interested in wood finishing after I acquired a house full of antique furniture. Most of it needed repair and refinishing, and I enrolled in an evening class where I was assured I would learn all I needed to know to restore my prized antiques. But I was displeased from the start with my instructor's approach. He was meticulous about preparing the surfaces, but then he would brush on a coat of colored plastic, and everyone would stand around admiring this shiny object. And if the next day you dragged your fingernail across the shiny surface, you'd leave a visible gouge. That wasn't what I was after.

I felt that a good finish should go into the wood and then build up a protective layer on the surface. I didn't like this business of applying plastics on top of the wood and then calling it a finish. The way this instructor liked to remove old finishes irritated me as well. Everything went. Good, bad, indifferent—it was all stripped away. I recall my shock one evening when a man brought in several strikingly beautiful pub chairs he had bought in Ireland. After some gluing and minor repairs he asked, "Now what should I do?" The instructor said, "Well, let's get that old finish off." At that point I'd had enough.

I found a day class with an altogether different approach to refinishing. My new teacher, Charles Kishady, was a most remarkable man, thoroughly in command of his subject and able to inspire his students. He came to this country at the end of World War II. Though his parents were Hungarian, he had spent four years in Germany as an apprentice restoring a 13th-century cathedral, and later he graduated from Heidelberg University with a degree in industrial arts. I told Mr. Kishady how I felt about furniture refinishing and what I wanted to do. He said, "Well, go ahead and do it and we'll see how you make out." He left me alone and would simply observe and make occasional comments, such as, "Wouldn't it look better if you did this...?" Or "Wouldn't it look better if you did that...?" I began to understand his suggestions and began also to develop an attitude toward wood that I had never seriously considered before.

As my relationship with this man deepened, together we decided to organize and teach a wood-finishing course at a professional level. But we wanted everything to be done as simply as possible, with all the frills knocked out. Though I'd never thought about teaching before, after a while I found what I had to communicate was extremely well received by my students. Once our program was under way, we tried to teach each student to respect the natural finish that was on

Oscar MacQuiddy, of Southgate, Calif., has taught antique restoration and refinishing for many years. Before he retired in 1968, he worked for Shell Chemicals. This article is the first of two parts, extracted by Alan Marks from lectures given at The Cutting Edge in Los Angeles; part two follows.

the article and to restore it when possible. It was really amazing the things we could bring back, and we were committed to saving the patina that develops on wood with time. When we used color, we tried to put it only where it belonged. We removed old finishes only when necessary, cleaned the wood and applied hand-rubbed oil finishes.

It is not necessary to remove old finishes completely, especially those possessing an attractive patina. It is often worth the effort to restore an existing finish, and really it is not that hard to do. Part of the secret is the ability to match the colors. There will be areas where the finish is totally gone, and sometimes these require almost heroic efforts, but they can be restored. Frequently, as when doing kitchen cabinets, all the surfaces will have to be cleaned. Scrub them thoroughly with TSP (tri-sodium-phosphate), which is probably the safest approach, sometimes adding a little household chlorine bleach to do some bleaching along with the cleaning; in this case, wear gloves and avoid splashing the liquid in your eyes.

When the old finish must be removed, methylene chloride remover seems a good choice. No remover is completely safe, but as available products go, it's one of the less toxic members of a highly toxic group called chlorinated hydrocarbons, and it has to be used with adequate ventilation. Ideally, a strong air current should carry the fumes away from the user. Once in the bloodstream, methylene chloride metabolizes to carbon monoxide. Breathing the vapors is harmful to healthy persons, but is especially hazardous to those who suffer from cardiac problems, and they should not use the product.

How do you choose a good brand? When you go to the store, pick up all the cans. The heaviest cans put to one side, because methylene chloride is the heavy ingredient. The can that is the heaviest at the lowest price is the best buy. Standard Brands makes good remover that's as heavy as Jasco. Jasco costs $12; Standard Brands costs $7 (1981 prices).

Methylene chloride is an efficient remover. When you apply it, use a brush with a natural wood handle because the remover will take any paint off the handle and stain your work. Working in a shaded area, apply a heavy coat by slopping it on. Don't brush it, just let it sit there. You paid a lot of money for it, so let it do all the work. Let it sit for 15 minutes and slop more on any dry spots that show up during that

From *Fine Woodworking* magazine (January 1981) 26:64-66

time. At the end of 15 minutes the finish will soften and lift, and you're ready to remove it. The instructions on the can will tell you to scrape it off with a putty knife or to use a rag or steel wool to wipe it off. None of these methods is effective. But if you have access to a supply of planer or jointer shavings, dump a handful in the middle of that table or on that cabinet door and start scrubbing, and you'll clean that surface flawlessly. The wood shavings will get into routed, grooved, relieved and carved areas. They will do a terrific job of cleaning without scratching the wood. With this method you'll be able to strip very rapidly and efficiently, and stripping can turn out to be not such a terrible job after all.

If you find you still have some old finish on the surface, there is an auxiliary method of attack. Get a can with a tight cover and fill it with planer shavings and then saturate the shavings with lacquer thinner or, preferably, acetone. If you can afford it, methyl ethyl ketone would be even better. Take a handful of the wet shavings and continue the scrubbing. The solvent has a paint-remover action and generally by the second application, you will have a surface almost clean enough to finish. These chemicals are highly flammable, so use them with great care. Work outdoors if possible, or use adequate ventilation inside.

This method of stripping is very simple, and shavings can be used several times. Even floors can be stripped this way, but you must pay special attention to ventilation. Afterward, how can you tell if your wood is clean? Sand the surface lightly with 150-grit finishing paper. If it doesn't clog, you know the work is done. If the paper loads up, clean the surface with 1/0 steel wool soaked in either lacquer thinner or a mixture of lacquer thinner and acetone or methyl ethyl ketone. This technique is well suited for cleaning around turnings. Occasionally a little picking will have to be done with a pointed tool, and sometimes a piece of heavy cord can be used to clean the bottoms of grooves. We have used abrasive cords, but they cut so quickly and so deeply that you have to be very careful with them, particularly on old finishes where you don't want to expose bare wood.

When working with paint removers and strong solvents, you must wear gloves to prevent skin irritation as well as possible poisoning from the absorption of toxic chemicals through the skin. Neoprene gloves are best because they hold up longer and are tougher than gloves made from other materials. But when working with oil finishes, it's better to use your bare hands, not only to generate heat necessary for good penetration but also for increased awareness of what is happening on the surface of the wood. During all my years as an instructor, I've seen only one case of dermatitis resulting from contact with an oil finishing product. If you should have an adverse reaction despite the odds against it, consult your doctor about it right away.

Clear finishes are of two basic types—penetrating finishes and surface finishes. It is possible, though, to build up a surface layer by using a penetrating finish that hardens in the wood. As far as penetrating finishes are concerned, you can use an oil that dries or one that doesn't. Non-toxic linseed oil is slow-drying, but it was discovered that by heating it and adding chemicals its polymerization rate could be increased. They used to put lead in it. Today they can't and have to use a cobalt drier, making the oil just as toxic as it was with lead. Originally I worked with linseed oil, but the drying time was slow and unpredictable. Now I use Watco Danish oil, and it

has become standard in my work and teaching. To make Watco they take linseed oil and convert it to a resin. They dissolve this resin in a solvent and add driers to make it penetrate, and this penetrating solution has the property of combining chemically with oxygen to become a polymerized solid. It saturates the wood and solidifies in the cell cavities. Watco oil is quite easy to apply, and the results that it gives are excellent. You just apply it on raw wood until it won't absorb any more and then wipe the surface dry. Repeat this procedure the next day. Watco does alter the color of wood and it does darken somewhat with age, characteristics it shares with linseed oil.

Pure tung oil—not to be confused with heat-treated (polymerizing) tung oil, which is actually a varnish for hand rubbing—is a product I use with reservations. Once applied, its effects are irreversible, though it never completely hardens. But it's a beautiful finish, often producing spectacular results and requiring little preparation, aside from original sanding. On light woods, you get about the same color change as you get with Watco; and on some dark woods, the color change seems to be even less. But heat-treated tung oil will turn other dark woods almost black. I worked once with a man who finished some redwood altars with heat-treated tung oil; they ended up extremely dark, and you couldn't recognize them as redwood. If he had used three or four coats of Minwax Antique Oil, the natural beauty of the wood would have been revealed. When I first began to work with Minwax Antique Oil I was skeptical—it seemed almost too good to be true. It contains such effective driers that it will congeal in the can if half the volume is airspace. You need never worry about it drying hard—it'll dry. You wipe it on the surface, and it acts as a penetrating sealer and sets very hard. I have diluted it slightly on occasion and sanded it in wet as I do with Watco. But you must work quickly because it gets tacky fast, and you wind up with a sticky mess if it's not wiped off in time.

One interesting variation of the penetrating-oil finish is the "salt-pork finish." It is non-toxic, and because the pork fat contains salt, it does not become rancid. I have used it several times to refinish very old raw-wood chests and the paddles bakers use to remove bread from ovens. It can be used to finish all wooden kitchen utensils. Mineral oil has also been used for this purpose; it is definitely a spreading oil. If you take a piece of warm metal and put a drop of mineral oil on it, the oil will disperse and coat the whole surface. Salt pork does the same thing. In the old days people apparently just recoated with it when needed, and it has been claimed that this finish was used by the Shakers.

A friend of mine with broad experience in antique restoration observed that often old kitchen tables were not finished at all; they were just scrubbed at intervals with caustics and water. He speculates that during washing, the oil and tallow spills on the wood surface were observed to resist moisture and to shine with rubbing. So the practice of oiling wood to preserve it was probably a logical development of this observation. The old oil finishes applied by our great-grandparents by way of maintenance perhaps account for the fact that their furniture has survived. The oil was enough to preserve the wood and prevent moisture penetration and moisture-related decay and degradation. I am quite certain that glue joints in old furniture owe their preservation to this application of oil.

In the old days people bought cedar oil, a mineral oil that

was colored red and scented with a cedar extract. Today we use lemon oil—the same oil but colored yellow, and scented with lemon. But we don't use it as generously as our grandparents did. Instructions on the bottle say to use only one or two drops. I suggest that you go to a drug store and buy a pint of light mineral oil and use it as a furniture polish. You'll be getting the same basic ingredient of "lemon oil" but paying a lot less for it. There would be nothing wrong with using this light mineral oil as a non-toxic furniture finish. If the furniture needs cleaning, why not add a small amount of vinegar to it and a small amount of turpentine? Some restorers of antique clocks recommend cleaning and reviving old clock cases with a mixture of turpentine and vinegar and mineral oil.

The first oil/resin mixture used for finishing was varnish. From the Orient came lacquer and shellac which, when mixed with alcohol, yields the formula for the "French polish." The French-polish finish is a beautiful high-gloss, durable finish that is very slow to create (see pages 72-74). It possesses poor moisture resistance, is very difficult to repair and is quite impractical for commercial use. In order to create a durable, rapid-dry commercial finish, nitro-cellulose lacquer formulations were developed, but because of their fast dry time, spraying was the required method of application. Some years later, Deft Inc. formulated a modified water/white-coconut-oil-base, nitro-cellulose lacquer with special solvents that proved to be an improved brushing lacquer. The product is self-leveling, non-yellowing and easily repaired; it quickly rubs to a beautiful satin sheen and can be applied directly to raw wood. Three coats are recommended, and will produce a bar top finish. Each successive coat melds with the preceding one. When brushing Deft, I prefer satin for a final coat, although gloss is the more durable material. If you are going to rub it out, you might just as well apply two coats of gloss before putting on the final coat of satin. The only mistake you can make is not to use enough finish for the job, but several thin coats are better than thick ones.

The original oil/resin varnish has undergone many formula changes. One of the more recent has been to replace the resin with a polyurethane, a plastic resin. The result is a highly versatile coating. Defthane, a brand of polyurethane varnish, can be applied to raw wood or clean metal, inside or outdoors. Three coats are recommended. Thirty minutes gives a dust-free surface, and you can recoat in six hours. The finish is hard and rubs to an elegant satin sheen. With Defthane, as with Deft lacquer, the best procedure is to start with two coats of gloss followed by a third of satin.

You might wonder, with such a tough, hard finish, how the second and third coats can be made to adhere. Since it will dry in six hours, at the end of four hours it is two-thirds dry. I put on the next coat before the end of six hours. If I rub the surface lightly with 4/0 steel wool and wipe it down thoroughly, the subsequent coat will bond tightly to the first. Buy a large can of gloss and a small can of satin. When the last coat, the satin coat, is thoroughly dry at the end of 12 hours—36 hours is even better—rub the surface with 4/0 steel wool and wax it with Trewax (50% carnauba).

It is at first unsettling to use a water clean-up finish in place of varnish, lacquer and oils. It's hard to believe that anything that can be dissolved initially by water can dry to a durable, non-water-soluble state. But this is true of the new water-wash acrylic finishes. They give excellent results, and I predict that eventually they will enjoy wider use, especially in areas with smog problems. One such product, Wood Armor, is easily applied with a rag, roller, brush or spray gun. It dries quickly, has a pale color, and is non-yellowing. In 30 minutes after application it's dust free, and it has a two-hour recoat time. It has no noxious odor, cleans up with water, and is a beautiful finish for fine paneling where a minimum color change is desired. It comes in gloss and satin, though I prefer satin. I feel that the inside of drawers, the underside of drawers and even the back should have a finish, and Wood Armor works well for this purpose. Cabinet interiors are done to advantage with it. If you want to remove the still-wet finish for any reason, wipe it with a damp cloth before it skins over.

Let us pick up at the point where a piece of furniture has been stripped and prepared for finishing by a light sanding with 150-grit paper. We selected for our purposes a penetrating sealer/oil finish because we're after a traditional look with a soft sheen that doesn't obscure the grain of the wood. Many experts advise rubbing the oil in by hand or with rags or steel wool. We found a method, in the course of instruction, that we believe to be superior to any of these methods.

Working with the grain, start by pouring a small puddle of Watco on the surface. Then wet a pad of 320-grit wet/dry carbide paper and start sanding in figure eights, beginning at a corner and working across the surface. Within a few minutes you will have a slurry of oil and very fine sawdust that is continually being worked into the pores of the wood, which is quickly filled with its own substance due to the sharp cutting action of the carbide grit. After it gets tacky (15 minutes), I wipe off the excess with a rag. The resulting surface possesses an almost glass-like smoothness. Finish sanding across the surface and then sand with long strokes in the direction of the grain to obliterate any cross-grain marks. Actually with 320-grit paper it's almost impossible to leave any such marks except in the hardest of woods. At this point, you have smoothed the surface with a minimum of sanding, prepared and applied a filler, and put on a penetrating sealer.

You really can't simplify it much more. I've done a lot of beautiful work using this method. When I first started using it I applied raw linseed oil, but I didn't like it because the drying time is unpredictable. Watco is relatively fast drying. I know with certainty that in four hours it can be recoated. I felt that it did everything a linseed oil did and did it better. When you consider the amount of sanding saved and drudgery eliminated in achieving this kind of finish, there is no better alternative. A small sandpaper pad will do moldings. It fits anywhere and it will not quickly wear out, because the oil lubricates the cut and keeps the paper from clogging.

Your second coat is applied after the first has dried for at least four hours, or preferably overnight. Rub the second coat in by hand, having again poured oil on the surface. The heat of the hand friction aids in the penetration of the oil. Let it sit for a few minutes, and if you see any dry spots, spread oil from the wet spots over them. Keep the surface wet with oil until there is no more absorption. It is very important with each successive coat to wipe away all excess surface oil. Because this is not a surface treatment, but a penetrating finish, everything on the surface must be wiped away or rubbed into the wood. Excess oil on the surface will become sticky and take a long time to dry. When the second coat has dried, preferably overnight, the third coat is applied similarly to the second, and during the third application, the question of coloring comes into play. And that's another story. □

Coloring With Penetrating Oils

A little dab goes a long way

by Oscar MacQuiddy

In my article on clear finishes (pages 34-36), I said little about the business of coloring wood, except insofar as a clear finish might darken certain woods, as in the case of oils. Color is a quality possessed by tiny particles of a substance. These absorb all wavelengths of light save those in certain portions of the spectrum, which are reflected and which we perceive as color. What makes a thing look green is its ability to absorb red. A stain consists of tiny particles suspended in a liquid or a paste. Because ultimately the test of a color's quality is its degree of permanency and how closely it approaches what you want it to do, I like to use readily obtainable universal colors.

These colors are standardized, and several brands are available. Also, they are inexpensive if you buy them in large quantities; I purchase them in pint containers. For class demonstrations I have pints of all the available colors, and I have never experienced any problems mixing them with any finishing product but lacquer. In my teaching I must use materials that are readily available where artist's supplies are sold, and the colors that are most easily and economically obtained are universal colors. Oil colors are slower drying than universal colors, and they don't burnish as well, probably because the particle size is larger. Universal colors are intended to be mixed with water-based finishes, including Deft Wood Armor. They can be used in varnishes and, most important, in penetrating oil finishes.

In case you think my preference uncraftsmanlike, you might be interested in a conversation I once had. I phoned one of the really fine antique furniture dealers. Saying I was an instructor of furniture finishing, I asked if I could speak with his refinisher. After asking the refinisher a couple of innocent questions to get the conversation going, I said, "Tell me, how do you handle your stains?" He told me that he used universal colors and thinned them with turpentine. Since then I have spoken with other commercial finishers and gotten more or less the same answer. The wide range of color available in universal colors provides professionals with the variety and versatility they need.

The stable earth colors we use are named after geographical areas. You may have heard of raw sienna. Sienna is a part of Italy. The earth there is an intense yellow, and it's used to make pine and maple stains. It has good transluscency although it can be too bright. Since this earth contains a lot of extraneous organic materials, Italians experimented with firing to purify it. It turned red, and became known as burnt sienna. That's the beautiful red we use on mahogany, but used alone it's too red. In another part of Italy, called Umbria, the soil is greenish-brown in color, and they'd use it when

they wanted to make a deep, cold walnut. When they wanted to deepen another color they put some raw umber in it. In purifying it they produced "burnt umber," a beautiful brown the natural shade of walnut. Working with these four colors—raw sienna, burnt sienna, raw umber and burnt umber—it is possible, in most instances, to match almost any color you see on wood.

Of course, you do have a wider choice of colors. The Spanish oxides are tremendously stable red colors. Sometimes French ochre, a light, more subtle shade of yellow than raw sienna, matches some of the early pines a little better. Or you can get modern chromium oxides, yellow and green. In my kit I carry the four stable earth colors and three additional yellows—a French ochre, a chromium oxide and a bulletin yellow for the places where I want to add a spot of yellow that's really alive. I carry three reds in addition to burnt sienna—American vermilion, Venetian red, and a tube of French vermilion, for the times I want a red shadow that is warm but not bright. For the greens, I have chromium oxide and permanent green, in its medium version.

In coloring wood, I prefer not to stain. I'm not knocking stains, but I teach students to see the color they want and to set out like an artist to make it. Stains simply don't give the effect I want, but they will give solid color, in particular the 5-Minute Watco stains, which come in nine wood tones and nine colors. I prefer to develop the color gradually with control, which produces subtle nuances and a high degree of transparency. Of course, compatibility with the penetrating oil finish is necessary. In choosing the so-called universal colors, nothing is compromised.

In using universal colors, I like to mix them with natural Watco Danish Oil because the color will penetrate the wood along with the oil and become tightly locked in. But sometimes I use Minwax Antique Oil (a polymerizing tung oil) as the vehicle for the colors, especially where I want a harder, glossier finish that has the appearance of being built up on the surface of the wood. One advantage of using Watco as the vehicle is that if you make a mistake, you've got 30 minutes to rub it off with a clean rag soaked in turpentine or thinner. You can remove close to 90% of it if necessary and you can start again within a few minutes. You have a marvelous leeway in developing color.

Let me emphasize that I'm not talking about dramatic color changes. You don't take ash and make it look like rosewood. This method just isn't practical for that, nor does it produce a uniform color. You use it to create shades of color where they enhance the overall piece. Let's say we have a piece of furniture that has some carving and turnings on it and we want to emphasize the designer's original concept. There will be shadows in the recesses of a carving and at the depths of a turning. First do the preliminary finishing. Then, using a piece of nonabsorbent cardboard or plastic as an

Oscar MacQuiddy lives in Southgate, Calif. This article, like the one on pages 34-36, was adapted by Alan Marks from MacQuiddy's lectures at The Cutting Edge in Los Angeles.

artist's palette, we put on it little spots of color (shadows do have color). If it's the shadow on a piece of walnut, burnt umber may approximate it. But perhaps we want a subtler shade. So we add spots of raw umber and a bit of red or yellow on the board. Pour on a tiny bit of Watco and take a ½-in. white bristle brush and capture a little puddle of the oil. Pick up some burnt umber and rub it into the oil. Say we want to go a little toward the red. Wipe off the brush in a rag, pick up a tiny bit of red with the tip and rub it into a little area of the brown spot. Now hold the spot next to the shadow. Say it looks all right, but it's not quite dark enough. Wipe off the brush and pick up a bit of raw umber. Rub it into part of the red-brown area to darken it. Now hold that next to the carving, and it looks mighty close to capturing the tone of the beautiful shadow.

Next, take a shallow catfood can and put in it a tablespoon of Watco, a teaspoon of burnt umber, a tiny bit of red and mix them, watching the tone as it develops. Get it about right and then add a tiny bit of raw umber to darken it. Now we have our shadow color. Using Watco as a vehicle to carry the color, we have produced a rather concentrated stain.

Take a small brush and go over those carvings, covering all the areas, and let it sit until it gets a little tacky. Then get a clean rag and try to remove it. You won't be able to get it all off, and the amount you leave is going to be exactly right. The whole area will accept the tone, and rubbing diligently on the convex highlight areas will expose them to advantage. Now you suddenly discover that you have added depth to this carving, making it appear as the designer once envisioned it, with prominent highlights and deep shadows. When it is thoroughly dry, give it another coat of clear oil rubbed in by hand; then wipe off the excess. This seals in the color. Waxing later will give it a translucency that will make it even more spectacular and will bring even more life to it.

Charles Kishady, my associate (a master antique restorer), suggests that when restoring fine antiques, you should use at least three colors in shadowed areas—a basic color, a lighter color and a darker color. The exciting thing is that you can warm a color with a spot of an analogous color or kill it by adding its complement. If you put on a red and you want to reduce its intensity, green will do it, making it go towards a brown. The tiniest bits of color achieve dramatic changes. You can have one color in the highlight area and introduce a trace of its complement in the shadow. This changes the quality of the shadow emphatically.

I recall refinishing a table with a lot of intricate carvings on the legs and two drawers in front. Because of the old finish, the carving was totally lost. You knew some kind of irregular surface was there, but you didn't have the foggiest notion what it was. I asked the owner, "How would you feel if that carving suddenly came to life and you could see it?" She indicated that perhaps it would be a good thing. So I took the table to my shop, put on a polyurethane varnish and rubbed it out to a durable satin finish. But first I mixed some dark, murky color and smeared it over the carved surfaces. Then I spent an hour trying to get the stuff off. Most of it I removed, but the carving had now dramatically come to life.

I once worked with a student refinishing a lovely little

AUTHOR'S NOTE: The only text I have found that treats the subject of color the way we do in our courses is H.W. (or W.H. in some editions) Kuhn's *Refinishing Furniture,* Arco Publishers, N.Y. (out of print; check libraries), and I recommend it highly.

cherry coffee table. It had a large white slash of sapwood across the top. A purist might say, "Well, since it is natural you'd expect that white slash in cherry." But all you saw was the white slash. Now I felt it belonged there, but wanted to alter it so your eye didn't stop at it but wandered on around to see the rest of the table. I made some shadow color and put an extremely light coat of the color on the white. It didn't change it much but gave it the general tone of the darker area. Then picking two or three spots along the white slash, I introduced a little more of it, slightly darkening these areas then fading off to a very, very light color. You still noticed the white area, but your eye moved on to look at the whole table. Still, I wasn't satisfied. It had gone a little cold, so I took a tiny bit of American vermilion and burnished it into the top of that table. That changed its entire character. Suddenly the table seemed to move off the ground.

In using this approach to finishing it is important to ask certain questions. If you are considering a chair, for example, do you see merely a chair or do you see a chair with one post that is different? Does it have some quality that makes its back stand out from the rest, or do you see the chair as a whole? Is the ornamentation conspicuous? Do you see shadows? Do you see highlights? Does the carving look like part of the piece or like an unrelated appendage? On an old chair, up for restoration, does it appear as though someone has been sitting in it, has rubbed the back slightly, has rested his arms in certain places?

You can approach furniture finishing as an artist would paint a picture over which he wants your eye to move in certain ways. But you should also be concerned with the effects of use and care. If it is a chair, the places where people habitually put their hands will be a little lighter than the rest. People wonder how to intuit this sort of thing. Let's say the chair you're working on belongs to a wealthy lady. She has a housekeeper who has a lot of work to do, and so cleans well only the places she knows her mistress will notice. She'll notice the overall appearance, but where the posts join the rails her housekeeper will leave a little dirt, and where the spindles join the rungs she won't be able to reach. When you decorate furniture with these things in mind, you discover you're creating authentic-looking antiques.

I had one student who had made many trips to the East Coast and had collected some very beautiful cherry furniture. We restored all of it eventually, but when we first started she said "I don't want any of that stuff [color] on my furniture." But when she saw some finished pieces, she began to do the same with hers; and when she finally completed her work, she was convinced of the merit of shading. Her beautiful cherry tables were all shades of color. When the appraiser came to evaluate them, each was assessed at a top price. The man said he'd never before seen restoration done so well.

As I said in my first article, you don't have to remove old finishes completely when you want to preserve their original patina. After cleaning the surface with TSP, just take a small can of natural Watco, or if the wood has been stained a dark color, pick one of the darker shades of Watco, and a small pad of 4/0 steel wool. Wet the pad with Watco and rub softly with the grain. This will remove any loose finish, and the oil will penetrate into areas where finish is missing. Start by doing a small portion to find out how quickly it is going to dry and how fast you can work; then wipe this area thoroughly with a clean rag. Frequently you will find this surface now almost completely restored. You may have a problem in several spots where color is missing. Since you already know how to recognize what this color consists of, you can match it, and then burnish the color into these spots. And now the piece is thoroughly restored.

In class after my lecture on finishing, I bring in a piece of furniture in sad shape and tell the students, "I am going to restore this piece, and in 20 minutes it will be acceptable to sell." Of course, no one believes me. I pour some Watco into a container, and with some 4/0 steel wool I quickly rub the piece down. I squeeze out some universal color on a palette and show them how to match the color. Then I pick up some more oil, rub the color into spots where it's missing, and presto, the job is 95% done. In two or three places it may be necessary to come back the next day and rub in some more, but it's essentially done at that point. Minwax Antique Oil also works well. Most antique dealers could restore furniture without altering anything, or ruining the original patina. But instead, they usually work their hands to the bone putting on varnish or something else and make a mess of things.

If you need to clean the furniture, rub it down lightly with a mixture of vinegar, turpentine and mineral oil. If the finish is thoroughly dried out, as some old varnish finishes are, you can use linseed oil instead of mineral oil. When working with oil, you must wipe off everything you put on, and you must dispose of the rags properly. To prevent a fire don't throw them in the trash, but spread them out to dry.

I would like to say a word or two here about lacquers. On woods requiring a minimum change in color or texture, water-white lacquers are satisfactory, especially when speed is important. You can put on three or four coats of lacquer in one day. But in working with lacquers, color is sometimes a problem. However, vinyl stains work very well with lacquer, though you don't have the freedom you do when using the penetrating oil finish. But using the vinyl stains and very carefully shading or highlighting before applying the lacquer produces good results.

The 5-Minute Stains made by Watco are aniline dyes dissolved in methanol, and they work very well. Watco is completely compatible with urethanes and acrylic finishes. They will go on over a Watco/universal-color mixture, and the Watco/universal-color mixture can be applied over them. Let this dry, and apply a finish coat of urethane or acrylic to lock it in. You can blend two or three colors to get special tones. Minwax provides aniline dyes in other forms, more subtle in color. In working with stains, stay within the family. If you start with Minwax, work entirely in the Minwax line. If you are using Deft, stay within the Deft family of products. You may avoid some costly errors.

One of my students had built his daughter some walnut cabinets for her kitchen and bathroom. He wanted to finish them so that moisture would be no problem. He'd worked too hard on them to have them spoiled. He said to me, "I want them to look oiled. Can we do it?" I said I could see no reason why not. He brought in some samples of his walnut and we experimented a little. We put on two coats of Watco for the oiled appearance, and we followed that with two coats of satin urethane varnish. When it had thoroughly dried, we rubbed it with steel wool and wax. It resulted in a soft, subtle oil finish, and the wood was completely washable.

I usually finish off with waxing. Of the waxes available, I prefer a hard wax finish that is easily maintained, having to

Oscar MacQuiddy touches some tone into a shadowed area of chair's arm. He mixes earth colors with Watco oil on a cardboard palette to create just the right effect in restoring antiques.

be done perhaps every six months. I call my method the "three-rag approach." Take three clean rags and a can of Trewax, which is comparable to bowling-alley wax or similar to any one of the hard carnauba-wax products. Thoroughly saturate the first rag with wax. Rub that saturated rag on the surface to be treated and attempt to load it with wax, putting on as much wax as you possibly can. Set rag #1 aside and wait about one minute. Then take rag #2 and try to remove every trace of wax. Scrub, rub, get that wax off. Wait five minutes, and take rag #3 and lightly burnish the surface. This procedure may seem unduly complicated, but it works. You put the wax on, thoroughly saturating the surface. You rub it off, and you will have no difficulty burnishing to a soft, shiny, smooth surface.

If you have a problem surface, one not quite as smooth as you would like, particularly when you've applied polyurethane and dust particles have contaminated the finish, another approach is necessary. Take some 4/0 steel wool and after applying the wax, rub the surface with long straight strokes, removing the wax as outlined above. You will smooth the surface and get rid of the excess wax at the same time. Upon wiping the surface down, you will have achieved a beautiful satin finish with a protective wax film. All the dust particles will have disappeared, and you can count on compliments from people who see your work.

The exciting part of teaching these methods of finishing has been being able to communicate my enthusiasm to others, helping them develop an appreciation for fine work, helping them to understand that with simple materials it is possible to work miracles. You don't need to use exotic preparations. You can use things that come off the shelves of discount paint stores. You come to know how it feels to work directly with your hands and to know the effects you are capable of producing.
☐

Finishing and Refinishing   **39**

Stains, Dyes and Pigments
The wood grain should remain readable

by George Frank

We all love wood because of its endless variety of grain. To put the natural markings of the wood in evidence is the true task of anyone who tries to beautify it through finishing. Concerning beauty in woodfinishing, I have set up a rule for myself: The first requisite of a beautiful finish is that the wood must remain "readable." This means not only that the grain must be clearly visible after finishing—that is self-evident. It also means that from the grain of the wood, qualified people can read the whole history of the tree: its origins, age and environment, its fights for survival, its adventures.

Woodfinishing is the stepchild of the woodworking industry. Even its vocabulary is poor and misleading. We use the word "staining" when we refer to a chemical action that changes the color of the wood, to a process where a dye brings this change about, or to a process where we cover the wood with a colored film, or a thin layer of colored pigment. Only this last method should rightly be called staining. The first two should be called dyeing. The difference between dyeing and staining is like the difference between getting a deep suntan and using makeup to imitate one. While stains always reduce the readability of the wood, they have great merits, especially on the production line. Ease of application is one, but far more important is that stains help to achieve uniform coloring, and this, especially on the assembly line, is a fair compensation for the reduced readability.

Chemical action

Cuban mahogany has the color of raw steak. Sponge it with a solution of potassium dichromate, a yellow crystal, and its color deepens considerably. Not only does it become a dark rusty red, but the contrast between the light and dark markings becomes more accentuated. This chemical process, wrongly called staining, really enhances the beauty of the wood. Napoleon's craftsmen often used this process, and most French Empire furniture is "stained" by this method.

It is a well-known fact that wheat-colored oak becomes brownish-grey when sponged with ammonia. Here is a short story about another chemical action: In 1938, a Pennsylvania manufacturer imported a shipload of timber from Europe. To mystify the competition, he gave it a name—palazota. It looked like bird's-eye maple, but was whiter and had more eyes in it. He made bedroom suites of it and sold them successfully. By 1942, the market was saturated with white palazota bedrooms, and dealers asked for something new. Since he had over two-thirds of his lumber still in stock, he tried stains. His stains obliterated most of the delicate markings of the wood, and the stained palazota did not sell. That is when I was called in. After three weeks of experimenting, I found the answer. A weak solution of ferrous sulfate brought unbelievable changes to this wood. The miniature eyes opened

See pp. 44, 60, 63, 65, 102 for more on George Frank.

up considerably, while the flat areas remained almost unchanged. The wood seemed to acquire a third dimension, depth. When I added some coloring dyes to the ferrous chemical, I produced a whole new gamut of decorative effects. Regardless of whether the palazota was tinted grey, brown, gold or red, its markings always came out loud and clear. Three years later, the manufacturer did not have a single board left in his factory.

A simple example illustrates the possibilities: Apply potassium dichromate solution to a piece of birch or maple and the wood becomes pleasantly dyed a rich yellow color. Apply it to a piece of oak, and the wood becomes a dark rusty brown. So far so good. Now imagine that you can get somehow a cake of logwood extract, more scientifically called extract of campeche wood. Dissolve one ounce in a pint of water, and with this wine-like brew you sponge the three pieces of wood you are experimenting with. Let dry, sandpaper lightly and apply the potassium dichromate solution. After an hour you will find that the birch and the maple have become rusty brown, and the oak a rich chocolate color.

Potassium permanganate is a common chemical. One ounce dissolved in a pint of water will stain most hardwoods a pleasant brown. But the tint will fade and change color—from brown-violet to brown. If the color you get is too dark, wash down the wood with a fairly strong solution of sodium thiosulfate (available from photo-supply stores as hypo solution). You will get a nicely bleached wood.

Another woodfinishing concoction can be prepared by mixing equal amounts of ordinary vinegar and water, then throwing in all the rusty iron you can find—old nails, screws, hinges, tools and so on. Let sit for a week, then filter through a piece of cloth. The resulting liquid will produce a silvery grey color on oak. It won't be so effective, though, on woods lacking tannic acid. This can be remedied by prestaining with a mordant made of an ounce of tannic acid in a quart of water. Obviously the vinegar mixture is rather iffy, since its strength depends on the amount of iron the liquid will absorb. Ferrous sulfate dissolved in water (about 1½ oz. to one quart water) will produce a more positive and very pleasant grey color on oak.

Dyeing

Until about 1870, dyes for textiles or for wood were always extracted from plants, insects or animals, and rarely from minerals. For example, to obtain one pound of the dye called Tyrian purple, Mediterranean fishermen had to bring up close to four million mollusks (*Murex branderis*), break their shells individually and carve out a small sac from their bellies, which contained the coloring matter. The price of this dyestuff was so high that in ancient Rome, its use was reserved by law to royalty and to the princes of the church (hence its popular name, cardinal purple). Another red dye was brewed

From *Fine Woodworking* magazine (September 1978) 12:58-59

from a little bug, *Coccus cacti L.* Seventy thousand of these bugs had to give up their lives so that men could brew one pound of dye from their dried bodies. Only a hundred years ago, England imported seven million pounds of these dried insects annually. Tea is not only one of the most popular beverages in the world, it is also an excellent dye, used mostly on antique reproductions, since it conveys to the wood a pleasant golden hue, characteristic of many fine antiques. There are a few hundred of these natural dyes that can be used on wood, but progress has relegated them mercilessly to obsolescence.

A little over 100 years ago, W. H. Perkin accidentally came across the first aniline dye. Others were discovered in rapid succession and the era of synthetic dyes began. Between the two wars, a giant industry was born in Germany, the manufacturing of colors and dyes. A huge company, I.G. Farben, had almost a monopoly, and its subsidiary, Arti A.G., specialized in dyes for wood. There were no wood-coloring problems in Europe during the 1930s because Arti always had the answer. They had simple dyes that would give the selected color to nearly any wood. Other dyes involved two applications, a prestain, or mordant, which was followed by the dye, resulting in deeper penetration and more positive coloring. The most important tools in any woodfinishing shop during this period were a pharmacist's scale and a graduated glass to weigh and measure the proper amount of dye and water. All these dyes were properly numbered and matched a master color chart. Arti also supplied dyes to be dissolved in alcohol or in oils, for special needs. Before World War II, Arti tried to gain a foothold on the American market, evidently without success. I do not know of any manufacturer here that markets dyes for wood with proper color samples and reliable instructions. This does not mean that American-made dyes are inferior to European. I simply deplore that they are presented in a very haphazard way.

Pigments

Any solid substance that can be reduced to powder can become a pigment. With the proper carrier and a binder, it can become a pigmented stain. All pigmented stains have the same formula: pigment, carrier and binder. Again, let me give you an example from my past. The first person who ever sought my professional help was a small-town manufacturer of a line of children's furniture, such as playpens and high chairs. The local lumber he used varied so much in color that he simply could not obtain a uniform light finish. I mixed for him equal amounts of powdered chalk and French ochre powder, and stirred the mixture into a pail of lukewarm rabbit-skin glue solution. This simple stain not only solved his coloring problem, but also acted as a sealer on his wood. In this instance the chalk-ochre combination was the pigment, the water was the carrier and the glue was the binder.

The most popular and the best-known pigment-stains are the commercial oil colors. They contain very finely ground pigments mixed into the oil (the carrier), to which a drying agent is added (thus the oil becomes the binder, too). Almost always, the carrier in this mixture is extended with turpentine or other paint thinner. Pigment stains in general do not change the color of the wood. But even after the most thorough wiping off, some of the pigment remains on the wood and adds its own color to it.

There appears to be a clear-cut difference between the three ways of changing the color of wood. The reality is far

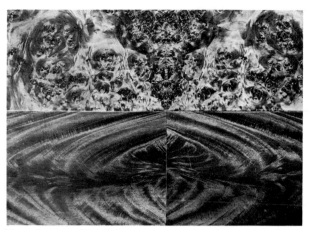

Top, ferrous sulfate brings out contrasting figure in 'palazota' maple, Bottom, mahogany treated with potassium dichromate gives illusion of great depth.

more complex. The three methods can be and very often are intermixed. My story about coloring the palazota illustrated how chemicals can be combined with dyes to create new horizons in changing the color of the wood. But that is just one story out of thousands. Chemicals can be mixed to dyes, dyes can be mixed to pigment-stains, and all three can be combined together to improve the quality of the finished products, this time correctly called "stains." Nearly any stain purchased in a paint store contains pigments, dyes and some chemicals (for deeper penetration), and all do an adequate job for the amateur, even for the average professional. The fine woodworker sticks to chemicals, natural dyes maybe, or accepts synthetic dyes to color the wood, but seldom uses pigment stains in spite of their great advantages and simplicity.

Application

Waterstains, dyes and chemicals should be generously applied with a sponge. The area to be dyed should be thoroughly soaked and then the excess should be taken off with the same sponge, squeezed out, to leave the wood uniformly moist. The stronger the concentration, the more potent the stain or dye. Chemical dyes, more than aniline dyes, should be used in weak concentration and applied repeatedly, since they show their final effect only after thorough drying, and it is far more difficult to lighten the wood than to darken it.

Some dyes can be dissolved in alcohol or lacquer thinner. Therefore, a liquid shellac can be further diluted and tinted with colored alcohol and the resulting colored shellac when applied would convey a tint to the surface. The same goes for the lacquer—if the thinner is colored, it becomes a tinting lacquer. Wax, varnish, shellac and lacquers can be tinted with dyes dissolved in their respective thinners. They can also be "loaded," that is, some finely ground coloring matter can be mixed into them—a fourth way of "staining" the wood. These four ways are very much like the four strings on a violin. The melodies one can play on these four strings are really endless, but the beauty of the melody depends on the person holding the bow. □

EDITOR'S NOTE: H. Behlen & Bros., Rt. 30N, Amsterdam, N.Y. 12010 makes and sells a wide range of stains, pigments and dyes. Their products are also sold by Constantine, 2065 Eastchester Rd., Bronx, N.Y. 10461. For chemicals, check the Yellow Pages under headings such as Hobby Supplies, Chemicals, and Photo Supplies.

Q & A

Mixing oils for color

Can Watco and Minwax be mixed to get a finish of a different color? —*David Dike, Norfolk, Va.*
OSCAR MacQUIDDY REPLIES: No, don't mix the two types of oils. Stay within finish families and use color as the manufacturer recommends. If you start with Watco, stay with Watco. Watco stains are strong colors and I dilute them 50% with methanol until I get the color I want. Remember, wet color is different from dry color so experiment on a scrap piece of wood.

Bleaching finishes

I've recently completed a sculpture in butternut and I am troubled by a dark grain blemish that is visually disturbing. Is it possible to apply a chemical or preparation to the distracting area to blend it with the adjacent area? What method should be used to avoid a reverse problem? I have had no experience bleaching woods and therefore have no idea of what to expect.
—*Paul S. Twichell, Keene Valley, N.Y.*
GEORGE FRANK REPLIES: The arsenal of bleaches we woodfinishers use is rather poor. The most important are chlorine bleach and oxalic acid. The only way to find out how to eliminate the disturbing color in your sculpture is to experiment. Start with the oxalic acid. It is available from paint stores in crystal form and must be dissolved in alcohol. Apply the solution with a brush and allow the alcohol solvent to evaporate. You may wish to alternate the acid treatment with ordinary chlorine household bleach applied in a similar manner. When using these chemicals, beware: use a chemical filtering mask and ventilate the area well.

If these chemicals provide no relief, you may try peroxide bleach. The peroxide may do a better job than the others but it may also completely kill the markings of the wood. Whichever solution is used, a thorough washing with a fairly strong laundry detergent, used warm, may increase the effectiveness of your bleaches.

Finally, if all else fails, you may have to camouflage the problem area under a veil of pigmented finish—in plain words, paint the desired color over the unwanted one. This requires a certain amount of skill and, surprisingly, the need for such skill frequently uncovers its existence.

Chemical dye

For years, I've been using a concentrated solution of potassium dichromate to darken cherry so that it appears aged after finishing with linseed or Danish oil. Am I correct in assuming that this is harmless to the wood and that it is not a stain? —*E. Jeff Justis, Memphis, Tenn.*
GEORGE FRANK REPLIES: To my knowledge, potassium dichromate is completely harmless to wood and it isn't a stain but a dye. On woods with no tannic acid, it may convey its own yellow-orange hue; on woods with tannic acid, potassium dichromate can produce a great variety of colors. When using it, be sure to work in a room with good ventilation and wear eye protection and gloves.
EDITOR'S NOTE: Several readers report they have been unable to find small quantities of potassium dichromate crystals (suggested by George Frank for chemically changing the color of wood). Companies listed under "Laboratory Equipment and Supplies" in the Yellow Pages are more likely to deal in small quantities than companies listed under "Chemicals." If your phone book doesn't have these listings, try asking the local high school for the name of the company that supplies the chemistry lab. If you can't find a nearby source, a company that will sell small quantities of potassium dichromate crystals by mail is American Scientific and Chemical, 2019 Walker Ave., Box 18116, Houston, Tex. 77003.

There is also confusion about the safety of using potassium dichromate. Dr. Michael McCann, of the Art Hazards Information Center in New York City, says it can cause skin ulcers and severe allergic reactions. He advises wearing goggles and rubber gloves when using it. Some chemical suppliers say that selling the chemical to hobbyists is forbidden by Food and Drug Administration regulations, but an FDA spokesman said that potassium dichromate—neither food nor drug—doesn't come under its jurisdiction. One chemical salesman said companies who sell industrial chemicals in large quantities are often reluctant to sell to hobbyists because they might hurt themselves and sue. Many companies also find it easier and cheaper to sell only 100-lb. sacks or boxcar loads.

For those who plan to experiment with potassium dichromate, George Frank suggests the following procedure: If you dissolve 50 grams of potassium dichromate crystals in a half-liter of (preferably) rain water, you will have a concentrated solution. Keep this in a bottle and experiment on scrap wood with more dilute solutions. To start, take another half-liter of water and add to it two-tenths of your concentrated dichromate. Saturate the wood. Take up the excess liquid with a well-squeezed sponge and let the wood dry thoroughly, for half a day at least. Then check how close you are to your goal. Be patient and know that the greater part of woodfinishing is experimenting.

Dyeing hardwoods

How can I dye hardwoods, mostly red oak, different colors? I want a deep black finish that allows the grain to show through. I'd also like some bright reds, blues and greens as accent colors. —*Kurt Martinson, Coeur d'Alene, Id.*
OTTO HEUER REPLIES: There are three kinds of dyes that can be used to stain oak: water-, oil- and alcohol-soluble aniline dyes. All three should be available in a well-stocked paint store, though you may have to special-order them. Some dyes are carried by H. Behlen and Bros. (write them at Rt. 30N., Amsterdam, N.Y. 12010, for local distributors). All of these dyes can be brushed or wiped on, or sprayed on with a pump-type sprayer of the type used for insecticides.

Water-soluble aniline stains are the most lightfast. In a plastic or glass container, mix about 4 oz. of dry stain powder in a gallon of hot water, allow it to cool and strain it through a triple layer of fine cheesecloth or muslin. Vary the application rate to get the color you want. Water-soluble aniline stains should be freshly prepared for each application, and they shouldn't be stored in metal containers.

Alcohol-soluble aniline stains will produce bright colors, but they are likely to be light-fugitive, especially the reds. To mix them, add 2 oz. to 6 oz. of powder to 1 gal. of a mixture composed of 8 parts methanol and 2 parts denatured alcohol.

Oil-soluble aniline dye mixtures can be made by mixing 2 oz. to 6 oz. of stain powder to a gallon of toluol, xylol or any other aromatic petroleum solvent. Agitate the mixture well, let it settle, strain it and apply as above. Avoid breathing the vapors from this mixture and don't work around open flames—the solution is extremely flammable. To bring out the colors of any of these dyes, especially the blacks, you may need to add a top coat of semigloss or gloss lacquer, or reduced white shellac.

Staining poplar

I'm making kitchen cabinets for my parents' home using poplar that has a fair amount of green color to it, which stains darker than the surrounding wood. How can I create an even color? What kind of finish would be durable enough for a counter made of the same wood?
—*Dan Snellenberger, Cloverdale, Ind.*
OTTO HEUER REPLIES: Poplar has light-colored sapwood and a darker, green-tinged heartwood that can present problems in staining. But by bleaching the wood, you can even out the

undesirable streakiness staining often produces. I would suggest an application of type A and B wood bleaches (available from the Klean-Strip division of W.M. Barr Inc., PO Box 1879, Memphis, Tenn. 38101). Follow the recommended instructions for the bleach, use rubber gloves and apply it with a fiber brush. A cheaper alternative is ordinary household chlorine bleach straight from the bottle. Be sure to wash the wood well before attempting to stain it.

Before staining, you may want to use a washcoat of one part 4-lb. cut white shellac to 7 or 8 parts alcohol. When this has dried, sand lightly and apply a coat of linseed oil to the end grain of the doors to prevent excessive stain absorption. I recommend a pigment wiping stain that does not contain any aniline dyes. As a top coat, you can use a Danish oil or perhaps a urethane varnish or any other surface finish that meets your requirements for gloss and protection.

I'm sorry to say that poplar is not a good choice for a countertop because it is so soft and dents and damages easily. A better choice would be a plastic laminate counter or a harder wood. But if you must use poplar, a tough two-part urethane varnish will help protect the wood.

Staining black walnut
Can you help me find a way to get the grain to show through on black walnut? I've stained several scraps of it, and I'm not pleased with any of the results. I've heard of water-base stains but don't know where to get them or how to use them. I once read about using chemicals to bring out the grain in crotches and burls, but now I can't find the article. —T. Bennett, Woodland Hills, Calif.
Your mistake is trying to stain it at all. There is no reason walnut needs stain, unless it is painted on in thin coats with a brush to even the tone of sapwood and blend it into the heartwood. Otherwise, its own color is truly beautiful without further manipulation.

Stain for oak
Do you know of a mixture of coal tar and kerosene that will produce a good stain for oak? I have a table that is supposedly stained with such a mixture, and its top is beautiful. My problem is that I have to stain some chairs to match the table, but I can't find anyone who knows the proper mixture of the two ingredients. Can you help?
—Peggy Gefellers, Greenville, Tenn.
DON NEWELL REPLIES: I suspect that the mixture you're referring to is a mixture of asphaltum and kerosene. The asphaltum (or asphalt) supplies the color, and the kerosene is merely a solvent.

Though I have used dissolved asphalt as a wood stain, it has one major drawback—it never hardens permanently or polymerizes as it ages and can always be dissolved by an organic solvent. The result is that the subsequent application of a lacquer or varnish will lift the stain and thereby lighten the wood. It will work as a stain, but it's a trifle difficult to get the exact color desired.

I would never use kerosene as a solvent. Use mineral spirits, which dries much more quickly and more dependably than kerosene. Obtain asphalt from a hardware store: a small can of asphalt roofing or gutter paint, without any fillers or additives. Thin a teaspoon of asphalt paint in two or three ounces of paint thinner. Try it on a scrap of wood, thinning or thickening the mixture to get lighter or deeper shades.

When you have the color you want, brush it on in fairly wet coats, let it soak in and lightly dry the surface with a paper towel. After an hour or two, you can apply the finish—a good satin varnish is a safe choice.

Honey-tan stains for pine and maple
I would like to share two good honey-tan staining methods. The first is perfect for pine because it doesn't darken the end grain more than the surface. Buy a bag of chewing tobacco and soak it overnight in a quart jar filled half-and-half with ammonia and water. Decant it and it's ready to apply.

Because the stain is weak, I use ten to twelve applications, but I can do three applications on a winter evening. The stain is transparent and unaffected by subsequent wetting. It raises the grain, so I steel-wool after every three or four coats.

Final finish for this stain is the woodworker's choice. I generally use wax or urethane.

My other finish formula is apparently unique to maple. I oil the wood with bacon fat and place it in my barbeque smoker with a small green twig in one corner. After half an hour the maple turns brown-black. Wipe it clean and seal with linseed oil. I tried this with pine and it turned a horrible yellow color, so I conclude that maple darkens through chemical action.
—P.L. LaMontagne, New Britten, Pa.

To make a honey-tan pine stain, buy three tubes of artist's oil paint: burnt umber, burnt sienna and yellow ochre. For an antique pine I use 60% to 90% burnt umber, with most of the balance burnt sienna and a touch of yellow ochre. A stronger portion of yellow ochre should yield a honey color.

Mix the colors you want in a bowl. Then mix turpentine and boiled linseed oil, half and half, in another bowl. Finally, take an old rag, dip it in the oil and turpentine, then dab it in the paint and rub it on a scrap of wood to test the color. The oil mixture can be used without paint to thin out areas on the wood.

When you are ready to begin staining your piece, be sure you have enough paint mixed to do the job. You will find that it is almost impossible to make a second batch the exact shade as the first.
—Eddie Trerillian, Columbia, S.C.

Yellow finish for red woods
I am making a small round extension table for a dinette, using Brazilian cherry, a fragrant wood with grain and color similar to mahogany. I would like its final color to be beige rather than ruddy brown, and it would be nice to retain the fragrance if possible.
—Louis O. Heinold, Warwick, R.I.
GEORGE FRANK REPLIES: To make a red wood blond you have to get rid of the red. You may be able to camouflage the red and come up with a beige-brown finish by putting hints of green into the stain (if you use any), into the filler and into the finish. Or you may have to bleach the wood by washing it two or three times with the strongest chlorine bleach you can find. Let the wood dry between washings, sandpaper when dry, and wash off with white vinegar to neutralize the bleach. If the red is gone, you are ready for staining and finishing. Peroxide bleach would surely remove the red, but would also eliminate all the beauty of your wood.

Your problem is far more difficult than you realize. You must be willing to experiment on samples, don't hope for an easy solution, and be sure to treat both sides of the boards the same way.

It is very unlikely that you'll be able to retain the fragrance. It will not resist repeated washing nor will it come through the finish.

Fernan Banks on Ammonia

No time for restaining?

by George Frank

Since no one could pronounce his name—Ferdinand Schnitz-span—his customers simply called him Fernan. We, his workers, addressed him as "Patron." He was a giant Alsatian and in the early 1920s he ran a good-sized woodfinishing shop in Paris. All his men liked him; I, then a youngster of 21, loved him like a father.

This was the time when France was rebuilding after World War I, and the Banque de France was Fernan's best customer. New branch offices were being built and opened up in every important town. The furnishings of these banks were made in Paris, and Fernan had the contract to finish them. The style was always the same, and the wood was invariably oak. The only allowed difference was in the finish, or, more exactly, in the staining. The architect could select one of four colors, ranging from No. 1, which was the lightest, to No. 4, the darkest.

Early in June we shipped out all the woodwork for a bank to be installed at Lisieux, a town closer to Deauville than to Paris. This branch was supposed to open up on July 16, just after the Bastille Day holiday. Around July 10 there was a big upheaval in our shop. The telephone did not stop ringing, telegrams arrived, people were coming and going like chickens without heads, and all of us sensed that something was amiss. By noon the secret was out—the Lisieux bank was stained too light. Fernan had made an error. His order had called for color No. 3, but he made us use No. 2, a lighter one. The architect was adamant: He wanted the color he had specified and told Fernan in no uncertain terms to come and darken up the bank before the opening date.

Fernan had a car built to carry four people, but the next morning he and six of his best men somehow squeezed into it, along with all the material needed, and headed for Lisieux. We arrived around 9 A.M. and entered the bank. There was no question about the error nor about the size of the task on our hands. Even if we worked 24 hours a day, it would still take 10 to 15 days to restain and refinish the bank. After hashing over every possibility, Fernan and his men decided that the situation was hopeless—the job simply could not be done in the remaining few days.

There was one fellow who did not open his mouth, me, but whose mind was working furiously. Although I was the youngest and the least experienced member of the group, I had had more school learning than the other six combined. In evening courses I had studied woodfinishing for two years. Now, when doom settled on our small company, I touched Fernan's sleeve and very timidly said, "Patron, I think I can do the job by tomorrow night. . . ."

Six pairs of eyes looked at me, not knowing whether I was joking, dreaming or trying to be funny. I explained that the job could be done by gas. If we could create a strong enough concentration of ammonia gas in the bank, there was a great chance that it would go through the thin layer of finish and react with the tannic acid in the oak to darken the wood.

Since there was no other choice, my plan was accepted. We sealed all doors, windows and openings. Then we made about 30 simple alcohol burners, consisting of a board about 10 in. square, with a small bowl containing about a half pint of alcohol in the center. Three long nails held up a small pail over the bowl. With wet towels over our faces, we poured the strongest ammonia we could find into the pails, lit the alcohol and scurried out of the bank, leaving all the lights on and closing and taping up the last doors. By the time the alcohol had burned out, all the ammonia had evaporated, and there was such a concentration of gas in the room that no living thing could remain. Then we went to sleep.

Sleep, no one could. We played cards and drank an awful lot of Calvados, a local apple brandy. Every hour we checked whether the gas was working. It was not, at least not fast enough for us to see. But the next afternoon the architect joined our group with a sample in his hands. Peeking through the window he was shaking his head approvingly and said: "This is it. Please don't make it any darker."

It was not easy to re-enter the bank and to get rid of the ammonia gas. Our noses and eyes were running, but my tears were tears of joy. We touched up the small areas that were unaffected by the gas, and the bank opened up as scheduled.

But I was not there to see it. Fernan said, "You, fellow, I don't want to see you for a week. Go and have a good time at Deauville," and stuck about a month's pay into my hand.

On July the 15th I lost my last franc at the roulette table. Luckily I had my return ticket, and on the 16th I was back and happy at my workbench.

Q & A

Shoe-polish finish

My father returned from Mexico with a beautifully carved quail in ironwood. I was admiring the finish, a fine semi-gloss with depth, and imagined oil being rubbed in with care. Smiling, he said it was shoe polish. Immediately I tried neutral shoe polish on a damaged marquetry piece, over Watco. It is beautiful. Something has to be wrong; it's too simple. —Gary Wright, N. Conway, N.H.
GEORGE FRANK REPLIES: You can apply the best possible finish to roughly sanded wood and you will not be proud of the effect. On the other hand, you can apply shoe polish (which usually is composed of fine waxes) to a well-sanded piece, and feel it is so beautiful that something must be wrong. No, fine finish nearly always can be equated with superior smoothness. Try to finish an unsanded piece with shoe polish and you will agree.

DON NEWELL REPLIES: Nothing is wrong with shoe polish as a finish for surfaces not subjected to wear. It starts out and stays harder than most other wax finishes and buffs up nicely. Eventually it will soften, and it will have to be renewed to maintain a soft luster.

Tung Oil
Quick-drying finish is handsome and tough

by William D. Woods

If you haven't used tung oil, and you're tired of worrying about stain and filler colors, primers, adhesion, drying time, runs and drips, checking and water marks, it may be time to give it a try. While there's probably no stage of woodworking easier to mess up than finishing, it's hard to go wrong with tung oil. It yields a finish with contrast and depth, and is readily available and easy to use. It also builds well, dries quickly, and is water- and solvent-resistant.

Tung oil is an aromatic natural drying oil extracted from the nuts of the tung tree (*Aleurites montana* or *A. fordii*), which is native to the Orient but now cultivated in the Gulf States. The color of tung oil ranges from golden yellow to dark brown, depending on the amount of heat used during extraction. The oil takes its name from the Chinese word "tung," or stomach, because it has a purgative action when taken internally. The properties of the oil are almost proverbial, and the preservation of the Great Wall has been attributed in part to tung-oil treatment of the masonry. In modern varnishes, tung oil is often used as a drying oil, giving elasticity and durability to the film.

Tung oil (sometimes called tung-oil varnish) is commonly available in two forms: the "pure" or unthinned state, which has about the viscosity of glycerine, and the volatilized or thinned state, which is watery or sometimes a little thicker. Although manufacturers are loath to reveal their "trade secrets," the odor suggests that the vehicle is mineral spirits or something similar. Pure tung oil can be thinned with paint thinner or turpentine; however, the commercially thinned oil, which probably contains a drying agent, dries faster than tung oil mixed with paint thinner alone. In general, the commercially thinned oil is easier to use and more versatile than the pure oil. The pure oil is also becoming harder to find.

The characteristics of tung oil are unlike those of most "oil" finishes. In fact, the name "tung oil" is misleading, because it produces not only a soaking finish but also a building finish. If brushed on like any other surface finish and left to dry, it will harden into a glossy film much like varnish. If used as an oil finish, it will build quickly and effectively consolidate the wood surface; furthermore, it will yield a much better sheen than any other oil preparation I know of.

Cured tung oil is tough. When I first encountered this oil, I conducted some experiments to compare it to other finishes. I found that a dried tung-oil film is considerably more flexible than a lacquer or varnish film—it is possible to bend the film sharply double and then flatten it out again without breaking it. Although a tung-oil film is not as resistant to abrasion as urethane varnish, tung oil soaked into the wood is incredibly resistant to marring. It also shows good solvent resistance, even against a short exposure to acetone. To test tung oil's resistance to water, I made up a sample of Honduras mahogany with three soak coats of tung oil, drying it in the sun and overnight. I then applied a large drop of water to one section of the sample and kept that area wet for an entire day. At the end of the day I dried the sample off, and with 4/0 steel wool burnished away the mineral ring left by the water. I couldn't detect any damage. My uncle, a gunsmith, claims similar results on gunstocks. He says that tung oil puts the more commonly used linseed oil "right out on the back porch." Tung oil is often used on salad bowls, butcher blocks and other wood surfaces exposed to water, acids, oils and food residues. When used on eating utensils, the oil should be allowed to dry thoroughly before using. Polymerized tung oil contains metallic driers; check to see if the product meets federal standards for use with foods (see page 49).

In my experience, tung oil is easier to use than any other wood finish. It will prime any raw wood I have tried, including rosewood and vermilion, without delayed drying and without bleeding the color. The first coat is applied immediately after finish-sanding or scraping—use a brush, your fingers or a rag. I use thinned oil because it flows and soaks better without filling the pores, but for maximum build or a final coat pure oil is suitable. You can make thinned oil as thick as you want by exposing it to the air in a shallow pan. The oil should soak into the wood anywhere from 30 seconds to about 10 minutes, depending on weather conditions, the properties of the wood, and the particular oil being used. It may be beneficial to rub the oil into the wood with the hand or a pad. After soaking, wipe off all the excess with a clean rag. If the oil has become tacky, wipe it off with a rag moistened in fresh oil. Clean up brushes and spills with mineral spirits or lacquer thinner.

Each coat of oil should dry at least an hour, longer if it is very humid. I have sometimes recoated within 20 or 30 minutes on warm dry days with no trouble. To hasten the drying, the project may be set in the sun to cook. Tung oil does not seep out of the wood and "bead" on the surface, since it dries quickly, supposedly from the inside out. It usually does not raise the grain, and a quick rub with 4/0 steel wool after the first coat will ensure a smooth surface. Otherwise, it is not necessary to rub between coats.

The number of coats required depends on the porosity of the wood, the thickness of the oil, and the desired sheen. For protection, two coats of thin oil are often enough, although I would recommend three coats for the best durability and an

Burl bowls of ponderosa pine, 8 in. and 3½ in. in diameter, made by the author and finished with tung oil.

attractive satin sheen. After drying for a day, the surface may be burnished with 4/0 steel wool for a more even sheen. All subsequent cleaning and polishing of the finished surface should be done only with lemon-oil treatment. Although I have used tung oil as a surface finish in experiments, I do not recommend it as such, because it is not as durable as varnish or lacquer and poses the same application problems as any other surface finish.

Tung oil can also be used as a filler finish, because it will build with repeated applications. Apply the oil in the usual fashion, but let it dry until it becomes viscous (from 5 to 30 minutes). With the palm of the hand or with a rag, rub the gelled oil into the open pores of the wood much as you would a regular filler, then wipe off the excess. It will be necessary to dry the project for a day or more, because more than the usual amount of oil has been applied. Filling the pores completely may require five or more applications. Remember that the oil in the pores will shrink, so thorough drying is essential before any rubbing. This method is more laborious and time-consuming than the apply-and-wipe method.

Like many wood finishes, tung oil tends to skin over and finally to congeal if stored in a container less than about three-quarters full. If thickened tung oil is not too far gone, it can be reconstituted by adding mineral spirits and straining; however, always test such oil before using it. The problem of storage can be overcome by using a variable-volume container like a flexible polyethylene bottle. As the oil is used up, the bottle is squeezed to drive out all air before being capped. Better yet, obtain two or three of the refillable plastic food tubes made for hikers (they look like large toothpaste tubes). Cap the tube, then fill it with oil through the large open end, leaving enough room to fold the tube over and install the retaining clip. As you use the oil, squeeze the tube to eliminate the air. As for the storage life of tung oil, I have not had opportunity for a long-term experiment. It has a shelf life as good or better than traditional varnishes, if kept from temperature extremes and direct light in a nearly full, tightly sealed container.

Tung oil, because it soaks into the wood, heightens contrast and deepens color. Its finished sheen is warm, yet it permits easy view of the wood without any disturbing glare. And the disadvantages? Undoubtedly, the price of tung oil has been a deterrent to potential users—the unthinned extract is about $9 a pint, the thinned variety about $6 a quart (1978)—but a little goes a long way. One quart of thinned oil will easily finish three or four medium-size pieces of furniture. Considering the properties of tung oil, the price becomes rather insignificant. Because tung oil emphasizes most subtleties of graining, it may infrequently be found objectionable as a primer for light softwoods (spruce, for example) where the revelation of peculiar grain patterns may spoil the even, creamy color. With these woods, a test sample is in order. Personally, I think nothing looks better on wood than tung oil, because in finishing, I prefer to alter the wood as little as possible. I seldom use stains and usually make no attempt to fill the pores, which I feel are part of the wood's natural beauty. Above all, I want to see the wood, so I avoid glossy finishes. Tung oil agrees with my sense of esthetics. □

Bill Woods, of Phoenix, Ariz., refinishes furniture part-time, makes guitars, and has worked for several years as a professional woodworker.

Oil/Varnish Mix
Making oil more durable

by Jere Osgood

There is a basic decision to be made when choosing a finish for a piece of furniture. Would you prefer a matte oil finish or a glossy varnish or lacquer?

For many years now, a matte oil finish has been very popular because it penetrates the wood and becomes part of the surface, and because it is easy to put on. But it is not really durable, especially for often-used table tops. On the other hand, a good water and alcohol-resistant finish would mean a varnish or lacquer which is more of a surface finish, frequently glossy, and much more difficult to put on. The various varnishes or lacquers also require a fussy environment—warm, ventilated and dust-free—for application.

If you do prefer an oil finish, you have several choices—including an oil/varnish mix that I have found to be particularly effective.

Linseed oil is of course in wide use as a finish. But it has a long application time (a matter of weeks), requires continual upkeep, and is not water-resistant. Its advantage lies in the fact that it is easy to apply, though time-consuming. A ruined spot is easy to repair with a little wet rubbing, using a rag dipped in oil and thinner. It is also pleasant to use, is easy to clean up and can be put on in a dusty, slightly cool shop if absolutely necessary.

Various synthetic penetrating oils, and Watco oils in particular, are a tremendous improvement over linseed. Watco is more water-resistant and can be used on tables if they are treated with care. The other advantage is that you can deliver your work in three days, instead of the three weeks it takes for linseed oil. Watco oil used to be a little hard to locate in some areas, but many of the mail-order woodworking supply houses carry it.

Oil and Varnish Mix

The best general finish I have had experience with is the oil and varnish mix. I can't claim to have originated it but I have pushed its use. It seems to have a long history, and variations of it are used by many furniture craftsmen because of its durability where an oil finish is needed. Its advantages over Watco are that I find it slightly more water-resistant, easier to obtain, and it has more of a body to it (but still penetrates like an oil). It doesn't need any special shop environment or equipment. A little dust or another piece being worked on nearby will cause no difficulties, though a clean, dry shop would probably be best. And the ingredients should be available at most local paint-supply stores.

The piece to be finished should have all planing, scraping or sanding completed so that a later wet-rubbing step deals only with raised grain or unevenness in the finish.

You need a pure, boiled linseed oil with no driers or additives. Parks brand is pure and widely available; Behlen's is also pure (write them at Rt. 30N, Amsterdam, N.Y. 12010 for local distributors). Pure turpentine is also required: Do not use mineral spirits or other substitutes. Also needed is a good-quality synthetic varnish. Try for a minimum of 50% alkyd resins (the resins are the solids) in the varnish. Use a gloss varnish so it won't contain flattening agents. The two brands I have found to be good are Valspar Gloss (50% alkyd resins) and McClosky's Ultra Spar Marine Varnish (52% alkyd resins). Clean, absorbent, lint-free rags are required—an old diaper is perfect. Also needed are 400-grit silicon carbide wet-or-dry paper for wet rubbing and a small cork or heavy felt rubbing block about three or four inches square. Mixture proportions are one part pure, boiled linseed oil, two parts synthetic varnish, and three parts turpentine. Mix a minimum of one quart the day before if possible, so it can "make" overnight.

Application steps

First day: Flood the surface of the piece using a brush or rag. If you see dry spots, apply more. Keep the surface saturated. After two hours, check for tackiness and wipe off with a rag if the finish has started to thicken. Thickening may take two hours or all day, depending on wood species, humidity and temperature. In any case, the surface should be wiped off before being left overnight. If you let it get too tacky, it will be difficult to wipe off and will leave crusty spots.

Second day: Generally a repeat of the first application but don't apply quite so liberally and watch carefully for thickening, because there is not as much absorption by the wood. The time it takes to become tacky will be much shorter than with the first coat—even as short as an hour or less. When it does, wipe it off with a rag.

Third day: Flood the piece (or a section if it is very large) with mix and do the wet rubbing. Pour some of the mix into a pie plate or other flat dish. If there are some slightly crusty spots from the previous day, it might be better to thin the rubbing mix half-and-half with turpentine. Put a few pieces of 400-grit wet-or-dry paper in the plate to soak. Wrap one of these on the block and rub evenly back and forth, with the grain only, until the whole surface is covered and is smooth everywhere. This will flatten the raised grain, eliminate crusty spots and smooth out to an even thickness the finish that has been put on. Curved surfaces can be rubbed using a folded leather pad behind the paper. After this wet sanding or rubbing is complete, the piece should be vigorously buffed clean and dry. Do this by hand with clean rags, not with an electric buffer, because this finish does remain soft for a period of time. An electric buffer might possibly take too much of the finish off.

The piece is finished now, but with some woods I have found a slight sweating occurs, i.e., "mix" comes out of the pores. If this happens, it can be taken care of by a treatment on the fourth day—a light moistening application of mix, and then buffing it dry immediately.

You can use the wet sanding technique as a rescue for a dried or gummy oil finish at any stage. Add a lot of thinner to the mix if it is a big disaster. For wet sanding you can

Hickory wine locker by the author was finished with an oil/varnish mix over a three-day period.

The third-day application of the oil/varnish mix involves wet rubbing with sandpaper to flatten the raised grain and smooth out the finish.

substitute very worn 220-grit garnet paper for the 400-grit wet-or-dry paper, but it disintegrates quickly. You can also use 4/0000 steel wool, though it tends to shed particles that can lodge in pores or corners. Damaged spots in this finish can be repaired easily by scraping the bad spot and/or wet sanding with some of the mix (depending on how bad the spot is), then reapplying more finish.

While this oil and varnish mix can't compete with the durability of a varnish or a lacquer, it does meet some of the demands for a more durable oil finish. □

Oil/Varnish Finishes
Experiment to find the right proportions

by Don Newell

Most finishers have probably experimented with mixtures of boiled linseed oil and varnish in an attempt to produce a better finishing material than either oil or varnish alone. Whether the resulting finish is really better depends on what is needed in terms of drying time, hardness, luster and film build. Because no information exists on the properties of specific mixtures of varnish and drying oils, the finisher must continue to experiment. To give the would-be experimenter some data on which to base the experiments, I ran a series of tests under controlled conditions, eliminating as many variables as possible.

The oil/varnish homebrew mix — I chose a typical soya alkyd varnish (because most varnishes on the market are of this type) and a commercial boiled linseed oil as the base ingredients. I blended the varnish and oil samples into mixtures of the following proportions: 100% varnish, 90% varnish/10% oil, 80%/20%, 60%/40%, 40%/60%, 20%/80%, 10%/90% and 100% boiled linseed oil. The 100% varnish and 100% oil samples were the standards against which I compared the various mixtures. The 90%/10% varnish-to-oil and oil-to-varnish mixtures were used to determine how a mere trace of oil changed the properties of pure varnish, and vice versa. The other formulations were varied by 20% steps

to keep the total number of test mixtures manageable.

I drew out each of the mixtures on a piece of chemically clean glass to a uniform wet film .009 in. thick. The drying times are shown in the table. The only real surprise was that the addition of 10% boiled linseed oil to varnish produced a substantially softer film than one might expect, and that a 10% addition of varnish to oil produced a harder film. In the other mixtures, each material's properties were modified by the other's properties to about the same degree as the amount of each component present. In practice, this means the more oil you add to the varnish, the slower the film will dry and the softer it will remain.

Although I evaluated alkyd varnish and boiled linseed oil, any drying oil can be mixed successfully with varnish. Polyurethane and phenolic varnishes will work well in place of alkyd types, as will tung oil in place of linseed. But whatever the makeup of a given mixture, its overall properties will probably vary as the proportions of its components vary.

Only experimentation will provide answers. However, a 50%/50% mix of whatever components the finisher chooses is an excellent starting point. Chances are the finisher will never need to experiment with other proportions.

I didn't use thinner in testing because it would have introduced a variable without changing the ultimate results. In

Drying times of mixtures of soya alkyd varnish and boiled linseed oil. All samples drawn out on glass to a film thickness of .009 in.

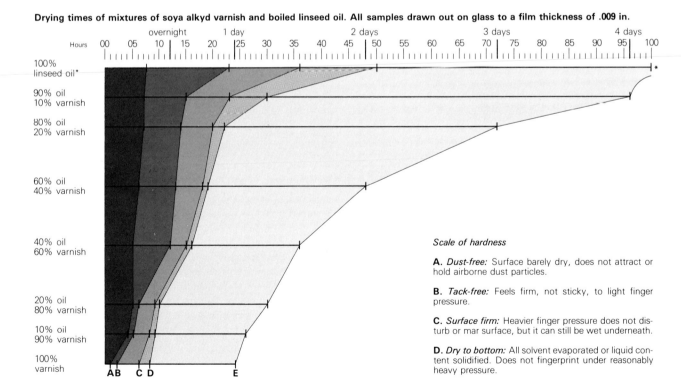

* Still soft after a week, never really gets hard.

Scale of hardness

A. *Dust-free:* Surface barely dry, does not attract or hold airborne dust particles.

B. *Tack-free:* Feels firm, not sticky, to light finger pressure.

C. *Surface firm:* Heavier finger pressure does not disturb or mar surface, but it can still be wet underneath.

D. *Dry to bottom:* All solvent evaporated or liquid content solidified. Does not fingerprint under reasonably heavy pressure.

E. *Maximum hardness:* Hardening reaction completed.

From *Fine Woodworking* magazine (November 1979) 19:76-78

actual finishing, however, such mixes are often thinned with either mineral spirits or turpentine.

Thinning helps the first coat penetrate the raw wood and seal its pores, but probably has no effect on subsequent coats. In most cases, the thinner present in the varnish as it comes from the can provides adequate penetration. But if you want to thin the first coat, mix equal parts of thinner and oil/varnish mix. Keep in mind that the more a mixture is thinned, the lower the solids (film-building) content. Consequently, you'll need more coats of a thinned mixture to produce the same film thickness as an unthinned mixture.

As mentioned, tung oil may be used to replace boiled linseed oil in the oil/varnish homebrew mix, and in fact it will produce results superior to linseed. To this end, I ran another test comparing a 50%/50% mix of polymerized tung oil and the same alkyd varnish. Chart 2, right, shows the results. Though the tung/varnish mix remained fluid long enough to rub out well under hand pressure, the film dried hard all the way through in the same period of time it took the linseed/varnish mix to become only tacky.

The three faces of tung — Tung, or China wood oil, has been used as a binding agent and finishing material for centuries, and many finishers consider it the ultimate material for the classic hand-rubbed oil finish. Tung is available in three forms: plain (so-called pure) tung oil, tungseed oil and polymerized tung oil. Plain tung is oil pressed from the nuts of the tung tree and filtered to remove impurities. Tungseed is basically the same as plain tung, but it is dissolved in thinner to provide maximum penetration of the wood. It contains about 21% oil solids. Polymerized tung is the most useful form. This is tung that has been heat-treated to initiate the polymerizing process (molecular cross-linking by which the oil dries to a solid film) but remains in a sort of holding pattern. Such oil need only absorb oxygen to complete the hardening process. Polymerized tung usually comes thinned to about 49% solids to make the oil fluid enough to penetrate the wood surface.

Any of the tung oils is suitable as an in-surface finish. Generally, two or three coats are applied by hand, rubbed in well and allowed to dry. This leaves the pores and grain structure of the wood open, yet protected by the oil film.

Tung oil films are about twice as resistant to moisture passage as are linseed oil films. In fact, they can stand up to a dilute solution of household lye that will completely strip away an equivalent film of aged boiled linseed oil.

While tung in any form dries faster and harder than linseed, the speed of drying varies among the three different forms. One indication of the differences in reaction speed can be seen on the shelf, assuming half-empty cans of each type. Tungseed oil is the most stable because 79% of the contents are thinners, which do not react with air. Yet tungseed oil will gel solid within 60 days when stored in a half-empty can. Plain tung oil absorbs oxygen from the air in the can more quickly, creating a gelled layer on the surface of the oil within a few days. Polymerized tung oil, however, is much more reactive. It is so hungry for oxygen that a solid layer can form overnight on the surface of the oil in the can.

Drying speed — In tests on wood and on clean glass, tungseed appears to dry a little faster than polymerized tung and much faster than plain tung (chart 3, top right). This is

Comparative drying time for 50%/50% polymerized tung/varnish and 50%/50% boiled linseed/varnish

	Dust free	Tack free	Surface firm	Dry through
Tung/varnish	55 min.	1½ hrs.	2 hrs.	6 hrs.
Linseed/varnish	6 hrs.	13 hrs.	16 hrs.	18 hrs.

Comment: The tung/varnish film was much harder at through-dry time than was the linseed/varnish film. Even after a week of drying time, the linseed/varnish film remained much softer than the tung/varnish film.

Comparative drying times of tung oil types

Type of oil	Dust free	Tack free	Maximum hardness
Plain tung	12 hrs.	20 hrs.	30 hrs.
Tungseed oil (20% solids, 80% thinner)	2 hrs.	4 hrs.	15 hrs.
Polymerized tung (50% solids, 50% thinner)	3 hrs.	6 hrs.	20 hrs.

Safe Finishes for Toys and Food Utensils

Finishing toys and utensils used for food service poses special problems for woodworkers. Many conventional clear finishing materials normally used for furniture and other interior wood surfaces contain compounds which, if ingested, are dangerous.

Driers pose the greatest threat. Ordinarily they are composed of metals or metal compounds; driers containing lead are the most dangerous, but no amount of any metal can be considered absolutely safe. Drying oils such as linseed and tung and most varnishes contain metallic drier compounds. Even though the actual quantity of metal in a given amount of finishing material is small, little by little it can accumulate to dangerous levels in humans.

In the case of wooden toys, a child can quickly strip and ingest the finish by chewing or sucking. Wooden dishes and utensils in food service are not so likely to be chewed, but with continuous exposure to foods and liquids the compounds can be leached out of the finish and carried into the human system together with the food.

Countertops and food-preparation surfaces can safely be finished with most varnishes, because food is less likely to remain in contact with the finish for long periods of time, and the potential for drier compounds leaching out is reduced. Nevertheless, because the possibility of a hazard exists, the woodworker has a responsibility to select the safest possible finishing materials.

A report by the Safety Products Division of the U.S. Food and Drug Administration indicates that their major concern is with the presence of lead and mercury in a finishing material. The report concludes that as long as lead or other metals are not present, a finish can be considered nontoxic and acceptable for food service and toys.

Consequently, finishing materials that fall into this nontoxic classification are clear woodfinishing lacquers, both spraying and brushing types, and water-based or "latex" varnishes. Among the finishes approved by the FDA are Behlen Salad Bowl Finish (Woodcraft, 41 Atlantic Avenue, Box 4000, Woburn, Mass. 01888); Wood Bowl Finish (Craftsman Wood Service Co., 1735 W. Cortland Court, Addison, Ill. 60101); and Wood Bowl Seal (Constantine, 2065 Eastchester Road, Bronx, N.Y. 10461). The Watco-Dennis Corp. maintains that Watco oil leaves a solid, nontoxic finish, but stresses that at least 30 days should elapse between finishing and use of food utensils and children's toys to ensure complete polymerization. This is not the finish to use on Christmas eve for next-morning toys.

One other material particularly suited to finishing the end-grain wood of butcher blocks is plain paraffin wax. Melt the wax and pour it over the surface, then literally iron it down into the end grain with a hot electric iron. When cool, scrape the surface residue off, down to the wood. Such a finish remains soft, making it unsuitable for finishing any surface other than porous end grain. It can be renewed at any time simply by ironing in more wax.   *D.N.*

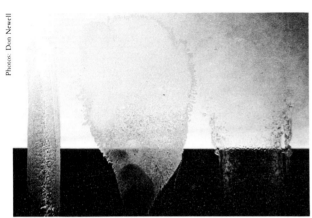

Tests on clean glass show that plain tung oil (left) dries to a badly wrinkled, opaque film. Tungseed oil (center) dries to an opaque film with tiny wrinkles. Polymerized tung oil (right) dries to a fairly glossy, transparent film.

Plain tung (left), tungseed (center) and polymerized tung (right) films dried on cherry wood. As with the glass test, tung dries totally flat, whereas tungseed can be steel-wooled to a low gloss. Polymerized tung has a high sheen after only two coats on unsealed wood.

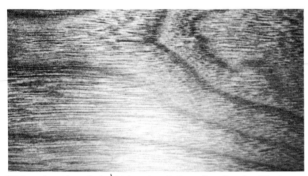

Walnut board sanded, whiskered and given three hand-rubbed coats of polymerized tung oil. The clear finish permits the grain to show with good contrast, and the medium luster enhances the appearance of the well-figured wood.

somewhat misleading in that upon evaporation of the thinners from tungseed, only a thin coat of the oil is left. This thin coat will harden faster than the heavier-bodied forms, but it takes many more coats of tungseed to equal the thickness of one coat of either plain or polymerized tung. Plain tung takes about four times as long to dry as either tungseed or polymerized tung.

Penetration — To test the three forms of tung for depth of penetration into two different woods, one veneer and one solid, I flooded three adjacent areas of wood with the oils,

allowed them to set for ten minutes and then wiped them dry. On 1/32-in. cherry veneer, plain tung oil penetrated through to the back in spots. Tungseed penetrated completely through at all points. Polymerized tung penetrated less than tungseed, but more than the plain oil.

I also tested the oil on 1/4-in. solid walnut. After wiping it dry, I sawed the wood through the center of the test areas. Plain tung oil at first showed little penetration. Tungseed showed some penetration (about 1/64 in.) and polymerized tung showed the deepest initial penetration (at least 1/32 in.).

However, several hours later I observed that plain tung continued to penetrate slowly, darkening the wood with its still-wet presence, though polymerized tung did not. Tungseed oil penetration could not be seen at all, perhaps because the high thinner content of tungseed had evaporated out of the wood, leaving a thin, virtually transparent film of oil behind. It's also possible that the polymerized oil had continued to penetrate, but because of its high reactivity had hardened to a more or less transparent state.

Surface appearance — Plain tung oil dried on the wood to an extremely dull film composed of countless microscopic wrinkles. No amount of polishing or rubbing improved the luster. Tungseed dried to a semivelvet surface that was also wrinkled, but because of the thinness of the film, the wrinkles took on the appearance of a haze. Repeated coats, with drying between, produced a satin luster which, with judicious steel-wooling, was quite attractive. Polymerized tung oil dried to a hard, transparent film with a high luster, without a matte or hazy appearance.

Film thickness — The thickness of any given finish is a function of the solids content of the material in liquid form. The three forms of tung were drawn out on clean glass to a wet film .009 in. thick. After drying for 24 hours, the plain tung oil film was .0005 in. thick, the tungseed oil film was .0001 in. thick, and the polymerized tung film was .0007 in. thick. The bigger the number, the thicker the film and the fewer coats necessary to achieve the same degree of protection. Seven coats of tungseed oil or about one-and-a-half coats of plain tung will produce a film the same thickness as one coat of polymerized tung.

Storage and handling — Tung oil in any of its forms should be treated as a highly reactive (oxidizing) material. Any papers, cloths or rags wetted with tung must be stored in covered metal containers to eliminate the possibility of spontaneous combustion.

Because in partially empty containers of tung oil there is sufficient oxygen present to react with the oil, often within just a few hours, always store it in full containers. Dropping pebbles or marbles into the storage can as the liquid is used, bringing the liquid level up to the neck each time, is one way to do this. Another is to obtain a quantity of small plastic or glass containers and transfer your stock of oil to those. Any spoilage thus will waste only small amounts of oil at a time. A third approach is to obtain squeezable or collapsible plastic containers and squeeze out the air after each use, prior to capping the container. Collapsible containers are used in photographic chemistry and sold by photo suppliers. □

Don Newell is a former paint and varnish chemist.

Varnish Finish That's Rubbed On

Sanding is the way to a glass-smooth surface

by Joe Thomas

When I first started working wood, I read a lot about finishing. The more I read, the more confused I got. There are literally hundreds of stains, dyes, varnishes and fillers around—some soluble in water, some in alcohol, others in oil. It seems to me, you ought to have fun working with wood without having to build a chemical processing plant. So I experimented and developed my own finishing method using paste rubbing stains and varnishes. I'm sure it's not the most sophisticated in the world, but if you follow my procedure, you'll get a silky smooth, alcohol- and water-resistant finish.

The secret to good finishing is to prepare the wood properly by careful sanding. Actually, wood preparation should begin even before you reach the sanding stage. I carefully choose the wood for a piece I'm building. I love distinctive grain and knots, so I try to use them to good advantage. If you prefer clear wood, work around the defects, or position them where you won't have to give them extra sanding later. If possible, don't use wood with planer snipes—ugly gouges caused by improperly adjusted planers. Even if sanded smooth, the glazed wood of a snipe will sometimes show as a streak. Another way to save sanding time is to chisel off the glue squeezed out of joints instead of wiping it off with a damp rag, which just smears it around. Let the glue set for about half an hour, until it's rubbery, and it will slice right off with a sharp chisel.

You will need a good-quality finishing sander. I have a Rockwell orbital that isn't made anymore, but of the half-dozen other sanders I've tried, I think the Black & Decker #7430 (which takes a third of a sheet of sandpaper) and the Makita block sander (a quarter of a sheet) are both good buys. Whichever sander you use, cut a stack of sheets to fit it at one time, so you won't have to stop sanding in the middle of a project to cut more paper. For inside curves, tight spots and end grain, I have a drum sander that fits my ¼-in. portable drill and accepts small sheets of regular sandpaper instead of sleeves. I got it from Singley Specialty Co. Inc., PO Box 5087, Greensboro, N.C. 27403.

Before I begin sanding, I clear my bench of all tools—if you drop a sanded piece on a sharp tool, the small nick that results will look like the Grand Canyon when you stain. I start orbital-sanding with 180-grit aluminum oxide paper until all the scratches and tool marks are gone. To check for missed blemishes, I view the wood obliquely, with the light in front of me. If none are visible, I give the piece a thorough once-over with 220-grit. What do I mean by thorough? It's no 15-minute ordeal. If you're working a 5-in. by 12-in. piece with 220-grit, for example, you ought to see the surface improve after 30 seconds to one minute of sanding. More sanding at that grit won't give you a smoother surface. Switch to a finer grit. Once you learn to find flaws by viewing the wood correctly, you'll know when to stop. If you're progressing too slowly, start with 120- or 150-grit, working up to 220. If you must, use a belt sander to smooth large flaws, but never use a belt coarser than 100-grit.

Now I'm ready to raise the grain for the first time. Raising the grain causes loose wood fibers to stick up from the surface of the wood so that they can be removed with steel wool. Dampen an old washcloth—not dripping but wet—and wipe the wood surface with it. After the wood dries, the surface will feel fuzzy. Now with a loose ball of 0000 steel wool, take a swipe over the wood in each direction. The wool will hook the loose wood fibers and pull them free. Vacuum away any strands of loose steel wool that may remain.

With a fresh piece of 220-grit on your sander, sand the surface again, checking for defects as before. Repeat the grain-raising process, hit the piece again with steel wool, vacuum, then switch to sanding with 320-grit paper. At this point, I protect the wood from marring with an old towel on my bench. By now, the wood should feel smooth as glass. Give it a quick polishing with 600-grit wet-or-dry paper and then wipe off the sanding dust with a tack rag, a sticky cleaning cloth sold by paint stores.

Next comes the exciting part: staining and finishing. I don't always stain, though. If the wood is already the color I want, I just go ahead and finish it. When I do stain, I prefer oil paste wiping stains. The Bartley Collection, Ltd., 747 Oakwood Ave., Lake Forest, Ill. 60045, (800) 227-8539, is one good source for these stains. I've been happy with the finish I get without using any of the paste wood fillers that are on the market, but I don't see why they wouldn't work.

I use the stain right out of the can. Spoon a few blobs into an aluminum pie tin, dip a terry cloth pad into it, and rub the stain firmly and briskly into the wood, going with the grain. When you run out of the small amount of stain on the pad, briskly polish the stained area with a larger piece of terry cloth. Now go back for more stain, blending it into the already stained area and polishing again. Continue this way until you're done, allowing the work to dry for 24 hours.

I use either of two kinds of varnish: the paste varnish sold by Bartley, or McCloskey antique polyurethane. Both are rubbed on and polished just like the stain. If you prefer the McCloskey, or any other store-bought polyurethane, thin it 1:1 with mineral spirits. Apply four or five light coats, allowing 24 hours' drying between. Don't try to get away with one or two thick coats, or you'll wind up with a blotchy, ugly film that you'll just have to sand off.

When the final coat has dried, polish it with 600-grit wet-or-dry paper lubricated with mineral spirits. Wrap the paper around a scrap-wood block and wet the grit with spirits, dribbling a few drops on the varnished wood while you're at it. Now begin sanding, with the grain. On the first pass, you'll feel the paper sort of bumping along the relatively rough varnished surface. On the second or third pass, it will feel like a vacuum is sticking the paper to the surface. At that point, quit. You're done. Buff the surface with a soft, dry rag, and sit back and admire the beautiful finish you've created. □

Joe Thomas works wood in Tucker, Ga. He published his own book about finishing, called Silky, Sensuous Wood Finishing *(61 pages), which is available for purchase from him at PO Box 1158, Lilburn, Ga. 30247.*

Q & A

Tung oil caution
In "Tung Oil" (pages 45-46), William Woods states that tung oil is often recommended for use on salad bowls, butcher blocks and other wood surfaces exposed to water, acids, oils and food residues. However, in "Oil/Varnish Finishes" (pages 48-50), Don Newell states that tung oil is not suitable for surfaces that may come in contact with food or children's toys. I would like some clarification.
—Michael McGrath, East Dubuque, Ill.

DON NEWELL REPLIES: While tung oil is often recommended for salad bowls and children's toys, the possibility also exists that your particular brand of tung oil may contain some metallic driers. The reason I do not recommend tung for the above applications is because I think it is much better to be absolutely sure you have a lead-free or mercury-free finish wherever there is a possibility of its being ingested.

Finish toxicity
Are there any nontoxic finishes that are tough and durable? On page 49, Don Newell mentioned three nontoxic finishes. I have tried two of the three and found them unsatisfactory. The Craftsman finish, a lacquer type, is so soft it is scratched and made unsightly by crisp snacks such as Fritos and pretzels. The Woodcraft finish is no tougher, and it dries too slowly. The polyurethanes and moisture-cured urethanes are tough and quick-drying. Do you know if any are suitable for contact with food?
—Thomas A. Laser, Springfield, Va.

DON NEWELL REPLIES: Sorry the woodbowl finishes didn't work for you. The recommendation was based on freedom from toxicity rather than on working properties. Though I haven't used either the Craftsman or the Woodcraft finish on bowls, I'm surprised to learn that they are too soft for dry snacks. I would try either a standard polyurethane or a moisture-cured urethane. No manufacturer I've contacted will recommend his finish for use with food or toys because of liability problems—this is understandable.

The question of toxicity arises mostly where a finish is exposed to liquids long enough or often enough to leach metallic compounds out of the finish and into the food. For only occasional use, even with liquid food, I would anticipate no problems with polyurethanes. They are very chemical-resistant, once they are thoroughly dry. Watco Danish Oil might also serve your purpose, as long as you let it cure for about 30 days to complete polymerization.

Follow-up
Shortly after writing you, I wrote to United Gilsonite Laboratories in Scranton, Pa., the makers of ZAR polyurethanes. I was happy to hear that ZAR is nontoxic and suitable for bowls and other food utensils.
—Thomas A. Laser, Springfield, Va.

Metallic drier toxicity
Don Newell's discussion of oil/varnish finishes was instructive but I am still confused by the toxicity question (for toys and utensils). Are the metallic drier compounds added during manufacture or are they integral to the raw oil? If added, does that mean that "pure boiled linseed oil" is not pure?
—Scott Lowery, St. Paul, Minn.

DON NEWELL REPLIES: Metallic drier compounds in drying oils are added during manufacture. This means your "pure" boiled linseed oil is pure only in the sense that it probably contains the things that commercial boiled linseed oil should contain and nothing more. Commercial boiled oil is supposed to have metallic driers in it to aid drying. Hence, your "pure"

oil conforms to commercial specifications for purity. Commercial boiled linseed is not actually boiled, since boiling does not improve its drying properties appreciably.

Epoxy varnish for salad bowls
I just carved a large, free-form bowl from a locust burl. I meant for it to be a salad mixing and serving bowl, but hesitate to use it for this because I am not confident about what finish to use. Those I have tried in the past begin to develop a rancid smell with use and age. Do you know of a good oil or sealer that's odorless, colorless and safe for salad bowls?
—Ray J. Gormly, Prior Lake, Minn.

R. BRUCE HOADLEY REPLIES: There are several good bowl finishes on the market. Clear epoxy varnish applied in successive coats makes a hard and durable finish and it will not react with food or drink or dissolve in vinegar. Some craftsmen use plain mineral oil, though this finish requires a periodic reapplication of oil. My favorite treatment for bowls is Behlen's Salad Bowl Finish (available from Woodcraft, 41 Atlantic Ave., Box 4000, Woburn, Mass. 01888). I prefer to rub in a couple of thin coats to seal the wood, though you can use the stuff more liberally if you want a built-up finish. I burnish the bowl to a soft luster. Light recoating is required from time to time, depending on the thickness of the original film. I've never had any problems with rancid smells using this finish, although I've never made salad bowls from black or honey locust, either.

Finishes for butcher-block countertops
How do I finish a butcher-block countertop to seal and protect the wood yet be nontoxic? The top is birch, glued with plastic resin.
—Van Wagner, Trenton, Mich.

GEORGE FRANK REPLIES: I finished my butcher block with polyurethane varnish. Cut the first coat three parts to one of thinner, apply it generously to all sides of the block, let set for about ten minutes and rub off vigorously with a cloth. Let it dry overnight. Then brush on two coats of varnish diluted about two parts to one of thinner, without rubbing it off. This produces a thin coating but still a solid protection, and no smell whatsoever. Or, mix two parts of boiled linseed oil with one of turpentine and one of some good brand of spar varnish, apply three or four coatings and energetically rub off the excess each time.

Butchers use melted paraffin. Paint the surface of the block with the paraffin; remove excess wax with a cabinet scraper. Repeat three or four times. Then rub a little mineral oil into the surface from time to time to keep it looking beautiful. To clean, scrape lightly and wash with hot water and ammonia.
—Eric Rasmussen, Berkeley, Calif.

Finishing countertops—several views
What finishing techniques are recommended for solid wood kitchen countertops? My objectives are durability and avoiding food poisoning and staining. Also, I work with some wide boards and flitches and have heard that I should place relief cuts in the unexposed faces of these pieces to eliminate warping. How does this work?
—Brad Miller, Bangor, Maine

GEORGE FRANK REPLIES: Would you apply today's technology—as 90% of kitchen builders do—you would cover most of your countertop with plastic laminate. It will very durably prevent food stains and food poisoning. You could reserve an area about 24 in. square in your countertop (or anywhere else in your kitchen) for a butcher block. This could be either the commercial variety from the lumberyard, or the professional type, where end-grain maple is the working surface. For finishing, buy some paraffin wax (the kind mother used to seal her fruit preserves), melt it and coat your block with this melted wax. It will gel quickly. Then, with a dull scraper, scrape off as much of the wax as you can. The remaining thin coat will offer a safe protective coating to your butcher block. The process could be repeated as the need arises.

TAGE FRID REPLIES: For finishing a kitchen counter, I use linseed oil, letting it dry 24 hours between coats. For the first coat, use one-half raw linseed oil and one-half turpentine, and soak the top. For the second coat, use boiled linseed oil. Leave it on for about two hours, sand it with the oil on, then wipe off the excess. For the third coat, mix half boiled linseed oil and half Japan drier, but be careful not to coat too large an area at once because all of a sudden it will get tacky and dry quickly. Remove excess oil by scrubbing with a piece of burlap across the grain to force the mixture into the pores of the wood. Clean with a dry cloth, then rub with steel wool, and the countertop is finished. (Don't leave the oily rags inside the house; they may start a fire.) This finish doesn't stain easily, but don't leave a wet beer can on it overnight. It is an easy finish to repair: Just scrape and sand the mark out and oil it again. I know linseed oil is not recommended for salad bowls, but for countertops it's fine.

I would not put relief cuts in the bottom of the board. It is not necessary. Just be sure the underside of the counter is sealed.

EDITOR'S NOTE: Japan drier is available from Mohawk Finishing Products, Rt. 30N, Amsterdam, N.Y. 12010.

George Frank . . . suggests that kitchen countertops be covered with plastic laminate. Solid spruce countertops ⁵⁄₄ in. thick and 26 in. wide in one piece were in the house where I grew up, and these were treated periodically with linseed oil and are still in good condition after fifty years. Two houses I had built had no plastic laminate anyplace. In one I used glued-up birch for counters, in the other, alternating strips of walnut and maple. Both were treated with linseed oil. My only suggestion is to avoid mitering corners and to detail the installation to accommodate the almost continuous expansion and contraction, a measurable quantity in a board 2 ft. wide. —Wesley V. Korman, Beaverton, Ore.

For finishing a wood kitchen countertop, how about using moisture-curing urethane such as is used on bar tops/bowling alleys/gymnasium floors? Wood must first be sealed properly with a compatible lacquer sealant. Check out products of Hughson Chemical Company, Erie, Pa. 16512. They're tough but flexible and the glass-like surface does not mar easily. Alcohol resistant, too. . . . —C. Haber, Huntington Beach, Calif.

I have found that household paraffin wax is a super finish for breadboards and butcher blocks. The secret is to heat the item to be coated to just above the melting point of the wax. Then rub the piece with wax: as the piece cools the wax will be drawn into the wood, darkening it and leaving a low-gloss sheen. I heat small items in the oven and larger items with a heat lamp.

I would never use boiled linseed oil with Japan driers on anything that might come in contact with food. Warnings on containers caution against ingestion. A customer deserves the highest possible consideration; it is not ethical to do anything that has even a remote possibility of causing harm. —Mike Graetz, Lakeland, Minn.

Durable finishes for kitchen cabinets

I do a lot of kitchen cabinets and have tried various finishes—in particular, polyurethane, lacquer thinned 50/50 and Watco oil followed by wax. I like both the look and the working properties of the lacquer and oil better than polyurethane, but which finish is most durable? —Claire O'Meara, Washington, D.C.

DON NEWELL REPLIES: A good polyurethane should be the most wear-resistant because it leaves behind a thick film upon drying. Polyurethanes have a higher solids content than either lacquer or Watco oil, so more material is left on the surface when the solvent evaporates. However, refinishing with polyurethane may lead to problems of poor adhesion.

Lacquer (Deft) thinned 50/50 produces extremely thin coatings. Try using it straight from the can, brushing it so that laps and bristle marks don't show. A little thinning might be necessary, but 50/50 is way too much. Lacquer produces a good, wear-resistant finish, but you need two or three coats to build up a decent thickness. This will probably stand up as well for your purpose as polyurethane.

Watco oil penetrates more deeply than either polyurethane or lacquer, and builds up a protective coating in the wood rather than on the surface only. Because it helps toughen and stabilize the wood, it also delivers excellent wear resistance. I'd use at least two coats, with a couple of days' drying time between. Using wax as a final treatment over Watco is a good way to give you the luster you want, though it will require cleaning and rewaxing at intervals.

For a durable interior finish, start with spar varnish thinned 50/50 with turpentine. Apply this first coat with a clean, lint-free cotton cloth shaped like a French-polishing rubber. The second coat is thicker (75/25) and is applied with a bristle brush, followed upon drying by light sanding to remove dust and flecks. Then apply a third coat (gloss or satin) full strength with a foam-rubber brush. If any surface irregularities appear, they can be smoothed out with a light touch from a cabinet scraper. Then I rub with 3/0 steel wool, followed by vigorous rubbing with a cotton cloth. Finally, I apply Trewax with 3/0 steel wool, buffing it just prior to drying. A second coat of wax will give a higher luster, but this time it should dry completely before it's buffed. —Richard C. Ollig, Maryville, Tenn.

Five years ago I made kitchen cabinets and finished them with two saturation coats of Watco followed by three applications of Minwax Paste Wax. They still look good.

However, tabletops and other pieces that receive lots of wear I spray with Deft lacquer before waxing. As for brushing Deft—forget it. If the humidity is high, it blushes; if it's hot, it dries too fast and develops little dimples and wrinkles; if it's cold, it takes forever to set. Thinning Deft results in lap and brush marks, which are hard to eliminate.

For those who do lots of finishing and don't own a spray outfit: Get one. The time saved and the superior quality of the finish will quickly offset your initial investment in a compressor and spray gun. I recommend spraying Deft reduced about 10% with lacquer thinner. Spray at 55 PSI, at 3 CFM to 5 CFM to produce a fan pattern about 4 in. wide. Hold the gun 10 in. to 12 in. from the surface. Two consecutive wet passes give about the same film thickness as one brushed-on coat. I spray on a third coat about 30 minutes later. Then I steel-wool (4/0) the surface and wax it with Minwax paste several times, buffing each application with a chamois. —J.E. Gier, Mesa, Ariz.

Q & A

Dining-table finish

I'm making a dining-room table, and would like to learn of a finish that would be tough and touchable.
　　　　　　　　　—John Millerd, Pemberton Meadows, B.C.

MORRIS SHEPPARD REPLIES: There are as many finishes for tabletops as there are finishes. But the one I have found to be both durable and attractive combines a prime coat of Watco Danish oil with following coats of Deft lacquer. Here's the method: Brush on a sloshing coat of Watco over the prepared surface, let it soak in and then wipe it thoroughly with a clean, absorbent lint-free cloth. Let it sit for at least 24 hours, and then rub it down with 4/0 steel wool, taking care to rub in the direction of the grain. Allow it to sit for another two to three days, depending on the humidity, until the Watco has gotten fairly hard and won't interfere with the adhesion of the Deft to come.

Now spray or brush on a thick, wet coat of Deft lacquer, as much as the surface will take without developing runs. When this coat is completely dry, sand it in the direction of the grain with 220-grit paper, using a padded block. Spray on another full coat, and when it is dry, sand with 400-grit paper. Repeat this step. The fourth coat is also a full-strength application, but it should be steel-wooled, not sanded.

An alcohol-resistant bartop finish

I'm finishing a restaurant bartop with an oil finish and can't seem to come up with one that is alcohol-resistant. I've tried oil and turpentine and tung oil, to no avail. The customer insists on an oil finish. Any suggestions?
　　　　　　　　　—Alexius R. Robben, San Antonio, Tex.

GEORGE FRANK REPLIES: Bartops can be finished with oil, but the finish is not alcohol-proof and it will need frequent renewal if you want a decent-looking job and some degree of protection from alcohol and moisture. I'd suggest a good alcohol-proof lacquer or varnish that can be dulled to an oil flatness with steel wool. Contrary to what many believe, you don't have to build up many coats to protect the wood; two coats of lacquer or varnish should offer excellent protection, in most cases.

OTTO HEUER REPLIES: If the customer insists on an oil finish, I would apply a mixture of equal parts of tung oil, japan drier and mineral spirits, and let this dry 32 to 48 hours. Sand lightly and apply a second coat, allowing it to dry about 36 hours. Dispose of any rags used with this mixture, as it may produce spontaneous combustion, or store them in a fireproof container. Alcohol-resistance can come from a product such as Varathane, made by Flecto International, 1000-02 45th St., Oakland, Calif. 94608. Thin this finish with two parts of the proper reducer to one part of varnish, and brush on a thin coat. A mixture of two parts tung oil, two parts mineral spirits and one part phenolic spar varnish might work as well. Apply two coats at 36-hr. intervals, sanding lightly between coats.

Tung oil for finishing gunstocks

I'm an amateur woodworker and make stocks for my own rifles. I've used linseed oil a number of times, and recently tried polyurethane as a stock finish. I'd like to know if you have any thoughts on tung oil as a gunstock finish. How does it compare to varnishes and to other oils?
　　　　　　　　　—Ralph Gustin, Brookings, S. Dak.

DON NEWELL REPLIES: Tung oil is the best finish for a gun you use in the field. It is a better moisture shield than any other drying oil, and is probably better than the commercial varnishes and penetrating oils, for the same reason.

You can use pure tung oil (sold by Sutherland Welles, 113 Main St., Carrboro, N.C. 27510 and Woodcraft, 41 Atlantic Ave., Box 4000, Woburn, Mass. 01888) or polymerized tung oil, which Welles also sells. The pure tung oil dries to a dull finish, and I've never found a way to get a decent sheen. I prefer polymerized tung, which gives you a much higher sheen. You get a decent gloss, especially if you apply several coats thinly, well rubbed in by hand.

Thin down the first coat of tung with mineral spirits. Use about 75% oil to 25% thinner by volume so that it penetrates deeply. Apply it fairly wet, particularly on end grain at the butt, at the fore-end tip and the pistol grip. Soak the inside of the inletting. Where end grain soaks it up quickly, apply until no more soaks in. Then wipe it all down and let it sit for 48 hours. Don't let it build up on the surface during this first seal coat or you'll get uneven gloss later.

After it's dried for a couple of days, start rubbing in by hand a thin coat of the oil, unthinned. Let it dry 24 hours, and repeat. What you're doing now is building up a thin layer on the top of the wood. One seal coat followed by two thin coats should give you a moisture-resistant, durable finish that resists abrasion, handling and perspiration.

Watco Danish Oil should work well also, as should Waterlox Transparent Seal, Minwax Antique Oil, McCloskey's Tungseal Danish Oil and ZAR Wipe-On Tung finish. They all are excellent products and should do what you want if you treat them as penetrating-type finishes and not surface varnishes. This means using a thinned-down first coat followed by a well-rubbed second coat. Don't let the oil build up in the checkered areas. You'll never get it off once it dries.

Avoid using water-base finishing products on gunstocks, as they will introduce water into the wood. This is a good way to warp the forearm and change the point of aim, as the warped wood will bear against the barrel.

Revitalizing dried-out walnut furniture

I have a fine set of walnut dining furniture, which has aged considerably in the 3½ years I've owned it. The wood, which I treat with lemon oil, appears dried out and lighter than it did when new. How can I return it to its original color?
　　　　　　　　　—Susan Melwing, Bourbonnais, Ill.

OTTO HEUER REPLIES: Try removing some of the finish in an out-of-the-way place, such as inside a chair leg, with fine steel wool. Then apply an antique or Danish oil such as Watco, which can be colored to your liking with oil-based tints sold in tubes at paint stores. If this method restores the color, you may wish to treat the entire surface after removing the old finish or having it commercially removed. Incidentally, lemon oil polishes are somewhat like the famous pork and beans, that is, mostly beans and little pork. Typically, these products are very light mineral oil in a petroleum base with 0.4% to 2% synthetic lemon oil. The lemon oil is there only as a perfume, and it has little beneficial effect on the finish.

Polishing brass and copper

I am looking for a book or any information on polishing brass and copper. I have trouble having black come off on the piece when I buff it on a drill press. I also need a typewriter platform that folds under the desk and springs up when needed. The type I am looking for fits into the bottom right side where drawers would normally be.
　　　　　　　　　—Hap Aames, Lincoln City, Ore.

ANDY MARLOW REPLIES: For buffing, try different grades of rag wheels and a coarse to fine rouge. For the typewriter platform, contact an office furniture supply house. They can order what you want from the manufacturer.

Fine-Tuning Color Finishes
Get lustrous depth with transparent top coats

by Don Newell

Most woodworkers use a clear finish such as varnish or oil, particularly when working with fine, well-figured hardwoods. Many craftsmen probably have never considered using anything other than a clear finish. But there's a time and place for everything. When the wood you're working with is lacking in figure, or you're building a piece from undistinguished pine or mixed woods, or you want the piece to stand out in an otherwise monochromatic room, a color finish may be just the ticket.

A color finish—paint—is merely a clear finish with pigment mixed in. The familiar store-bought antiquing kits work, but they come in unimaginative colors with variations limited to wiping on different shades of toning inks. For your next project, why not select a color that sings, or at least hums a little? Orange or purple might be a bit much, but a small object such as a side table done in viridian green or alizarin crimson can add a dramatic touch to a room decorated mainly with the brown and sienna tones of traditional clear-finished furniture and cabinetry. Modern latex paints—the same ones you'd use on walls and trim—are a good choice and they're available everywhere. But whether you use oil-base or latex paint (semi-gloss or satin) is really not important.

A color finish requires as much surface preparation as a clear finish. Even though the color finish is opaque, imperfections in the surface of the wood will show through when the finish dries and shrinks. A color finish, however, hides sanding scratches somewhat. Where you might final-sand the wood with 240-grit paper for clear finishing, often you can get away with 180-grit under color.

Should you fill the grain under a color finish? Not necessarily, but you can. With close-pored woods such as pine or birch, you wouldn't use a filler anyway, even in clear finishing. On open-pored woods such as oak or mahogany, however, a filler is mandatory if you want to produce a smooth surface. This is a matter of personal preference, however. Since you're using color for its aesthetic value, there's nothing wrong with having the wood structure show. In fact, wood grain often lends interesting texture.

Use a tack rag on the surface and stir the paint thoroughly. Apply a moderately heavy coat as evenly as possible using a clean brush. Brush with the grain, particularly on unfilled, open-pored wood. Let the paint dry overnight.

Now for the step that makes the difference between a fine finish and just a finish. Run your hand over the dry finish and examine the surface in a strong sidelight. You'll see and feel brush marks and specks of dirt or lint. Those, plus the graininess of the suspended particles of flatting agent used to pro-

duce a satin surface, must be removed. Using 320-grit wet-or-dry sandpaper (coarser is too coarse and finer takes too long) and plain water, wet-sand the entire surface to remove irregularities without cutting through to the wood. Wet the surface well with water and, using a light touch, sand the surface in long, overlapping strokes. Use a pad of felt or rubber behind the paper to evenly distribute finger-pressure. And always keep the work area wet. The water acts as a lubricant and keeps the paper from loading up with paint particles.

Frequently dip the square of sandpaper in the water to wash off accumulated sanding residue and keep turning it to present a fresh abrasive surface to the paint. Remember, a light touch does it. Periodically wipe the sanded area dry with paper towels or clean rags and inspect it. If the brush marks and dirt particles have disappeared, you've gone far enough.

If you do cut through to the wood, don't panic. When the surface is completely dry, clean off all sanding dust. It's difficult to repair just one spot, so recoat the entire surface, then resand. The piece should now have a uniform, matte appearance and is ready to be given the final, lustrous touch.

For both protection and beauty, apply a high-quality, durable clear film over the color coat. Since your color coat will be either latex or alkyd (enamel) paint, a clear varnish is the material to use. You could rub in tung oil without damaging the color coat, but its ultimate appearance and film thickness are not nearly as satisfactory. I've tried both gloss and satin varnishes and found that the satin polishes more uniformly. Don't use polyurethane. It will not adhere well to any substrate containing a flatting agent, which most satin or semi-gloss paints contain.

Almost any good brand of standard interior varnish will work well, especially if the information on the label indicates it can be used for furniture, trim or the like. Look for the words ''alkyd'' or ''modified alkyd'' on the label. This type provides excellent adhesion, good wear characteristics, and good rubbing or polishing properties.

Wipe down the sanded color coat with a damp cloth to eliminate all traces of sanding dust. One medium-heavy coat of varnish (just as it comes from the can) is preferable to two thin, drier coats simply because a heavier coat will flow better, leaving fewer brush marks to correct when the varnish has dried. Since this coat of varnish is the final coat, let it dry a full 30 hours rather than merely overnight. You want to give the thinners in the varnish time to evaporate so that the film is hard clear through.

To brighten the luster of the clear coating and to polish out any airborne dust or dirt that may have settled onto the surface, fine steel wool works well. But lightly wet-sanding with 400-grit or 500-grit paper is even better. Follow this by hand-rubbing the surface with rottenstone or automotive polishing compound. Finally, polish the clear coating with a sheepskin buff chucked in an electric drill. This will impart a

---

Don Newell, of Farmington, Mich., is a former paint and varnish chemist, and an amateur furnituremaker. Several of his articles tackling general and special finishing are included in this volume (see pages 2-5, 17-18, 48-50, and 57-58).

beautiful sheen, an appearance impossible to duplicate straight from the can. In fact, the luster will be close to that of a fine rubbed and polished clear lacquer.

Why not simply wet-sand, polish and buff the paint film itself? Two reasons: first, the paint film is much more susceptible to marking and scuffing than the tough clear coat of varnish, so it's less durable; and second, a clear coating over a color coat produces great depth and clarity.

Lacquer—While the paint-and-varnish system is the simplest to use because you can buy the materials at any paint outlet, lacquer produces equally beautiful, functional results. The basic technique—a color coat (over either filled or unfilled wood), followed by a clear protective film—is the same in either case, but the details vary.

Bare wood should be coated with lacquer sanding sealer for optimum adhesion. The sealer, color coat and final clear coat should be from a knowledgeable supplier. H. Behlen & Bros. (write Rt. 30N, Amsterdam, N.Y. 12010 for local distributor) sells brushing and spraying lacquers, both colored and clear, as well as sanding sealers, all of which are compatible.

Why not use a spray can? Simply because aerosol materials are heavily thinned to permit spraying under the very low spray-can pressure. The resulting film is extremely thin, so you have to apply many coats to build up a reasonably heavy layer. You can't rush it either: if you apply too many coats too soon, before the previous coats have had a chance to dry hard, the finish will remain soft for days. Stick with brushing lacquer if you don't have a good spray outfit.

Apply a sanding sealer and wet-sand it to a smooth, clean surface. Because lacquer shows coarse sanding scratches, all wet-sanding should be with wet-or-dry sandpaper of 360-grit or finer. Now put on several coats of color lacquer to build up a good film, lightly wet-sanding between coats to remove brush or spray marks. Then apply two coats of clear lacquer, allowing sufficient drying time in between for the thinner to evaporate. After the final coat of clear lacquer, let the finish dry for at least 72 hours before you polish it. Even though lacquer may appear hard on the surface, a substantial amount of solvent still remains in the film, and as this evaporates the film will continue to shrink.

To produce maximum sheen without gloss, rub the surface with fine-textured automobile rubbing/polishing compound, or with fine pumice or rottenstone. Then give the piece a final polishing with a dry sheepskin buff.

The result, whether you use varnish or lacquer, is superb. If you've ever seen a custom-finished car with coat after coat of semi-transparent paint hand-rubbed to a mirror gleam, you'll recognize the difference between merely finishing *with* color and clear-finishing *over* color. □

The aesthetics of clear finishes

Thinking of a finish only as a protective skin misses its aesthetic impact. The finish you apply becomes an inseparable part of the object and visually represents it. The right finish is a matter of function, appearance and historical precedent. All three must be considered if the finish is to complement the construction.

Consider a small rosewood music box inlaid with antique ivory and adorned by an heirloom cameo let into the lid. It will not be harshly handled, so the finish need not be extremely rugged. Moisture resistance in such a small piece is not a major consideration either. In fact, with this box, as with most small, cherishable objects, the meaningful consideration is aesthetic: does the finish help achieve, or amplify, the artisan's intended effect?

In this box, the maker used rosewood and ivory for their rich, nostalgic character. The finish should heighten this effect, and be one with the object. The grain and color of the rosewood should be allowed to show.

A drying oil such as boiled linseed or tung, hand-rubbed, will produce a dull surface. A gloss varnish will glare. And lacquer, rubbed and buffed, will give a high luster without shine.

Water-clear lacquer would be my choice. It can be wet-sanded between coats to eliminate brush or spray marks, and it yields not only a protective film that is completely transparent but also one that brings out color to the maximum. The final film can be rubbed and polished to a high luster.

Why not use varnish or drying oil? You could, but to me a drying oil's comparatively matte finish reduces the visual drama. A good rubbing-type varnish could probably serve as well as lacquer, but the clarity of lacquer is more jewel-like. It is compatible with the rest of the materials in the music box and their actual and subjective functions.

In contrast to the box, consider an oak desk—large, obtrusive and utilitarian. The wood, as beautiful and striking as its grain may be, was chosen to be used, and used hard. So it calls for a working finish. But the finish needn't look as though it was slapped on with a whiskbroom. Even a workhorse desk is entitled to face the world with a smooth coat. I'd use a sturdy satin varnish. Why varnish? Just as rubbed and polished lacquer expresses delicacy and refinement, so varnish projects a shirt-sleeves character. Historically, strong oak and durable varnish go together. A craftsman who makes or buys a desk of oak rather than of metal or laminate-covered particleboard is tying himself to a tradition. And for the same nostalgic reason, a mellow varnish is the logical choice. Gloss varnish would feel wrong. Its glinty, shiny surface begs attention, thereby embarrassing a working-class desk. Satin varnish, on the other hand, is comfortable on the desk and lets the wood come through, because there is no shine to interfere. The subdued luster also implies that the desk has been well used, its finish dulled by time and wear.

In another case of matching perception to function, consider a fine walnut gunstock. Historically, gunstocks have been finished with rubbed-in linseed oil, a material of countless shortcomings and only two possible virtues: it is easy to apply, and it is capable of producing a soft, pleasing luster if rubbed often and long enough. This soft sheen is generally believed to be a clue to a gun's quality, a perception that the gun is better made than one whose stock is not hand-rubbed. Ironically, for durability and moisture resistance, linseed oil is not a good finish for a gunstock. Tung oil, the popular Danish oils and certain penetrating varnishes can be made to look about the same as rubbed oil, and are far more durable. Yet even today, with these other materials available, a "genuine, hand-rubbed linseed oil finish" still sells guns. —*D.N.*

To Finish the Finish

Rubbing out dust, lint and brushmarks

by Don Newell

When it comes to finishing the finish, the type of material you're using will dictate which problems you face. Brushmarks and unsightly particles trapped in the hardened surface film, the bane of the wood finisher, are the most universal problems. Lacquer and shellac, which dry quickly, tend to show brushmarks, while varnish, which dries more slowly, is susceptible to dust. Fortunately, both problems can easily be solved by using the rubbing technique described here.

But first, where do the particles come from? The most obvious source is dust and lint settling out of the air, and sawdust kicked up from the shop floor. Second is dried particles of varnish released by inadequately cleaned brushes. Third is pinhead-sized clumps of varnish resin (called seed). These can be found in new, unopened cans of varnish, but are more common in partially used cans from the finisher's shelf.

Clean conditions are probably more important to good finishing technique than anything else, yet cleanliness is often neglected. The ideal finishing environment is a section of the workshop equipped with a filtered air-exchange system, but such a system is costly and takes space, and therefore is unavailable to most finishers. The practical alternative is a portable vacuum with hose and extension tubes, and a clean outlet filter. Before you open a can of finishing material, vacuum everything—the floor, the benchtop and the work itself. Then vacuum the ceiling, walls, tools and the tops of the lighting fixtures. Don't overlook your own hair and clothes. Many woodworkers mop the floor before finishing, but use only a damp mop. Too much humidity will interfere with drying of the finish, and excessive moisture will actually condense on the surface of freshly applied shellac or lacquer. This is the usual cause of "blushing" or "blooming," hazy white areas visible when the finish hardens.

As for dried particles from dirty brushes, even a good soaking in pure varnish solvent won't remove varnish that may have worked up into the heel of the bristles. The solution is simple. Obtain a wide-mouth glass jar with screw lid. Wash and dry it thoroughly, then nearly fill it with a half-and-half mixture of automobile engine oil and mineral spirits. After varnishing, use a rag to squeeze as much residual varnish as possible out of the brush. Briefly dip the brush into the oil/thinner mixture and squeeze it out again. Then leave the brush, with its bristles completely immersed, in the bottle overnight. The mineral spirits dissolves the varnish from between the bristles while the motor oil keeps the varnish fluid until it is removed.

After overnight soaking, mix up a concentrated solution of liquid soap and water in a coffee can. Squeeze out the brush and wash it thoroughly in the soap solution. Work the bristles vigorously between your fingers from heel to tip, again and again. Swish the brush up and down, then squeeze it dry. Using a fresh batch of soap-and-water solution, repeat the process. Then rinse the brush well under running water while working the bristles between your fingers.

If the brush is absolutely clean, there will be no odor of oil. If the brush smells or feels oily, wash it again. Then let it dry and wrap it in paper to keep it clean.

If brush-cleaning doesn't appeal to you, use a sponge-rubber applicator instead. These are sold in various widths, complete with wooden handles, at most hardware stores, or you can make your own from a small block of clean foam rubber. Used once and thrown away, these eliminate the dirty-brush problem. They handle differently from a brush though, so practice on scrap before tackling a real finishing project.

Particles of varnish resin, called seed, which come from the new or partially used can of varnish, are not so easily eliminated. Straining the varnish through a double layer of cheesecloth removes larger particles, but smaller ones pass through the mesh. If your varnish is seedy after straining, buy new varnish or plan to rub out the finish.

The rubbed finish — In the furniture industry, the process of adjusting the sheen of a finish to the desired degree of luster by abrading the dried film is called rubbing. Rubbing also eliminates specks and surface imperfections. It is totally different from the classic pumice-and-rottenstone varnish-rubbing technique many old-timers swear by.

Most hardware stores and all auto-repair shops carry carborundum or 3M brand abrasive finishing paper in a range of grits. The objective is to smooth the surface of the finish and cut off protruding particles embedded in the hardened film rather than to remove a measurable layer, so get a few sheets each of 400, 500 and 600-grit paper. One brand of 400-grit paper may feel much coarser than another—stay with a specific brand for uniformity.

Cut each sheet into small sections, say 2 in. by 3 in., and fold a section around a felt or rubber block. The block distributes the pressure over the entire surface of the paper,

To rub out specks and imperfections, lightly stroke abrasive paper that has been wetted with mineral spirits across the surface in the direction of the grain.

From *Fine Woodworking* magazine (September 1979) 18:75-76

Finishing and Refinishing **57**

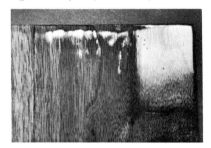

Mineral spirits acts as a lubricant, keeping sanding particles from clogging the paper. If a coat of sanding 'mud' appears (above) you're not using enough. The shiny unsanded section of the panel (below, right corner) is the original varnish surface. Shiny spots on the edge show that the sanding block tipped as it passed over the edge, leaving an incompletely sanded surface.

Solid walnut panel shows effect of rubbing polyurethane gloss varnish (right half) and alkyd satin varnish (left half). The shiny strip at far right is original, unsanded polyurethane, loaded with specks and lint. The strip at far left is original, unsanded satin alkyd, equally full of specks and lint. After identical rubbing and sheepskin-wheel buffing of the two inner sections, the alkyd (left center) came up to a highly attractive but not glossy sheen. But the polyurethane finish (right center) has a visible scratch pattern from the sandpaper, and the luster did not improve with buffing.

minimizing the danger of rubbing completely through the finish at any one point.

Pour a small amount of mineral spirits into a flat dish. Starting with 400-grit, dip the block-backed paper into the liquid. Gently rub the finish in long strokes. At the end of each stroke, lift the block clear, return to the starting point, and start the next stroke parallel to and slightly overlapping the previous stroke. The danger with back-and-forth sanding is in cutting completely through the finish. Remember, gently, lightly, does it.

The surface of the finish must be kept wet at all times with the mineral spirits, which acts as a lubricant and keeps the sanding particles in suspension. Frequently dip the paper into the mineral spirits to wash the surface clean and to bring new thinner to the area being rubbed.

Periodically wipe the surface clean with a paper towel wetted with clean mineral spirits. Let the surface dry and examine it in a good light. If it has been abraded evenly, and there are no shiny spots indicating skips or misses, change to the next finer grit and repeat. Then go to the finest paper and stop. Even when cutting with grit as fine as 600, corners and edges must be treated carefully because it is easy to cut completely through the finish.

When all specks and imperfections have been cut down evenly, wipe the surface once again with fresh mineral spirits and a clean cloth, turning constantly to pick up all remaining traces of the sanding mud. Let the surface dry completely— half an hour or so.

If you like an almost matte surface, nothing else need be done. If you prefer moderate luster and the appearance of greater depth, one or two passes with a sheepskin buff chucked in an electric drill will suffice. If you're partial to a waxed finish, though it isn't my cup of tea, this rubbed and buffed surface will respond beautifully.

Different finishing materials react differently to the same treatment. Gloss lacquer generally sands and buffs out to a finish of outstanding beauty, with a rich luster that no ready-mixed satin formula can equal. Shellac surfaces can be sanded glass-flat, but if shellac is to be buffed, keep the buff moving constantly. Shellac is comparatively heat-sensitive and a stationary buff can quickly soften and distort the film.

Each varnish responds to this treatment differently. For example, a typical satin (low-gloss) soya alkyd varnish sands easily under thinner-lubricated abrasive paper. When it is dry-buffed with a sheepskin wheel, it develops a highly attractive, even luster. The ability of the luster to reflect an image is about halfway between that of the original (unsanded) material and that of a standard gloss varnish. Apparently, alkyd varnish is buffable because it flows under the friction of the wheel just enough to even out the fine scratches left by the abrasive paper. Yet its flow is not sufficient to generate the harsh shine normally associated with gloss varnish.

On the other hand, a typical high-gloss polyurethane varnish rubbed with abrasive papers and dry-buffed with a sheepskin wheel exhibits a haziness or grayness, and retains fine scratches. Unlike alkyd films, polyurethane varnish doesn't flow under the buffing wheel.

If polyurethane and other hard finishes are to be rubbed to a scratchless luster, one further step is necessary. After rubbing with the abrasive paper, clean the surface with mineral spirits and let dry. Then hand-polish using a good compound such as an automotive polishing compound sold for polishing out a clear finish. It should contain a fine, friable abrasive compound such as tripoli, which breaks down more and more finely as polishing proceeds. ☐

Don Newell, of Farmington, Mich., is a former paint and varnish chemist and an amateur furnituremaker.

Q & A

Stripping paint from mahogany

I have a five-piece bedroom suite made of mahogany, and I want to refinish it. Many years ago the furniture was covered with a thick coat of white paint. What should I use to strip the paint, and once done, how should I refinish the set? —Robert Dalbo, Dubois, Pa.

GEORGE FRANK REPLIES: Modern paint removers are formulated so as not to harm or affect the wood underneath. However, some of the nonflammable, water-rinse types may change the color of the mahogany. A water-rinse type would probably do a better job in your case; therefore, you should first experiment on an unimportant piece or area. If it does stain the wood, use a solvent-base, flammable remover.

Your greater problem will be how to clean the wood once you've removed the paint. You'll probably find a varnish finish underneath the paint, and under that a pore filler. To do a proper refinishing job, all that must come off. This is the most important and most delicate part of the job. Use a good, strong laundry detergent in warm water and scrub the pieces repeatedly, until all the varnish and filler have been washed away. I repeat: Experiment first on an unimportant piece, and if you are satisfied, proceed with the main job. The choice of what finish to apply will depend on your personal preferences.

Stripping safely

How dangerous are chemical products used to strip old finishes? Many over-the-counter stripping mixtures contain toxic chemicals, and a flood of mail shows that readers are concerned about possible risks to their health. Generally, commercial strippers are available in two types—nonflammable (usually based on methylene chloride), and flammable (usually a mixture containing benzene, toluene or methylene chloride). We recently suggested methylene chloride as a safe replacement for benzene, but readers (some enclosing clippings from Consumer Reports *and the* Journal of the American Medical Association*) say otherwise. We put the question to Dr. Michael McCann, president of the Center for Occupational Hazards in New York City, whose reply appears below.*

When using any volatile compound, always keep safety topmost in mind. Wear gloves and goggles. Follow instructions on containers to the letter. Make sure your work area is well ventilated, or work outdoors.

MICHAEL McCANN REPLIES: Although benzene (benzol) has been known for decades to cause aplastic anemia (destruction of the bone marrow) and leukemia, it has been a common component of paint strippers (often more than 50% of the mixture). In recognition of these hazards, the Consumer Product Safety Commission proposed to ban benzene from consumer products on the basis that there is no safe level of exposure. Most companies have removed benzene, but some paint strippers containing it may still be found in workshops. Don't use any paint stripper containing benzene (or benzol).

Many people get confused between benzene and benzine. Benzene is extremely toxic. Benzine, on the other hand, is a petroleum distillate similar to naphtha, mineral spirits, gasoline, paint thinner, etc., differing only in its boiling point. It is also called VM&P naphtha (varnishmakers' and painters' naphtha). Benzine is moderately toxic; it and the other petroleum distillates can cause skin irritation and narcosis (dizziness, fatigue, loss of coordination, nausea) from inhalation. Ingestion is more serious and one can die if any of the solvent gets into the lungs (e.g., from vomiting). This is particularly hazardous with children.

Toluene (also called toluol), although related to benzene, is much less toxic. It does not cause aplastic anemia or leukemia. In the past, toluene was thought to cause these diseases, but this is apparently due to the presence of benzene as a contaminant. With the much lower levels of contamination permitted by the Consumer Product Safety Commission, and with better industrial practice, this problem should be eliminated. Toluene itself can cause narcosis, skin irritation, and liver damage. It has also been implicated as a cause of menstrual irregularities. Toluene was the solvent most commonly involved in glue-sniffing illnesses of the 1960s.

Manufacturers have been replacing benzene with other solvents, mostly toluene and methylene chloride. Methylene chloride has been implicated as a cause of heart attacks—including one known fatality—because the body converts it into carbon monoxide. This can tie up the blood's hemoglobin and deprive the heart of oxygen. Methylene chloride is also a lung irritant and narcotic, and, in the presence of a flame or lit cigarette, can decompose to phosgene, a poisonous gas.

Ink stains on oak

I recently inherited a solid oak roll-top desk from my grandfather and of course there is an ink stain on the writing surface. Are there any successful methods for removing or bleaching ink stains from oak? —Larry Sanford, Ypsilanti, Mich.

GEORGE FRANK REPLIES: Sorry, I don't know of any chemical that would tracelessly eliminate the ink spots. The only way to do it would be through scraping and sandpapering. If I did know about some magic chemical I would be loath to give it to you. To my mind a modern desk with inkspots is dirty, but an old desk without inkspots is not an old desk. You are lucky to have your grandpa's desk—leave the inkspots alone.

I also have a very old roll-top on which I am now writing. I also had the ink stains. I bought a small bottle of ink eradicator at a local office-supply store. It worked pretty well, although it took several applications and some very deep spots of color still remain. George Frank would be happy about that. —Ellis Rogers, Bloomington, Ind.

Dissolving wax

What is the proper solvent for carnauba wax? —H.B. Skinner, Seattle, Wash.

DON NEWELL REPLIES: If you want to dissolve an old wax film to remove it, you can use mineral spirits, dry-cleaning solvent (perchlorethylene) or lacquer thinner. If you want to soften or dissolve new wax to apply it to a surface, the same three solvents can be used, the only difference being that the finish will have different drying properties. Of the three, mineral spirits produces the slowest evaporating mixture, so a solution made with it will set slowest. Dry-cleaning solvent sets faster and lacquer thinner is the fastest of all. The final wax film will be the same no matter which solvent you use. Be particularly careful with lacquer thinner, though—it's extremely flammable.

Airbrush finish repair

I repaired a split in a mahogany-veneered card table, but sanding dulled the gloss-varnish finish on both sides of the repair... —Malcolm Garrett, Steelton, Pa.

GEORGE FRANK REPLIES: Use a fast-drying gloss varnish, thinner, and an artists' airbrush or a mouth sprayer (from art supply stores). Spray a light coat of thinned varnish on the strip (a little varnish will build up on the old finish) and let it dry. Gently level the overspray with very fine sandpaper. Build up 5 to 15 very thin coats this way and let it dry. Rub with a damp rag and pumice, then switch to rottenstone.

Elegant Fakes
34 chairs for the palace at Alexandria

by George Frank

The year was 1935; the place, my atelier in Paris; and the man who opened the door to my tiny office was Monsieur Sylvestre Baradoux, master cabinetmaker. Even though the late winter morning was cold and unfriendly, Baradoux was in his warmest mood—so much so that he agreed to buy a round at a nearby bistro.

Baradoux had every reason to be triumphant: an hour earlier he had met with an emissary from the Royal Court of Egypt and had received an order for most of the furnishings for a palace being built in Alexandria. The order would keep Baradoux and his crew of 40 craftsmen busy for at least two years.

My friend was blissfully ignorant of geography and had no idea where Egypt was, but as a craftsman he was a dogged and uncompromising perfectionist. After the third drink his smile faded, and I learned the real reason for his visit. It seemed that the Egyptian emissaries expected all the work to be of the first order, but in one room quality alone would not suffice—only perfection would be tolerated...or else. The contract made this clear in rather frightening small print. The furnishings of the Blue Salon, 34 chairs and two consoles, had to be so close in design, shape, construction and finish to genuine Louis XIV antiques as to confound experts. Baradoux was to build new furniture with the facade of authentic 300-year-old pieces...or else.

Now, my trade is woodfinishing, and I am as much a perfectionist as my friend Baradoux. Said he: "You have repeatedly deceived me with pieces of furniture that I would have sworn were genuine antiques. I have been stunned to learn that they were younger than my beard. Now tell me, George, can we meet these stringent specifications, or shall I refuse the order?"

I had already consumed four aperitifs and in my elated condition I felt I could carry out the contract with my hands tied behind my back. I replied, "Sylvestre, my friend, you are crazy. You have received that once-in-a-lifetime commission, an order that every cabinetmaker in Paris would sell his soul to have. Yet you dare to think of giving it up? If we cannot carry it out, who can? Who? Take it, take it, take it." And thus began one of the most difficult tasks of our lives.

The layman is amazingly ignorant about antiques. Any crudely built piece of furniture, shaped more or less in the style of the period it represents, beaten with a chain, mauled with a screwdriver, dropped from the roof of the shop and re-

George Frank, a master cabinetmaker and furniture finisher, is the author of 88 Rue de Charonne: Adventures in Wood Finishing *(The Taunton Press).*

paired with sawdust and glue, will probably pass at auction. Compound these mutilations with wormholes made with an awl, or with the legendary shotgun blast, and add a million flydroppings of dark shellac, spritzed on with an old toothbrush through a bit of screening—such a piece would fool half of the experts. But the specifications of the Royal Court left no doubt that such a hackneyed approach would not do. They wanted perfection.

We began by ordering two truckloads of the best horse manure and by making sure we could obtain enough old wood, for using aged wood is the first requirement in copying antiques. Baradoux had a lot of old beams in his warehouse, salvaged from demolished houses. He also knew all the wreckers. Although World War I had been over for almost 20 years, the salvage industry still flourished. While timbers of choice woods older than 200 years were becoming scarce, there still were plenty of excellent logs that had been removed from churches, ships, buildings and barns, all at least 100 years old and nicely weathered. Some even contained lively, hard-working worms in their bellies. The price was high, but so was the fee Baradoux was charging the Egyptians.

Using old wood in antique reproductions helps achieve the proper coloring, shading and finishing. But it also creates problems of strength. The function of a chair is to support sturdily and comfortably a person who may weigh more than 200 pounds. A new chair is built of sound, clear lumber that has been dried to a moisture content of 7% to 10%—wetter, and the wood will shrink, loosening the joints; drier, and the wood is dangerously brittle.

Since the chairs would have upholstered seats and backs, we could use new, kiln-dried lumber for the hidden parts. The partly exposed parts, such as the back legs, were made of sound old lumber, but not too old. We cut the pieces roughly to shape and buried them for three months under the mound of horse manure. From the manure they picked up alkaline juices, appropriate base coloring and the necessary moisture. The fully exposed parts, such as front legs and stretchers, got the same treatment, except they stayed in the manure only six weeks before being removed, cleaned, dried and shaped.

Our next problem was a basic one—we had to know precisely what it was we were copying. Fortunately, we both had done restoration work for the Louvre and other museums, and we could borrow a couple of chairs made during the reign of the "Sun King." We spent weeks studying these chairs, observing and noting every detail of their construction, carving, joining and finishing. We studied tools and working methods of the period, and once the wood was past the rough-cutting stage no machine or power tool was ever used. Baradoux went so far as to confiscate from his men some hand tools he deemed too advanced.

I made him disconnect the electric grinders the craftsmen used to sharpen their tools. We replaced them with an ancient *meule*, a stone 3 ft. in diameter that was turned with a foot pedal and revolved in a trough of water. Every man had to use this grinding stone, but no one except me was allowed to clean the water and the mud from the trough. I mysteriously saved this dirty water and mud.

Now it is early summer, 1936. Baradoux and I sit in my shop admiring the 34 chairs and two consoles. We agree that they are masterpieces, but Baradoux wants to know: "How will you copy the 300-year-old finish of the models?"

My answer hit him like a bomb: "The finish of the model chairs is less than ten years old."

Baradoux became red in the face. Then he icily removed the covering sheet from one of the model chairs, pointed to the brass plaque of the Louvre and said: "George, you don't mean to tell me this is a fake?"

"But no, all I said is that the finish is not old. I do not mean that it was refinished, but every time a servant polished it, waxed it or oiled it something was added to the original finish. So the original finish now is modified by 300 years of caretaking, carelessness, wear and accidents. These chairs were rewaxed very recently at the museum. Furthermore I will have to copy all these nicks, caused by rough moving between the shops. Now you see, the finish of these chairs is as old as the last addition to it. To copy all of it I intend to use the same ingredients, the same ways and means that caused the models to look as they do."

I had done much research on the coloring and staining of the wood and discovered some surprising facts. One of the great achievements of Louis XIV was the establishment of the *manufacture des Gobelins*. It was not only a huge workshop where the famous tapestries were made, but it was also a craft center where hundreds, maybe thousands, of skilled people found rewarding jobs. Joiners, carpenters and cabinetmakers worked not too far from the vats where the wool was dyed, and they soon discovered that most of those dyes worked well on wood too. The art of wood staining progressed amazingly fast. Colorants were derived from insects, trees, weeds, fruits and minerals imported from faraway lands and prepared with lye, vinegar, soda ash or alcohol to produce all the colors of the rainbow.

While the woodworker of the time tried out new colorants, in his own shop he usually stuck with the old proven methods of staining. The most important stain of the time was derived from the dried, green shell of the walnut. Brewed with some soda ash or a bit of lye and strained, this was and still is among the most popular and pleasant of stains. Today it is called walnut crystals or cassel extract.

The wood most frequently used in the shops at that time was oak, and the craftsmen knew that the water from the grindstone would turn this wheat-colored wood grey, or brownish-grey, especially when the grindstone water contained some urine, as it often did. In theory this iron-rich water worked only on oak, but some smart carpenter discovered and used mordants, or prestains. The simplest of these was a brew of acorns, which conveyed the necessary amount of tannic acid to any wood. Then the grindstone water would work well on it also.

I had saved every drop of water from Baradoux's grind-

This is an original Louis XIV chair, much like the one Frank and Baradoux borrowed from the Louvre to copy for the Blue Salon.

stone, hoping to use it to stain the chairs. But after three solid weeks of experimenting, the grindstone mud turned out to be useless. Finally I hit upon a prestain mixture of equal amounts of dried sumac leaves (a common American plant) and acorn cups, brewed and strained. Washing down the chairs with this liquid imparted enough tannic acid to the wood so it would accept my final stain. This was the classical *brou de noix*, or walnut extract, described previously, modified by adding a generous portion of strong ammonia. The proportions of each component mattered less than the process itself—endless experimenting with the original ingredients to find the correct combination of mordant and stain, then refinement of the mixtures to obtain the perfect deep, brilliant color.

Personal observation is by far the most important factor in learning this, or any other, trade. Let me illustrate:

While working for the Louvre around 1930, I detected the faint smell of perfume inside a cabinet that had been made by one of the masters of the Louis XV era. I attributed this to accidental spilling and paid no special attention. A few weeks later I came across the same sweet perfume inside another old chest. My curiosity aroused, I discovered the same scent inside many fine cabinets of the same period. Since perfume works by evaporation it was hard to believe these interiors had been perfumed on purpose, or that the smell could last through several centuries. My investigation drew a blank—no one could give me a clue about the mystery of the perfumed interiors.

In Paris every cabinetmaker makes his own *popote*, or polish, or has the secret of one. The *popote* is used to clean and restore the lustre of old furniture. At the cost of many aperitifs I learned a number of these secret formulas, most of them childishly simple. Generally they consisted of rainwater to which a few drops of oil and alcohol were added, plus some Tripoli earth, which is a fine abrasive similar to rottenstone. Bolder ones added a few drops of vitriol (a commercial version of sulfuric acid), to enhance the mystery of the product, not its efficiency. There was nothing earthshaking in any of this, until one of the old-timers disclosed that he dissolved some *benjamin* in the alcohol before adding it to the polish. This was new. I soon discovered that the proper name of the material was *gomme benjoin* (gum benzoin), and that it came in the form of pale, rust-colored, peanut-shaped lumps. When crushed, it had the very smell I had detected in the antique cabinets. From then on this subtle perfume became a trademark of my shop. In France I bought the benzoin in the paint store, but in America I had to order it from a large chemical company. The product I received was white, much like powdered milk, with no scent whatsoever. It had been refined out. To get the smell, one has to order unrefined gum benzoin, crush it and dissolve it in alcohol.

Observation, perseverance and a bit of luck also helped me find the proper lustre for my antique reproductions. I observed that beeswax applied to the wood long ago had a dry shine, while freshly applied wax looked greasy. I had to reproduce the dry shine, and I decided that the way was to dissolve the wax in water, rather than turpentine or some other greasy solvent. I asked dozens of chemists, but the answer invariably was the same: wax cannot be dissolved in water.

Still I never gave up. One day standing in line at the post office, I was able to help an embarrassed gentleman who had reached the window only to discover he had forgotten his money. A few hours later he was at my door with repayment, and we talked. He owned a small outfit that manufactured beauty products. He invited me to invest money in it and his pitch went something like this: "There is money in cosmetics, the cost is negligible, the markup is great and so is the profit. The base of 80% of our products is wax in water..." My heart stopped. Incredulous, I asked him to repeat what he had said: "The base of most of our products is emulsified wax." Here was the key—wax cannot be dissolved in water, but it can be emulsified in it. Not long after, I had my own emulsion, and triumphantly, the dry shine. It can be done in a blender.

This dry wax was the most important ingredient in the finishing of the furniture for the Blue Salon. With its help I could copy to perfection the shine and patina of true antiques. Moreover I could easily mix stain into my water-wax, to correct minor color deficiencies.

The remainder of the finishing secret involved some chain cloth from the armor of a medieval warrior, some old spurs, some sharkskin, bonesticks with rounded edges, and sunshine. The spurs reproduced spurmarks found on the models, very authentically. The old shops used sharkskin as sandpaper, and so did we. The chain cloth and bonesticks were used to burnish the waxed wood, and to achieve silky smoothness. And nothing can replace the rays of the sun when you want colors to fade.

To my knowledge the Blue Salon is still one of the most beautiful rooms at the Royal Palace of Alexandria, but Sylvestre Baradoux, one of the fast-shrinking clan of proud and true craftsmen, died in 1961. □

Q & A

Walnut stain
On page 61, George Frank refers to a walnut stain "brewed with some soda ash or a bit of lye." Could we have complete directions? —*T. Smith, Washington, D.C.*
GEORGE FRANK REPLIES: You can dissolve walnut crystals (also called cassel extract) in warm water. The more concentrated the solution is, the darker your color will be. This dye will have more penetrating power if you add to it some commercial ammonia (about one pint to a gallon of dye), or some soda ash, also called washing soda or sal soda (about 3 ounces to a gallon of dye), or some lye (about ½ teaspoon to a gallon of dye). Of the three, ammonia is the best for general use.

Walnut-husk stain
I would like to make my own stain from walnut husks and currently have about 20 gallons of black muck. If I can get my furniture to look like my hands, I'll be satisfied. Would straining the muck through burlap and mixing it with denatured alcohol be enough? And is there a way to extract the color from the shells?
—*Wesley Kobylak, Tuscarora, N.Y.*
GEORGE FRANK REPLIES: What you are trying to concoct is the famous *brou de noix* (literally, brew of walnut), the pet dye of all old-time French ébénistes. Since our professor taught us how to make it, brou de noix has been replaced by far better and easier-to-use aniline dyes. Still, maybe brou de noix has a nostalgic value and charm that some of us can still detect. I envy you your 20 gallons of black muck. Here's how we made the stuff into a wonderful stain.

The boss lady soaked the walnuts' green husks (not the hard brown shells or the edible fruit) in rainwater for a few days and then she put this muck over a slow fire, being careful not to let it boil. All the while, her hands became as pleasantly brown as yours. She added some soda ash (dry sodium carbonate) while brewing, approximately a heaping teaspoon per gallon, and let the brew simmer for two or three days. And that was it. She let it cool, strained it through an old linen cloth (the burlap you ask about would work just as well) and then filled green bottles with the filtered liquid. She kept the bottles firmly sealed and in a dark area until we were ready to use our brou de noix.

If you insist on using alcohol, don't put it into the brew, but into the brewmaster. Rye would do, but go easy.

Removing gray color from oak
When we stripped the varnish from an old oak wardrobe we own, the wood retained a grayish color. All our efforts to remove this have failed. Do you have any ideas on how we can solve this problem?
—*Pam Dillard, Savannah, Ga.*
GEORGE FRANK REPLIES: It sounds like you cleaned the wood well physically, yet the remaining gray color indicates that the wood may not be chemically clean. I suggest using a fairly strong solution of a good cleanser such as Spic and Span—a mixture of 4 or 5 ounces in a gallon of water should work—to wash down the piece. Use a good stiff brush and plenty of elbow grease. As I am a bit of a daredevil, I would use my trusty wire brushes and since this takes some skill you should first experiment on an unseen part of the wood. Scrub the wood well with the bristle brush and allow the cleanser to penetrate. Sponge off the excess water and use the wire brush in a sweeping motion, with the grain direction. Instead of the cleanser, you could use a weak solution of lye (1 oz. in a gallon of water). Rinse the wood clean with water after the lye treatment. When it has dried, a mild solution of oxalic acid can be used to restore the wood to its natural color.

The Way to Mecca

by George Frank

The ex-Khedive of a certain North African country had money problems—he had so much that he did not know what to do with it. He cared for his wife, their four children and his mistress in a manner befitting royalty. A *bon vivant*, he was a corpulent and jovial character, well into his seventies in 1939, the time of this story. His latest flame was the 18-year-old Yvonne. Court etiquette required that she be hidden, unknown, discreetly kept. A short time later, the Khedive purchased an estate about 90 miles south of Paris, complete with a 200-year-old manor. Yvonne adapted quickly and effectively to her new role as mistress of Ransonville and helped the Khedive spend money.

Since this is a true story, I have changed the names of some people and places. However, it is a fact that my atelier at the time was at 88 Rue de Charonne in Paris and that my office was a cubbyhole with a desk, three chairs and a filing cabinet. From there I did not see my two visitors alight from a Rolls-Royce. One of them, who introduced himself as Monsieur Boubli, asked whether I would care to do some woodfinishing—removing old paint in a stairwell to expose the natural wood. My affirmative answer was followed by a request for samples. My two visitors then had a conference of which I could understand not a single word, but eventually Boubli pointed to one of the finishes and said: "This is the one his highness would like you to produce."

Soon after, my crew and I started the job at Ransonville. In less than two months, the job was brought to a beautiful conclusion. The Khedive visited the worksite frequently, and many nights we shared a bottle of good wine with him. By the time I presented my bill, I was no longer Monsieur Frank, I was "my friend, George."

"My friend, George," said the Khedive, "I am enchanted with your work, but I have a favor to ask you. I invited some friends here for the month of Ramadan and they will be here in three weeks. Would you please do the same kind of work on the six paneled rooms of the manor?"

"Your highness," answered I with a question, "to do the stairwell took us nearly two months. How can I do six times as much work in three weeks?"

"I'll help you," said the Khedive. "I can rub the wood as well as your men can." There was only one possible answer. "The job will be done," I said.

Before I describe the operations that followed, I must go back about three months to when Boubli gave the contract to refinish the six paneled rooms to one of the leading interior decorators of Paris. He had about 20 men working on the job, not far from my four, busy in the stairwell. There was a great deal of teasing going all the time and some professional jealousy. My men even changed the labels on all our containers: the lime-water became angelmilk, the lye, laxative, and so on. The decorator's men finished first, almost a week ahead of us. The Khedive paid his well-padded bill without batting an eyelash and then asked me to redo the job.

The wood in the stairwell was silvery grey, much like hemp rope, and the shine, or rather the gleam, of it was the dry shine that I developed using emulsified waxes (see box below). We left some of the old paint in the corners here and there, but except for that all the markings of the wood were readable and well emphasized. Not so with the panelings. Their color was a nondescript yellowish brown, with far too much old paint left in the corners. The shine was the greasy glow of fresh beeswax, with which the work was overloaded. While the wood was fairly clean, it had no character.

By the next morning, four more men had arrived from my Paris shop with unusual equipment such as fisherman's hipboots, swim trunks and scores of brushes, half of them made of wire. Some of the men started to take the panelings from the walls, carefully marking every piece for easy replacement. Others lowered the water level in the brand-new swimming pool to about 2 ft., and I dumped in about 5 lb. of caustic soda (sodium hydroxide). The paneling was lowered unceremoniously into the pool, where the potent solution of caustic soda and my hipbooted men wielding wire brushes made short work of the finish on the wood. Removed from the pool, the panels oozed ugly brown juice, the sap, coming from the guts of the wood.

Men in swim trunks handled the next operation, washing the wood until the water ran clear. More than once the

Emulsified wax

I had sought, for many years, to find out how to impart to wood a hard, dry shine such as could be found on objects waxed centuries ago. I made up my mind that the key was emulsifying wax in water. This, however, was not so simple, and from professional chemists I had to learn the techniques. Hundreds of experiments later I arrived at the formula I give you now. It is the best, and the one I have always used.

In a nonmetallic container (enamel-coated is okay) heat a little over 3¾ liters of water (rain water is best). When it boils, add to it a little over 30 grams of triethanolamine, available from chemical supply houses. In another container, melt a little over 120 grams each of carnauba and candelilla waxes—I prefer the unrefined version of both, if available—plus about 190 grams of stearic acid. When melted, slowly add the wax mixture to the hot water. Let it cool, stirring frequently with a wooden stick. When cool, the waxes are emulsified, and will have the consistency of heavy cream. The color will be a pale green-grey-beige.

As I have said, this is the best formula that I know. But am I satisfied with my water-wax? The answer is no. I am far closer to the shine I am seeking, but I would be a liar if I said I was satisfied. The water-wax is far from being perfect. This is but one of the hundreds of woodfinishing problems that is open to research. —G.F.

Khedive and Yvonne joined the team. Helpers from the village wiped off the excess water and laid the panels on top of small brick piles, exposing the paneling to the sun (back first, face last). After drying, the panels were ready for the next step, the feeding with angelmilk—quicklime, freshly slaked in water. We painted this solution on the panels without much care because after drying we brushed and wiped off all the lime we could. A fine dusting of lime remained in the wood, however, accentuating its silvery-grey color. We did not use a single piece of sandpaper, yet from the scrubbing and brushing the wood was pleasantly smooth and had the beginning of a glow.

The second day was not yet over when the first panels began their trek back to their original positions. On the eighth day, the swimming pool was drained, cleaned and restored by a caretaker. My men shed their hipboots, donned overalls and entered the manor, where the first room was ready for them. Their immediate task was to repair the damage caused by the work done so far. A number of splits had developed and we glued wedges in them, but not before rubbing their edges with strong tobacco juice or with liquid nightmare, vinegar in which we had soaked all sorts of rusty iron objects. We did this to underline discreetly the fact that repairs had been made—we wanted the repairs to be visible. We used aged wood for wedges, and the fine brown or grey lines around them added credibility to their age. My carpenters used as few nails as possible to reinstall the panels, hiding most of them under the crown molding, the base or the chair-rail. The brads used to secure these were countersunk immediately and the holes filled with soft bread, moistened with saliva and tinted with powdered rottenstone. In two rooms we could not avoid visible nails, so I devised a tricky way to camouflage them. The frames of these panelings were held together with mortise-and-tenon joints, pegged at each corner with two wooden pegs. No one ever noticed that when we finished the job there was a third peg at each corner, a fake that just covered the countersunk nail.

At this point the paneling had a silvery hemp-like color but the general harmony was missing. The wood had not been selected to be exposed, and some boards contrasted sharply with others. To lighten the dark ones, we used a saturated solution of oxalic acid dissolved in alcohol (kept away from any contact with metal). On some pieces we had to repeat this process two or three times. After bleaching, we washed off the residue with vinegar, then with ammonia water. Boards that were too light had to be dyed with various strengths of "liquid nightmare," which added to the anemic boards a greyish hue.

I made up vast supplies of my emulsified wax, and we applied two thin coats of it to the panelings. After it dried, we shined up the first coat with stiff scrub brushes. We rubbed, or burnished, the second coat with chain cloth that originally came from medieval armor. By now the wood was silky smooth with full emphasized markings and a natural shine. Yet the job was not done. My wax had another quality. In a few days it lost its luster and settled down to a low, matte texture. Now my "stone wax" entered the picture. Unrefined carnauba wax looks like green-grey rock and is quite dull until it is rubbed, but then it acquires the most pleasant hard shine. I broke this wax into small pebbles, melted it over high heat in a double-boiler and then, away from all fire hazards, I poured lacquer thinner over it. In a short time the wax gelled

and became pastelike. With this wax, which dried to stone-hardness under my fingers, I coated the high points of the moldings, carvings and parts of the woodwork that were exposed to wear. A final buffing, this time with wool, helped us to achieve the finish that I consider the ultimate for this kind of work. The Khedive agreed and confirmed it in a letter that is still part of my treasured memorabilia.

The last day on the job was reserved for cleanup and for touchups. With a tray in my hand filled with stains and brushes, I strolled from room to room and found and corrected faults. One of the rooms was the Khedive's bedroom, furnished with austere simplicity: a huge bed, a few chairs and a single night-table. I walked in the room, stepped on a screwdriver left there by some careless workman, lost my balance and fell. The tray slipped out of my hand and the contents of one of my small jars spilled on the carpet, which was of a quality royalty can afford, woodfinishers never. My foreman, Richard, and I locked ourselves in the room and tried to clean up the spot. Two hours later we had to throw in the sponge: The spot remained. Then Richard had an idea: "Let's turn the bed around, and tell Boubli later about the accident." No sooner said than done.

The guests of the Khedive arrived the next day, and the reception dinner was scheduled for 6:00 P.M. Well before that time, I had received a message that the Khedive wanted me to "honor the reception with my presence." Sensing that a simple woodfinisher did not belong in the company of statesmen and political leaders, I tried to excuse myself, but Boubli, the Khedive's secretary, made it clear that the Khedive would resent my absence. Therefore, shortly after 5:00 P.M., I arrived at the manor in a hastily rented tuxedo, and was promptly put at ease by Yvonne and the Khedive. A few aperitifs helped to narrow the gap between diplomats and woodfinisher, and by the time the couscous was served I no longer felt that I was an intruder.

After cognac and cigars, the Khedive took the guests on a tour of the manor. Politely he asked my permission to use his native lanquage and I guess that they spoke about the paintings, furniture and rugs, which represented a small fortune. When the group reached the first paneled room, they looked at and stroked the wood, then looked at me with warmth. As new rooms opened up, the "oohs and ahs" of this appreciative audience increased. Finally, we entered the Khedive's bedroom. The bed was back in its original position, the spot was in full evidence, and my heart felt as if it had stopped beating. This time the Khedive spoke in French, addressing me directly: "George, my friend, under your magic fingers this lifeless wood has become a thing of beauty, like music or poetry. While performing your magic act, by accident you soiled my carpet. My intention is to keep that spot as it is, right where it is, to remind me of my indebtedness to you, who revealed to me the beauty that can be found in a piece of simple wood." The Khedive took me in his arms and kissed both of my cheeks. I had tears in my eyes and could not utter a single word. Then the Khedive spoke again, laughingly, pointing to the bed: "And remember, my friend, that a true believer can sleep only so that the line between his heart and his head points toward Mecca." □

George Frank, a master cabinetmaker and furniture finisher who left Europe during World War II and set up shop in New York City, is now retired.

Reproducing Those Old-Time Finishes

by George Frank

Several letters on my desk are awaiting replies. My policy is to answer inquiries promptly; these are unanswered because they all contain the same question and there is no simple answer. The question is: How can I reproduce those rich antique finishes?

There is no such thing as a single, standard, rich "antique" finish. There are as many antique finishes as there are antiques. If there is a basic rule for recreating an old finish, it is this: Have a sample. You must know the finish you are after. Beyond this, anything goes and any way is good as long as it brings you closer to your goal. There are no other rules, but there are a few tricks of the trade that may help. Before telling about them I want to relate three anecdotes.

In September, 1951, I was summoned to the office of a prominent decorator. He showed me a little wine table, commenting that it was a "genuine antique." They were used in elegant homes 150 to 200 years ago to rest the wineglass on, while the guest lounged in an easy chair. He asked me to make 12 copies of the small table to give his customers at Christmas. There would be no story had he not then said, "I know you cannot reproduce the patina of this fine piece, but do your best." Late in November I delivered the 13 tables, and even today he does not know which one is the original.

A few years later a decorator asked me to her store on 57th Street in New York. She had two antique doors from France, and she asked me to build an armoire incorporating the two doors. She repeated the other decorator's words about how I would be unable to reproduce the fine old finish. I took my time, and so it was nearly a year later when I asked her to come to the shop. She could hardly believe her eyes, and she thanked me for a magnificent job. Then, maybe thinking that she'd gone overboard, she added, "Of course, I can see the difference between the doors and the rest, but I doubt my customer ever will." Could she? I did not use her doors; in fact, I still have them. They were simply too far gone to use in the armoire. I wanted to give them back, but since she "recognized" them, I did not. If she reads these lines, she is welcome to pick them up.

In 1943 an apartment fire damaged a small Empire chest, scorching the finish and part of a door. The owner asked if I could salvage her "precious, fine piece," since "it was made by true craftsmen of the past who had pride in their work, unlike the woodbutchers of today." She also believed that quality and knowhow belong only to the past.

Two months later I delivered her restored cabinet. "Now," she said, "this masterpiece of ages past will again grace my home." I have her "masterpiece of ages past," and she has a copy, hastily made. Still, she made the best bargain. Her antique was a poorly made fake, while my replacement was made with far greater care—but I'll trade again, if she wants.

The point is that in each of the three cases I had a sample to go by, a color and a finish to copy. There are no products or set ways to reproduce antique finishes, but I will tell you about a few tricks. I do so reluctantly, since these ways are unorthodox, and I am practically discrediting myself.

The little table was made of Cuban mahogany. Its original finish was medium brown, by now mostly faded to blond.

The finish was varnish, finely rubbed, well aged. The grain was only faintly readable. Needless to say, my 12 tables were made of the same wood, carefully selected to match the grain of the original. All the details were precisely duplicated. To reproduce the finish I started with rabbit-skin glue. This glue comes in approximately 6-in. by 6-in. sheets, and it has a fantastic power to absorb water, which is the main reason I like it. The dry sheet has to be soaked for a day or so before being cooked into a thick soup. This soup, which gels when cold, is extremely helpful in imitating antique finishes. It can be tinted by waterstains, and it can be loaded with dry colors. This colored or loaded glue can be spread over the wood in incredibly thin layers. How thin? The volume of the noise made by a snowflake landing on the windowsill parallels the thickness of the coatings I work with.

To produce the faded look on my tables I coated them with such glue, loaded with chalk and French ochre. The rabbit-skin as a binder permits me to leave on the wood, after sanding or steelwooling the excess, just as much of the coloring matter as I want, exactly where I want.

The next operation is the application of the varnish, again not done by the book. I use fast drying, clear, glossy varnish, but I cut it drastically, especially at the beginning: Ten parts thinner to one of varnish for my first three or four coats. I let every coat dry thoroughly and sand between coatings. I keep on staining between coats, varying the stain according to my sample and my imagination. I know that waterstain will not go through varnish, but I use it. If the job needs it, I use a second, maybe a third coat of rabbit-skin glue, spiced with the shade the wood lacks. With each application I get nearer to the finish of the sample. In the meantime, I do not forget the distressings on the model. Bruises, scratches, dents, wormholes, spots, burns—you name it—are faithfully repeated, but I try not to overdo them.

As I progress, my coatings get heavier and my rubbing more thorough. When I am satisfied with the similarity, I apply the last coat of varnish full strength, and read the label on the can. If it says the varnish will dry in 12 hours, I time myself and 11½ hours later I go over it with a coating of rabbit-skin glue, this time a little more concentrated and containing no colorants. The next day I wash the glue off with lukewarm water, rub the varnish with pumice and later with rottenstone. By then my finish looks almost identical to the sample. The last, infinitely thin coating of glue produces cracks invisible to the naked eye, and microscopic dust fills them up.

The decorator's two French doors were made of walnut, stained chocolate-brown, with graying areas. My armoire was built entirely of old lumber, and in its construction I copied all the shapes and profiles of the antique doors, down to the most minute details. Finally the armoire entered the finishing room. I had on hand (from my Paris shop) some *brou de noix*, the classic walnut stain. (American walnut crystals are just as good, sometimes.) I made a fairly strong brew of it, added some soda ash, and dyed the armoire everywhere: inside, outside, over, under, front and back, as was done by the craftsmen of yore. After sanding I repeated the operation, and by then I had my basic color, lacking black and darker brown. The next morning I came to the shop with a tin of cocoa, mixed in some lampblack, and stirred it into semi-liquid beeswax (see "Brightening old black walnut" on page 33). Waxed with this creamy concoction, the finish improved. Wax finishes, at least the good ones, cannot be rushed. Three or four days later I rubbed down the armoire with burlap and muscle power. Then with some fine steel wool I started to work on the highlights. I repeated the staining, waxing and rubbing week after week, for ten weeks.

To add layers of color, I used my arsenal of dust balls. These are made of thick cloth, the size of a small handkerchief, made into a ball-like container and filled with rottenstone powder. I have about ten of these, the dust in each a different hue. To the rottenstone I add white, yellow, pink or black, or I forgo the rottenstone and use burnt or raw umber, or burnt or raw sienna powder.

As the armoire approached the look of the sample I stopped using my dark-colored wax. Instead, I dusted the wood with the dust I judged most appropriate and waxed over it, building up finish and color.

The finishing touch was again unorthodox. After letting the wax dry for a week I rubbed it out as hard as I could and padded a good layer of shellac over it. I know that one is not supposed to use shellac over wax, yet I did and it worked. The armoire acquired a pleasant, smooth shine, very close to the finish I was to match. The next day I cut the gloss of the shine using dry rottenstone on a rag and muscle power. When I achieved a very close match, I stopped.

So far I have been talking about reproducing antiques made mostly of solid wood. Other techniques are used for veneered pieces. Antiques with inlay or marquetry often used woods that were artificially colored before the logs were made into veneers. These colors frequently faded, and this is hard to imitate. I knew a manufacturer in Casablanca, Morocco, who left reproductions on the roof of his factory, exposed to rain and sun, to fade them. I worked in a Paris shop where we used a battery of lamps. Most shops, however, used chemicals like oxalic acid, chlorine, or a mixture of muriatic acid and potassium dichromate—dangerous if not handled carefully.

On the veneered antique there are more details to imitate than fading: The finish acquires, with age, a golden hue; the veneer cracks or develops minute warpings, and the original glass-smooth finish becomes wavy; and some veneers separate from their backings. The golden hue is comparatively easy to reproduce. Before finishing, we can wash the piece with a very concentrated brew of tea, or we may dissolve a minute amount of auramine (a modern aniline dye) in alcohol, and add a few drops of this to the shellac we use for French polishing. The cracking should be produced after finishing, by alternating exposure to dampness and to dry heat. A manufacturer in Orleans, France, stored his reproductions in his very damp cellar for a few months, and dried them in heated, well-ventilated rooms to produce these crack-ups. A faster method is to cover reproductions with mud, repeatedly, and dry them with a gas torch.

There is no way to describe all the tricks of the trade used to reproduce antiques. The Orleans manufacturer upholstered some fine chairs with costly damask and placed them in a chicken coop for hens to roost on. Horse manure was and still is used to age wood, and the smart craftsman uses only aged wood for reproductions. In this trade the rule is: anything goes as long as it gets you closer to the sample you are copying. There is no such thing as a rich, antique finish, there are only well-copied antiques. The most important tools are your head and your imagination. □

Q & A

Exposure-darkened cypress

I have recently purchased an old house in which the den walls are covered with cypress. It appears as if the walls were originally sealed with a thin coat of clear varnish. Where pictures have hung, the wood is lighter in color than the remaining walls, which have darkened through exposure. How might I blend these lighter spots into the remaining wall? —Furman B. Riddle, Jr., Greer, S.C.

GEORGE FRANK REPLIES: There is no simple answer, although someone specializing in photographic chemistry might be able to help you. I would take the boards off the walls and run them through the planer, taking off 1/64 in. Then sandpaper them and put them back. In the long run this may be easier than working with chemicals toward a very uncertain solution. Good luck.

Ebonizing maple

Can you suggest a method for ebonizing maple to give a high-gloss black surface that will wear well? —Daniel Symonds, Towson, Md.

GEORGE FRANK REPLIES: Ebony is a dark brown wood, irregularly striped with charcoal or nearly black markings. To ebonize means to copy such wood. This involves the use of a well-concentrated aniline dye, used repeatedly. When the desired shade is reached, it must be sealed with a wash coat of shellac. Then a nearly black oil-stain is spread over it evenly, and with a painter's graining comb (a cross between a comb and a rubber squeegee), about half of it is taken off, creating an irregular pattern, so the remainder will imitate the markings of ebony (one should have samples). When dry, the oil stain also has to be sealed with another, slightly heavier, coating of shellac.

However, if you were to ask the average woodfinisher to ebonize an object, chances are that he would say to build up a heavy coating of black, or nearly black, lacquer finish and for final rubbing he would use water and 4-F pumice stone, so that the finished surface would not be glossy, but rather would be satiny-smooth.

Workshop temperature and humidity

I refinish and repair furniture and recently built a new workshop. I strip or repair furniture in a room with kerosene heat, finish in a room with electric heat, and then store the finished pieces in a room with a concrete floor, which is unheated but insulated. Could you tell me if I will run into any problems with this process? —Steve Cole, Laceyville, Pa.

R. BRUCE HOADLEY REPLIES: I'll suggest a few things to watch for. Try to keep relative humidity in the 35% to 45% range, and beware of winter lows and summer highs. Avoid "hot spots," and put up barriers to protect pieces from strong, direct air currents. Stay within recommended levels of temperature for application of glues and finishes. Avoid moving a piece from a cool area to a warm area just before finishing, especially in humid weather, for surface condensation can be disastrous, and can take place without your noticing it. A bigger problem is with air expansion in the cell cavities as the piece warms up during finishing—each cell becomes a "bubble pipe," causing terrible bubbles in any lacquer or varnish-type finish, or pushing out droplets of penetrating finish. It is best to keep the temperature even, or move a piece from a slightly warmer to a room-temperature area to apply finish. In your storage area, beware of drastic fluctuations, especially when warm, humid weather moves in during spring. Condensation, especially on incompletely cured varnish, can ruin a finish.

Furniture Conservation
Historic objects can outlast us all

by Robert F. McGiffin

Hudson river valley kas, c. 1745.

Probably the greatest threat to furniture is man. Historical furniture is subjected to restoration abuse, misuse, damage and disfigurement by well-meaning individuals who are undoubtedly very proud of their work. Most of my work as a furniture conservator involves correcting theirs. I have seen many pieces of furniture damaged by modifications or inadequate repairs. It is all too easy to pick up a hammer or saw and go to work. I recently treated a Hudson river valley kas (large chest), c. 1745, whose shelves were originally large, single planks. At one point, probably within the last three decades, a section was cut out of one of the shelves to make room for a fire extinguisher, causing irreversible damage.

I feel that with luck, a piece of historical furniture will outlast all of us many times over, and we should do nothing to disturb it. Each of us should develop an attitude that we have no right to remove original material and evidence of an object's history, even if we own the object. This includes the aged finish. Unlike paintings, where darkened varnishes, scratches and later additions are considered disfiguring, historical furniture was designed to be functional, subjected to daily abuse and wear. Scratches, dents, stains and burns that may have occurred during its existence are part of its history.

Many times a beautiful and secure patina is dissolved in a stripping vat or is sanded and scraped away, because the owner, dealer or custodian of the piece is trying to "recapture the beauty of the wood" or to "return the piece to its original appearance." No one knows exactly how the piece appeared when new, although laboratory analysis may indicate what type of finish was used. We may even have some idea of the concentrations, but cannot tell for certain how the stain and/or the finish saturated the newly made object. We probably can't tell the degree of gloss or dullness that the finish originally had. Seasonal changes have made joints and moldings expand and contract, causing them to reach an equilibrium that is slightly different from when new. How about scratches, dents, abrasions and checks? Most can be minimized or camouflaged, but not all. Dents and scratches usually cause a traumatic shock to the wood fibers, obvious

under a microscope. What would be gained by removing a burn from a tabletop, caused by a trivet or kettle placed there sometime in the 18th century? Wouldn't a part of history be removed if the table's finish, along with the burn, were sanded or stripped away? I am not saying that today's cigarette burn on a piece of antique furniture is adding to its history—a modern burn is disfigurement, because the piece should be preserved from daily wear and tear.

Care of historical furniture — The treatment of the kas (photo, above) involved replacing the separated shelf portion, and a general cleaning. But this treatment won't work on all furniture. When you apply the following procedures to your own furniture, act with caution.

First, the surface of the kas was vacuumed with a soft brush attachment. Had there been cleaving veneer or upholstery, a piece of window screen, with all four edges covered with tape, would have been held between the object and the brush, to keep pieces of veneer or fabric from being pulled into the vacuum. To test the finish, a cotton-tipped applicator was dampened with distilled water and gently rolled over a small obscure area. The applicator picked up surface grime and didn't soften the finish. Whitening, which tells that the finish is reacting badly to water, did not occur after the area dried for a few minutes. Whitening may not be easily reversible—if it is visible, remove it, if possible, using the method described later, and continue cleaning not with water but with solvents.

A bucket was then filled with clean room-temperature distilled water, and the water applied with a clean, dampened (not dripping) sponge, by working in small areas and not rubbing too hard. The areas were dried with soft toweling to absorb any remaining moisture, then the entire process was repeated with clean water. The kas still had grimy areas remaining, so we repeated the steps with one teaspoon of

Robert F. McGiffin is conservator of the Collections Care Center, Bureau of Historic Sites, Waterford, N.Y. The Center is responsible for 35 state historic sites in New York.

Kas was irreversibly damaged when a section of one of its shelves was cut out to make room for a fire extinguisher.

Nails and screws where there were none originally can restrict wood movement, causing checks, or splits and disfiguring holes.

detergent stirred into a gallon of water. Use either a commercial woodwork detergent such as Soilax, or the anionic concentration, Orvus. Rinse away any detergent residue with a sponge dampened in clean water. We waxed the kas with a formula I will describe later. If you still have grime, further cleaning is possible with solvents. However, improper use of solvents can cause irreversible damage, and solvents are not safe for all finishes. The safer solvents are paint thinner (preferably odorless), turpentine and benzine (sometimes called petroleum benzine or VMP naphtha). Benzine is not benzene, which is toxic. Use these solvents in a well-ventilated area with no open flames or electrical sparks.

To test the solvent, dampen a cotton-tipped applicator with it, wring it out and roll it over a small portion of the grimy area. A lot of solvent on the surface can slow down evaporation and may soften the finish below the grime and wax, as well as surface wax, so be sparing. After removing some of the grime and wax from the test area, apply more solvent, making sure it is not softening the finish. Continue working in small areas with the cotton-tipped applicator and immediately dry the area with a soft, clean rag. At this point you have to decide if you are going to continue your grime removal to the point of removing old wax build-up from the entire piece of furniture.

Veneer cleavage — If there is veneer cleavage, you may be able to apply some glue under the veneer with a small brush. If you have a syringe, inject a little distilled water under the cleavage, clamp the area and wait a minute or so to let the original glue soften. Remove the clamp and wipe up any water that runs out on the finish. Dilute some hide glue 50% with distilled water and inject it under the veneer until it runs out. Wipe up the excess, then clamp. I prefer wooden cam-action clamps, such as the ones made by Klemmsia.

If you don't have proper clamps, hold the veneer down for about 24 hours with tape or a weight. Shield the veneer from the clamp surface with a small piece of Plexiglas, to keep the clamp from adhering to the wood and to prevent denting. Waxed paper will also shield the clamps from the glue. After the glue has dried, the Plexiglas may be stuck to the surface, but a gentle push from the side will pop it loose. Use hot hide glue or liquid hide glue, such as Franklin's. They are soluble

in water, easily removed many years later and similar to the glue used when the furniture was made.

Don't be fooled by white polyvinyl acetate emulsion glues. Although they are soluble in water when they come from the bottle, they are less so after aging. On drying, they form a continuous film by fusion of the polymer droplets present in the emulsion. They also penetrate deeply and once in, are almost impossible to remove. If you repair using a white glue and are dissatisfied, or someone wants to reverse it later on, damage could result. If a treatment involves reconstruction and perhaps the replacement of a missing primary support, such as a leg, hot hide glue is strong enough, yet reversible.

Wood fillers, losses and separated elements — If you have losses, or holes, don't plug them with commercial wood fillers. They won't look like wood and may shrink or fall out during the seasonal dimensional changes of the wood. If someone tries to remove them, damage may result to the surrounding areas. Under no circumstances should a separated element be reattached with nails and screws where there were none originally. Not only are they hard to remove, but the restriction of the movement of wood results in checks or splits. They also leave disfiguring holes after they are removed.

For a small area, say a nail hole, I often use a pigmented wax stick that matches the wood. If the loss was caused by a screw head, you can cut your own plug from new wood of similar grain. Dowels or some commercially made tapered plugs won't camouflage the loss unless it is in end grain.

If the loss is more extensive, let in a patch. Obviously, this is time-consuming. I do not remove original material around the area to be filled unless it has jagged edges or splinters. I first find a piece of the same kind of wood with similar figure. Various methods, such as rubbings or measured drawings, are used to transfer the loss configuration to the new wood. The patch is then cut out and shaped.

At this point, I test stains and finishes on the waste portion of the new wood until I can duplicate exactly the original appearance. Sometimes I can finish the patch before pressing and gluing it into place. If the color is wrong, it is safer to find out before the patch is attached. Usually, the patch is fixed in place, the profile is leveled off, and then the new color and finish are applied to match the original surrounding area.

Finishes — After cleaning and repairing, you may want to apply a new finish over the old. Instead of applying varnish, shellac or lacquer over the original, I usually prefer to use wax. Wax protects, and is easy to apply. It can look like a shellac finish, is generally harmless and can be removed at any time. I formulate my own wax recipe and you can do the same. It contains two parts Cosmolloid 80H (a microcrystalline wax) and five parts odorless paint thinner: for example, 20 gm microcrystalline wax and 50 ml paint thinner.

Weigh the Cosmolloid and melt it in a double boiler, bringing the water to a boil on a hot plate, not over an open flame. Keep checking the water to make sure it hasn't all evaporated. Work in a well-ventilated room. The wax may take about 45 minutes to melt. When most has melted, pour the thinner into a glass jar large enough to hold both the wax and the thinner, and place the jar in boiling water to warm for a few minutes. By now all of the wax should be melted. The thinner is heated so that when the molten wax is added it won't gel and form a lumpy mixture. Quickly pour in the wax. Remove the jar from the heat and let it cool. Apply the wax once every year or two, but dust the object once a week. Store the wax jar in a warm area.

You may wish to use another recipe if you don't have a double boiler, or simply don't wish to play around with hot materials. Use two parts by weight of wax plus five parts solvent. Simply place the wax in a jar and add the solvent. Keep tightly covered until a homogeneous mixture has formed. This may take several days with periodic stirring by rotating the jar, and it may be necessary to add a little solvent from time to time to keep the wax soft.

To apply, put a small amount on a soft cloth and rub in. If it seems to go on a little hard (some objects can't take hard rubbing because the joints might be loosened), dip the cloth in a little odorless thinner. Rub in a circular motion, followed by strokes in the direction of the grain. Do not overload the cloth with wax, which can cause the surface to remain sticky. Let the solvent evaporate a few minutes after the wax has been applied to the furniture, then buff in the direction of the grain with a clean, soft, lintless rag. You may want to buff again after 24 hours, after more solvent evaporates.

The wax formula may remain sticky for several days and therefore may not be appropriate for a piece of furniture that has daily handling. A useful product is Renaissance wax, which I recommend both because I know its ingredients and because it doesn't remain sticky. It's hard to buff on large areas, however, and will streak. Dampen the cloth in odorless thinner to overcome this. While polishing, watch for loose pieces of veneer, moldings or hardware that may be pulled loose, bent or broken by the cloth. In general, most conservators try to avoid commercial products because they can contain materials that, on aging, may undergo changes in color or transparency and become inseparable from the object to which they are applied. The Cosmolloid mixture and the Renaissance wax are not panaceas, and if there is wax build-up already on the surface, either may soften it and the surface could remain sticky. Wax build-up should be removed.

I would not use polyurethane varnishes on historical furniture. They are good moisture barriers, but never apply them over an original finish, because they are irreversible.

Avoid recipes for "feeding" the finish, a term from old wives' tales and 19th-century restorers' recipes. Feeding recipes, found in many books, often contain linseed oil, an irreversible drying oil that penetrates the surface, saturating the original finish or pigment particles. In a few years when the object becomes darker and darker, someone will try to remove it and may discover he must either leave it alone or destroy much of the original finish. Linseed oil changes chemically as it dries, forming a tough, hard film.

Some books suggest inpainting losses on painted furniture with oil paints, but never apply anything to painted surfaces. Oil paints discolor and are irreversible except by methods that may harm the original. Painted surfaces can be complex, and only someone with conservation experience should deal with them. Beware of "cure-alls." What may work for one treatment may be the opposite of what works for another. By not fully understanding the chemical and physical properties of a particular paint film, damage may result.

Furniture hardware — I don't use commercial emulsion-type brass polishes for hardware on historical furniture

Sloppy application of brass polish can damage a finish. White material around edges of pull is brass polish residue.

because repeated use can damage the hardware and, if you're not careful, the finish on the wood as well. I also stay away from copper brighteners or dip cleaners, the old home recipe of vinegar and salt, and steel wool or buffing wheels.

I use rubbing, isopropyl or ethyl alcohol to clean brass hardware, cleaning it on the object if the brasses appear original. If I can, I slip a piece of aluminum foil behind the brass to protect the wood, then wipe over the brass with a dampened cotton-tipped applicator to remove greasy fingerprints and allow a protective brown patina to form.

Whitening of finish — Water, condensation from a glass, or a fast-evaporating commercial cleaner can give the finish a milky-white appearance, but this is one area where we can rely on home remedies, moderately used. Try a little cooking oil mixed with cigar or cigarette ash. Rub on the whitish area with your fingertip for a short time, then wipe the area dry with a soft rag. If that doesn't work, try a little of the same oil and a small amount of whiting, pumice or rottenstone, or try wiping the area briefly with a little alcohol on a rag with your fingertip or cotton-tipped applicators. Be careful, because the alcohol may soften the finish, and can actually remove a French polish. If this happens, leave the area alone for a while to give the finish a chance to reharden. Any of these treatments may get rid of the white, but may make the area glossier than its surroundings. If this happens, rub a little 4/0 steel wool in the area. Pull off a small amount of fine steel wool from the pad and wrap it around a round wooden stick from a cotton-tipped applicator or toothpick. This can be followed by an overall waxing of the piece.

These treatments may also work on dark stains or burns, but make sure that the stain or burn is not relevant to the object's history. If the burn is recent, such as from a cigarette, use the same methods described for white rings. It may be a little deeper though and you might have to resort to 4/0 steel wool with a little turpentine or paint thinner. The finish will be destroyed in the area so you can tone with stains, or sometimes you can get by with acrylic emulsion paints or watercolors. Take a fine camel-hair brush and reapply a finish of shellac only in the damaged area. You may need to blend in the new shellac with 4/0 steel wool and wax. □

EDITOR'S NOTE: Orvus detergent, Cosmolloid 80H and Renaissance wax are available at Talas, 213 W. 35th St., New York, N.Y. 10001-1996. Pigmented wax sticks are available from Mohawk Finishing Products, Rt. 30N, Amsterdam, N.Y. 12010.

French Polishing I
The disappearing art of getting a fine shellac finish

by Paul Roman

To many woodworkers, the art of satin-gloss French polishing—the building up of a thin, fine shellac finish with a cloth pad—is a deservedly dying one. It takes not only much skill and experience to produce the transparent satin gloss that it's famous for, but also much elbow grease.

As a result, in this day of seemingly instant, effortless activity, French polishing is given short shrift, rarely or briefly mentioned in books on wood finishing.

To Anthony Arlotta, a former cabinetmaker and now a professional finisher and refinisher for many years in New York City, this is a sad state of affairs. He can understand why French polishing for commercially made woodwork has become economically impractical except for the finest antiques. But for the amateur craftsman, who has already spent dozens or even hundreds of hours making a piece of furniture or a marquetry panel, the extra several hours that French polishing takes, compared to the instant finishes, is well worth it. It gives a smooth, thin finish full of luster but without the thick high gloss associated with lacquer.

For refinishing work, it can be used over old shellac, but not over old varnish or lacquer because of the poor bond.

The advantages of French polishing over varnish and lacquer are not only its beauty, but also its relative practicality. That is, if the finish does get scratched or damaged, it's a relatively easy process to rebuild and blend in the new shellac buildup. In fact, Arlotta demonstrates this dramatically by

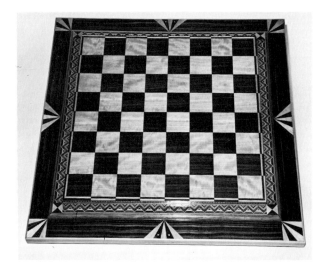

French polish gives chessboard by A. Miele a fine finish.

putting some 150 or 180 grit sandpaper to a finished piece, and then, in a few minutes of rubbing, getting rid of the intentional scratches.

There are disadvantages, however. Shellac is water resistant but not waterproof as some varnishes are. And, of course, it is not alcohol resistant, since that is the solvent for shellac. But given these drawbacks, there's no reason why French polishing can't be used for any fine furniture that is properly cared for, especially where the beauty of the grain and figure of the wood is to be highlighted.

For French polishing, Arlotta uses age old techniques, such as mixing his own shellac. (He considers ready-made French polishes inferior, but he does use them—on the undersides of furniture where it doesn't show.) He takes orange shellac flakes or crushed orange shellac buttons, fills a jar about three-quarters full with the dry shellac, and then fills the jar with methyl or wood alcohol, or columbine spirits, as it is sometimes called.

It takes about a week for the flakes or chips to dissolve. Every day he gives the mixture a stir or two; after a week the flakes have dissolved into an orange syrupy mixture. He strains it through cheesecloth if necessary, especially if the buttons were used.

Arlotta doesn't use bleached or white shellac because he's never sure of the impurities in it, and if it's the least bit old, it doesn't dry. Arlotta says the orange shellac has an indefinite shelf life if a skim coat of alcohol is poured over the top and the jar is tightly sealed. The color is not a problem because the shellac is put on in such a thin coat.

If the wood is to be stained before finishing, only *water-based* aniline dyes should be used. Otherwise the rubbing process of French polishing could lift up stains that have other base formulations.

In fact, to create a warmth and mellowness in the wood, Arlotta likes to stain all of his pieces (regardless of the wood) with a weak solution of yellow stain. If kept pale, the stain does not really turn the wood yellow, but does give it a warmth and depth that is hard to match.

(As always in the finishing process, it's best to do extensive experimenting beforehand, for instance trying various dilutions of the yellow stain on a spare piece of wood. And, of course, it's prudent to go through the whole French polishing sequence on scrap before trying it on a treasured piece.)

Water stain raises the grain, so wash with water, dry, and sand before you stain. After staining you should give it another light sanding with very fine sandpaper.

The first step in French polishing is to put on a very thin or light wash coat of shellac (two parts alcohol, one part shellac

Make up a pad (as described in the text) to work in the white pumice sprinkled on the surface, which will fill pores.

stock). This is done with a pad made up of a small ball of cotton wool or cotton waste wrapped into a larger square of cotton or natural fiber cloth and twisted into a ball. The shellac should not be put on heavily as its main purpose is to serve as a binder for the subsequent filling step.

After the shellac dries, usually in a half hour or less, Arlotta goes immediately to the filling process, using 4F pumice stone as filler.

A new pad is made up, this time with more rugged linen or tight gabardine as the pad material (because pumice is a strong abrasive). He sprinkles some pumice lightly on the surface of the wood, the pad is dampened with alcohol, and the pumice is rubbed hard into the pores. As with all French polishing steps, the initial rubbing should be in tight moving circles, then looser figure eights, and finally long straight strokes with the grain. Don't let the pad stop its motion, but keep it moving constantly. Otherwise, you'll get cloth marks where the shellac hardens.

What the combination of the alcohol and the rubbing does is to soften the shellac undercoat and imbed the pumice in it.

When the pumice has disappeared, sprinkle some more on, and add more alcohol to the pad. Keep on with this until the pores are completely filled, the surface seems absolutely flat, and the circular stroke marks have disappeared.

Then put it aside for a week. The shellac will dry completely and shrink slightly, exposing some of the pores again. Do another pumice filling sequence and again put it aside, this time for fewer days. When the surface stays completely flat, the wood is ready for the final polishing sequence.

(It's at this point, too, that any blemishes or defects in the wood would be fixed using wood powders.)

But assuming a blemish-free surface, a new cotton or wool pad is made up. Some shellac stock is poured onto the inside ball (the outer cloth then acts as a filter). The pad is squeezed to spread the shellac throughout, and flattened, and then just enough alcohol is put on it to make it lose some of its tacky feeling. A drop or two of lemon oil is touched here and there onto the wood surface (to act as a lubricant), and the padding process is begun.

Use the same small overlapping circles to put on the shellac. Glide the pad on and glide it off, but never stop its motion. Put enough pressure on the pad to rub the shellac in, but not so much that it takes off or "burns" the coat underneath. Recharge the pad with shellac and alcohol as needed. Add more lemon oil occasionally, and keep up the rubbing process, going from the circular strokes to the figure eights to the long straight strokes.

Repeat the process as often as you want, until you've built up the degree of finish that you desire. You'll know that you've rubbed enough when the stroke marks disappear. The longer into the padding process, the lighter the pressure on the pad should be.

At the end, you'll want to apply alcohol alone to the surface to take up the lemon oil and give the final polish. Arlotta uses a new pad that is barely damp with alcohol and uses straight strokes with very light pressure. Stop when you've got the surface to where you want it.

That's the essence of French polishing. After the filling step you can build up the shellac finish as many times as you want—once or twice for a really spare finish, to several or many times for a heavier build up. There is no drying time between steps and you can pause or stop anywhere in the process (as long as you glide the pad off).

And if the finish itself does get damaged, you can sand the affected area with fine paper and rebuild it to match the overall piece, provided you have no deep dents or gouges.

Unlike lacquer and heavy varnishes, there's no solid film to crack or chip off. There's only a very thin coat of shellac that has been padded or polished on.

After the final polish, you should wait a few weeks before you put any protective coats of wax (like butcher's wax)—if you want to wax it. But it's really not necessary.

Good polishing! Remember, keep that pad moving!   □

[EDITOR'S NOTE: If you cannot find the materials mentioned in your area, write H. Behlen and Bros., Rt. 30N, Amsterdam, N.Y. 12010 for local distributors.]

French Polishing II
Elbow grease and shellac build a fine finish

by Clinton R. Howell

By today's standards, French polishing is not economical for the commercial woodworker. It is virtually all sensitivity of touch, and it takes years to understand the nuances of technique, from knowing the precise amount of lubricating oil to put on a surface to sensing when the job requires a higher room temperature. It also takes time—the finish is built up of many thin layers of shellac. The maker of fine, one-piece-at-a-time furniture should not overlook French polishing, however, because of the warmth it gives a new piece and the patina it develops with time. The finish is also relatively easy to rebuild if it becomes marred, and can be applied over almost any existing finish. I have French-polished over oil-based varnishes, polyurethanes and acid-catalyzed lacquers with good results.

History — The development of French polishing is not well documented, nor is the first person to develop a good shellac for furniture known. The first mention of shellac in England can be found in *A Treatise of Japanning and Varnishing* (1688), by John Stalker and George Parker. Stalker and Parker treat shellac and the people who used it ("varnish dawbers") with disdain, but do admit that shellac was "commonly used by those that imploy themselves in varnishing ordinary woods, as Olive, Walnut, and the like." I believe that here they were acknowledging the nascent craft of French polishing and that their disregard for these varnish daubers might have been nothing more than a xenophobic reaction to the introduction of a new craft to England by immigrants.

The man who taught me how to polish, Herbert Burrell, of London, has been polishing for 45 years, and he also feels that alcohol-soluble finishes were used in England earlier than 1830, when French polishing is commonly thought to have been introduced. The difficulty is in establishing what is an unretouched surface, and whether that surface was originally French-polished. Burrell admits this is almost impossible to ascertain.

Formula — French polishes are generally shellac-based, though I have found formulas that include seedlac, sandarac, mastic and other resins. Stalker and Parker's formula of a gallon of spirit to 1½ lb. of shellac flakes is identical to one I found in the *Cyclopedia of Useful Arts* (1884), but I prefer to mix 2½ lb. of flakes with a gallon of ethyl alcohol. Both isopropyl and methyl alcohol will work, but to keep the solution free from water, use as pure an alcohol as possible.

I've used orange shellac, but the orange color does come through. Some people prefer this but I don't, except on light

woods like pine and maple, to which the orange shellac imparts a warm yellow tone. Bleached or white shellac has a short shelf life and I seldom use it. A shellac that works well for me is Angelo Blond from William Zinsser Co., 39 Belmont Dr., Somerset, N.J. 08873 (sold in minimum quantities of 10 lb.). I have not found an adequate ready-made American polish, though several are available in England.

Surface preparation — The most important step in French polishing is preparing the surface; you want the grain to lie flat. Shortcuts invariably lead to difficulties down the line, but if you use a water stain before finishing, save time by wetting the grain before staining. Use about as much water as you'll be using to stain. Allow the wood to dry about an hour or so, lightly sand and then stain. This is usually all that is needed to keep the grain flat.

Putting a sealer coat of polish on the wood is the first step in French polishing. The sealer will prevent the filler from working loose as the wood expands and contracts over time, as well as the discoloration that can occur when filler is applied directly to the wood. You can apply the sealer coat with a hardened fad (the piece of cotton wadding that makes up the inside of the rubber) or a brush. Don't use fresh cotton wadding because bits of it will come loose and stick to the surface of the wood. If you use a brush, thin the polish to avoid leaving brushmarks and lines.

Moisten the fad with polish—you want it to be about as wet as a squeezed-out teabag, not so wet that it drips. Move the fad in broad, sweeping strokes until the entire surface is covered with polish, then allow it to stand for 30 minutes.

The second step is filling the pores of the wood. While pumice was widely used in other countries, plaster (the hardware-store variety) to which color has been added is the traditional English filler. Improper plastering shows up as white flecks in the grain on antiques. For a dining table I'd use about half a cup of plaster and half a teaspoon of powdered color (contact H. Behlen and Bros., Rt. 30N, Amsterdam, N.Y. 12010 for local distributors). Experiment to find the right color for the piece you're finishing. As an example, for mahogany filler I might mix rose pink, yellow, orange and a touch of brown. Be conservative with the amount of color at first—what looks pale in the bowl will darken when wet.

Moisten a piece of burlap in water, dip it into the colored plaster, and apply with a circular motion. Lean down hard on the burlap—you want to force the filler into the pores of the wood. Wipe off excess plaster before it hardens. When the plaster has dried sufficiently, usually in three to four hours, remove the residue with a worn piece of wet-and-dry paper and linseed oil, then wipe the surface clean.

The next step is evening out the tone of the wood—in polishing, this takes the most skill. A good finish will allow the eye to travel smoothly over the surface of the piece without

EDITOR'S NOTE: *A Treatise of Japanning and Varnishing* (1688) by Stalker and Parker was reprinted by Alec Tiranti, Ltd., London, in 1960. It is often available in libraries or through inter-library loan, or your bookseller can order a copy for you.

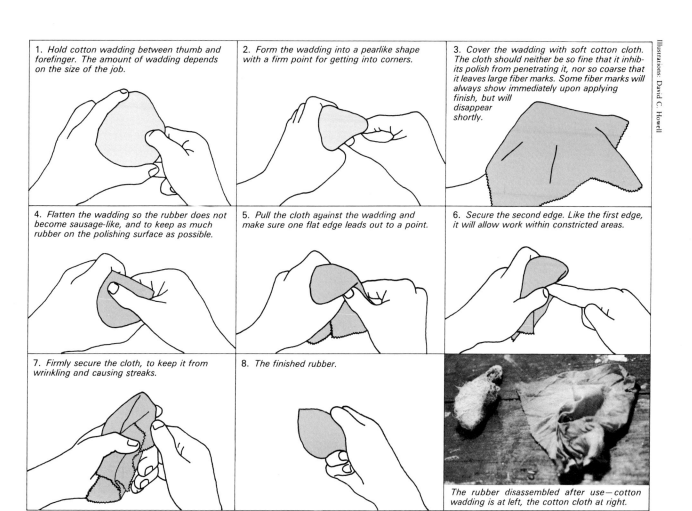

1. *Hold cotton wadding between thumb and forefinger. The amount of wadding depends on the size of the job.*

2. *Form the wadding into a pearlike shape with a firm point for getting into corners.*

3. *Cover the wadding with soft cotton cloth. The cloth should neither be so fine that it inhibits polish from penetrating it, nor so coarse that it leaves large fiber marks. Some fiber marks will always show immediately upon applying finish, but will disappear shortly.*

4. *Flatten the wadding so the rubber does not become sausage-like, and to keep as much rubber on the polishing surface as possible.*

5. *Pull the cloth against the wadding and make sure one flat edge leads out to a point.*

6. *Secure the second edge. Like the first edge, it will allow work within constricted areas.*

7. *Firmly secure the cloth, to keep it from wrinkling and causing streaks.*

8. *The finished rubber.*

The rubber disassembled after use—cotton wadding is at left, the cotton cloth at right.

Illustrations: David C. Howell

being jarred by splashes of bright color here and there. I use alcohol stains in two colors, black and Bismark brown (a red). Mix these colors well with about one part polish (for a binder) and three parts alcohol. In a year's worth of polishing I have used about half a pint each of brown and black—the equivalent of a teaspoon of stain in powder form. Black and Bismark brown can be adapted for use on almost any wood. However, colors such as chrysodine (another red) for maple, and green (good for making a red mahogany brown) are useful.

Always apply these colors patiently with a brush or hardened fad, depending on the size of the area being colored. Many thin coats are harder to detect than one thick one. Exercise caution when recharging the brush or fad with color. If the tool is too wet, drips will form marks on the surface, which then must be completely cleaned off with alcohol. It is disheartening when the job is nearly finished and an entire area must be reworked because of carelessness.

After staining, sealing, filling and coloring, the surface will look so beautifully flat and even that the novice will be tempted to stop. In truth, the work is just beginning.

Making a rubber — The rubber, unlike a brush, will apply the finish in flat layers, and is the principal tool in French polishing. It is wrapped into a pearlike shape to get into tight corners—the drawings above show how.

The medium-soft, all-cotton cloth that covers the wadding should be pulled together so that it will not wrinkle during use. Should streaks occur during polishing, examine and cor-

rect the rubber, then resume work. The streaks will disappear. Learning how to construct a proper rubber takes time and patience, but once it is mastered you will see that all other shapes are clumsy in comparison. I keep my rubbers and fads in airtight containers between jobs so they won't go hard, but if they do get a little stiff, pour in some alcohol.

Applying the finish — The best way to put on a high gloss is to work for three hours, leave off for a day, rub the finish down with worn, fine sandpaper and a bit of linseed oil, and

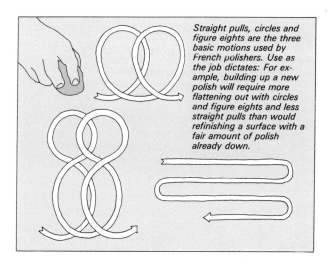

Straight pulls, circles and figure eights are the three basic motions used by French polishers. Use as the job dictates: For example, building up a new polish will require more flattening out with circles and figure eights and less straight pulls than would refinishing a surface with a fair amount of polish already down.

start anew. This was how pianos were finished before the advent of sprays, and the surface that resulted was phenomenally lustrous and durable. However, this was often done over a period of 60 days—certainly not economical today.

To get your layers of polish to lie flat, apply the polish with firm, steady pressure using the three basic motions shown on the previous page: straight pulls, circles and figure eights. If you were to do nothing but straight pulls, ridges would develop and mistakes, such as streaks, would be harder to eliminate. Generally, until this becomes second nature, it is best to do five or six straight pulls to each set of circles and figure eights. Never rub in a circle exceeding 8 in. in diameter, to avoid leaning too hard on the rubber. Both the figure-eight and the circular motions form whips in the polish, and these are difficult to remove when the rubber has been pressed down with too much force. Bearing down too heavily can also cause the polish to pick up previous layers.

Work as drily as you can while getting used to the surface. Too much polish too quickly will look good for a minute, but with subsequent rubbing the rubber will stick and pick up the polish. The way to keep the rubber under control is to charge the fad with polish a little at a time, removing the cotton cloth each time you do so. When the fad is charged, remake the rubber and squeeze out excess polish through the point of the rubber. When you accidentally put too much polish on the surface, let it dry for 10 to 15 minutes and then work straight over the streak, rubbing hard. You might need to add a drop of linseed oil to the rubber for lubrication.

Though oil keeps the rubber from sticking, the novice will find the use of oil difficult to master. Oil can fool you into thinking you have put a beautiful finish down, when in fact there is still plenty of oil to be removed. One way to tell is to blow on the surface—if it clouds there is too much oil. Leaving on excess oil will cause the polish either to crackle or go white. Sometimes this happens in a week, sometimes in a year, but eventually it will happen.

In England the traditional oil is raw linseed, though lemon oil can also be used. If you need it (and often no oil whatsoever is needed), apply about half a drop to the rubber, or flick a bit on the wood with a finger. The total amount of oil I used recently on a dining table was approximately a quarter-teaspoonful. If you put too much on you can either draw a rubber that is charged sparingly with alcohol across the surface with straight strokes, or work the oil out with the polish by rubbing (the dried oil will accumulate on the sides of the rubber). When the surface is free of oil, the rubber will begin to stick slightly, and you'll hear a faint squeak as you draw the rubber along.

French-polish whole surfaces at a time, such as an entire leaf of a dining table or the top of a sideboard, otherwise the surface will have ridges. Large surfaces are the easiest to polish because the "skin" in one area is drying while you're polishing another area. The hardest surfaces to polish are the smallest ones—it's tempting to polish incessantly, but work with deliberation and try not to speed up the routine. You will know when the job is finished when the surface is lustrous and free of streaks, specks and ridges.

As the polisher works, a residue of material will build up on the hands, but cleanup need not be a problem. A generous amount of baking soda dissolved in a container of warm water cleans well and is also reusable. Keep the solution in a pot and simply reheat it when you put down your rubber for the day. □

Clinton Howell is a furniture conservator, writer for such periodicals as Art and Antique Auction Review, *and former publisher of the* Antique Furniture Newsletter. *He currently deals in antique furniture in Pound Ridge, N.Y.*

Seedlac Varnish

by Sidney Greenstein

When you combine seedlac, the hardened secretions of the *Laccifer lacca* insect, with alcohol, you get a magnificent spirit varnish that was used for centuries past and is still used today by people in the know. Unfortunately, there are still too few people in the know, and seedlac is often left out of otherwise comprehensive literature about finishes, such as Don Newell's article, "Finishing Materials" (see pages 2-5). Seedlac is scraped off the twigs of trees; if it is melted down the result is shellac, but the heating and refining process robs the seedlac of many valuable properties.

Seedlac varnish is pale amber in color and, unlike shellac, does not tend toward opacity. Seedlac is also highly scuff- and water-resistant, and dries fast. You can apply it over any traditional water or alcohol stain, or tint the varnish itself with alcohol-soluble colors.

Seedlac varnish boasts a long, honorable history. The first definite reference in Indian writings to the use of lac resin occurs in 1590 A.D., in the *Ain-e-Akbari*, the official records of Akbar, the Mogul emperor. Details of using lac resin in "lacquering" and polishing wood in public buildings are given. One of the earliest references in the English language is to be found in *A Treatise of Japanning and Varnishing* by Stalker and Parker, printed in London in 1688.

The fine finishes we associate with 18th- and 19th-century French and English furniture are seedlac-based. The finishes of the old violinmakers of Cremona, Italy, may also be all or partly seedlac. Today's violinmakers argue whether oil or spirit varnish is best; proponents of the latter opt for seedlac and would never entertain the idea of shellac on a fine violin.

For years, tons of seedlac were imported yearly from India for uses in the paint, textile and medical industries, and modest amounts were available to artisans and small users. Political situations have stopped the export of seedlac from India, so it is currently very difficult to find. If you're lucky, you may find some stuck away on a shelf in a store or in a woodworker's shop. Otherwise, you can only check periodically to see if the situation has changed and export has resumed.

To shellac adherents: Forgo ready-mixed products and those you make from buttons and/or flakes; substitute seedlac any time you can find it. You'll have a superior material that can be brushed, sprayed or French-polished to produce a coating of much greater transparency, faster drying time and greater water resistance than shellac. □

Sidney Greenstein lives in San Diego, Calif.

Milk Paint
Colonial finish is cheap, charming

by Jon W. Arno

In reading books on early American and Shaker furniture I occasionally run across references to a paint used in Colonial times that was made of milk. I first thought it must have been a foul-smelling, short-lived, inferior finish, but a few months ago I mixed up a batch for use on a not-too-precious pine knickknack and found that milk paint has many advantages. It can be made as transparent or opaque as desired, and it dries overnight. Brushes clean up in water, and a batch can be mixed up in minutes for less than $2 a quart (1979 prices), including the pigment. It does have a strong odor, but this can be buried under a sealer coat of shellac or varnish.

The problem with making milk paint is the lack of literature covering it in detail. In furniture-refinishing books it is referred to, in passing, as that stuff on the bottom that defies paint removers. In the Colonial history books it is described as a paint made out of milk or buttermilk and colored with berry juice, blood or pigments made of burnt clay. Further coverage deals only with the coloring agents, assuming that any amateur can mix the base. When anything remotely like a formula is offered, it is usually a list of ingredients, often without proportions or explanation of the chemistry.

So that you need not cover the same ground I have, here is what works best for me. Reconstitute instant nonfat dry milk, using just enough hot water to dissolve the milk into a thick, smooth syrup. Add the pigment in small increments and mix thoroughly. Vary the opacity and color by adding either more hot water or pigment, testing the mixture from time to time on a piece of scrap. Apply to raw wood with a brush or rag while the paint is still warm. When dry, it will have an almost dead flat finish much like latex wall paint, but with a certain translucence all its own. For an antique look, use full-strength milk paint and rub it with a damp cloth as it dries: The opacity of the paint in the corners and crevices will contrast with the lighter finish of the rubbed surface.

Some books suggest limestone or quicklime was used but don't say whether it was a pigment, a thickener or a drying agent. With lime the paint seems to be a little more resistant to moisture, but it becomes grainy and dries more opaque and muddy. Vivid colors are harder to achieve.

You could probably use fresh whole milk, boiling it to a paint-like consistency, but I have experimented with neither fresh milk nor the canned evaporated variety. I have, however, experimented with a host of possible coloring agents. The pigments that produce colors like those seen in books and museums are the earth colors: burnt sienna, Venetian red and Indian red. The latter is best, but hard to find. Acrylic paints also work, and the choice of colors there is mind-boggling. I have even tried bloodmeal as a pigment, but it remained grainy and failed to go into solution. Prepared mustard produces a creamy yellow color, but the quantity needed for a vivid hue seems to affect the drying properties of the paint. Concentrated grape juice produces a blue-purple color depending upon how much water is added.

Only time will tell me of the resistance of milk paint to fading and its reaction to humidity. I have sealed the paint on the projects I have completed with shellac or varnish rubbed down to a satin finish. Orange shellac adds warmth and enhances the color of burnt sienna and Venetian red. □

Jon Arno, of Wayzata, Minn., is a business consultant and amateur furnituremaker. He spends most of his spare time tinkering in his basement shop.

Full-strength milk paint on pine stool hides most grain features.

Dilute milk paint on pine recipe chest is almost translucent.

Photos: Richard Levine

Q & A

Filler for French polishing

I am attempting to do some French polishing on dark walnut. What is the best filler to use? I have also heard about "open-pore" French polishing, although no one seems to know how to do it and it may be quite attractive. Do you know what it is? —E. Thomas Akyali, New York, N.Y.

GEORGE FRANK REPLIES: First, about the filler. If you would do real French polishing, you would use no filler at all. Part of French polishing is to work pumice stone into the surface of the wood with a special pad that the English call a "rubber," the French a "tampon." The tampon's heart is wool from old socks or sweaters. It is about the size and shape of an egg, that later will fit the inside of your palm, where you hold it quite firmly. The wool's role is to hold and to release slowly the alcohol, and later the liquid shellac. The wool is wrapped in a porous fabric—linen is best if you can find any—which covers it snugly and smoothly on the bottom. This bottom side becomes quite flat, since it will slide and slide on the surface of the wood.

You feed the wool with a few drops of alcohol at a time and sprinkle some finely ground pumice stone on the surface to be polished. Now, with broad circling motions, begin to force the pumice into the pores. The pumice first will fill up the small spaces of the linen, and being abrasive it will cut off invisibly small particles of the wood. Together these will slowly fill up the pores under the pressured rubbing of your fists. Since the pumice carries with itself the finest possible wood dust, it takes on the color of the wood. It thus becomes invisible, practically part of the wood itself. It is the finest method of filling the wood. (See pp. 70-71 and 72-74.)

However, not all French polishers go through this slow and tiring process. They use various kinds of fillers. One common recipe: Powdered chalk or simple whiting powder is the filling agent, colored with dry powdered colors to match the wood. The binder is rosin (or colophony), also powdered, and the carrier is mineral spirits. The spirits are frequently tinted (for dark walnut) with some asphaltum paint. The amount of rosin is about 10% to 15% of the colored chalk. Another recipe is talcum powder colored with dry pigment. The carrier and the binder are shellac and alcohol. This type of filler is difficult to use without skill and experience.

Open-pore French polishing was practiced widely in the first 20 years of this century. First the wood is sanded impeccably, then the dust is brushed or blown off, leaving all the pores open. The tampon is moistened with a few drops of shellac, further cut with a little alcohol. Again the rubbing begins, except that this time the tampon works with the grain, each passage leaving a breath of shellac on the wood. Repeat until a pleasant shine appears. No pumice is used, no attempt is made to fill the pores, and no oil is used either. The tampon should never be too moist, and each film must dry before the next one is applied. This type of French polishing does not have the bright glossy shine of the filled version, but it is far easier to obtain and still quite pleasant to look at.

Stripping milk paint

The process of restoring a 100-year-old farmhouse has revealed poplar baseboards and woodwork covered with a casein (milk-base) paint, with tooled varnish, defying all attempts to strip down. Have tried commercial strippers, ammonia, belt sander, scrapers and homemade concoction of lye, flour and water. —A.R. Zigan, Versailles, Ind.

According to a research paper delivered in 1972 by Prof. Seymour Z. Lewin: "A combination of the enzyme trypsin (available from biochemical supply houses and relatively inexpensive) and monosodium dihydrogen phosphate, dissolved in water, softens casein paints and allows them to be brushed away, no matter how old the paints may be." —John Greenwalt Lee, Annapolis, Md.

"Bix" furniture-stripping solution (Bix Process Systems, Plumtrees Rd., Bethel, Conn. 06801) works for me. —E.A. Franks, Silver Lake, Ind.

Cracked-paint finish

I reproduce antique furniture and distress my painted finishes to make them look old. How can I achieve the "alligatored" or cracked-paint finish, which involves placing a fast-drying paint over a slow-drying paint? —Robert J. Doolittle, State College, Pa.

GEORGE FRANK REPLIES: Varnish or paint will crack when a fast-drying coat is put over a slow-drying one before the slow-drying first coat is completely dry. You can buy crackling varnish in any good paint store. Crackling lacquer is available too, but it's a little harder to find.

We old-timers had our own way, which is more fun. Paint your piece and let it dry at least a week. Next, skim over the surface with the finest wet-or-dry sandpaper, making the surface as smooth as possible. On this dry, clean and smooth surface, apply a coat of varnish. If the instructions say that the varnish dries in 5 hours, do the next step in 4 to 4½ hours. At any rate, before the varnish dries, apply an uneven, irregular, ½-in.- to 1-in.-thick coating of good potters' clay. Keep your fingers crossed for the next two or three days . . . at least. When the clay is dry, it will chip off easily. If the timing was right, you'll get the loveliest cracks and "alligator skins." The potters' clay is a big gun in the antique reproducer's arsenal, but first experiment on scraps. Good luck.

Removing an oil finish

Several years ago, I finished an oak coffee table with Minwax Antique Oil. Since then, the table has been cleaned with furniture oil or a mixture of turpentine and linseed oil. This finish isn't tough enough to hold up under the abuse the table is subjected to, and I want to refinish with polyurethane. What can I use to remove all traces of the oil finish so that polyurethane will adhere to the surface? —John O'Leary, Northport, N.Y.

JIM CUMMINS REPLIES: Stripping your table may not be your best option. Minwax Antique Oil has several advantages, in my opinion, over polyurethane, and I'd suggest that you give it another chance. For one thing, I think it looks better—more like wood than slick plastic. For another, you can repair an oil finish easily, just by rubbing on more oil, whereas polyurethane doesn't adhere well to itself, and you may have to strip the whole table again the next time it gets scratched or wears through. You've just been treating your oil finish wrong since you first applied it: Furniture polishes, which are simply nondrying oils that impart a temporary gloss, won't help the finish. And the turpentine/linseed mixture is so much lighter-bodied than the Minwax—and takes so much longer to dry—that it won't do much good either.

Instead, if you finish a table with three or four very thin coats of Antique Oil and refresh it with a thin coat whenever it shows wear, you'll probably be well pleased. For scratches, you can sand the old finish around the scratch to a feather edge and apply more oil—it will blend right in. For routine maintenance, rub on a fresh coat every few months. This will clean superficial grime off the surface, and should make the finish last indefinitely. Two-year-old oil can look fresh as new, but two-year-old polyurethane will show every scar.

Gilding With Metal Leaf
Fit for a frame or a fleur-de-lis

by Erwin O. Deimel

While there is no doubt that genuine burnished gold leaf is the ultimate in gilded finishes for frames, furniture and ornaments, there is a much less costly alternative. Schlagmetal, thinly beaten metal alloy, is the material used on most picture frame moldings and other gold-leafed articles. The result is meant to look like the burnished-gold leafing that was extensively practiced during the Renaissance, but which, due to cost, is seldom done today. Schlagmetal is much easier to handle than real gold, which is beaten so thin that it is transparent when held up to the light—you can touch schlagmetal without having it disintegrate.

As a picture framer who finishes most of his own moldings, I use a process not much different from that used by commercial molding companies, who gild thousands of feet a day. This process, however, can be adapted to small scale, using brushes instead of air guns, and not requiring such elaborations as spray booths; in short, adapted to the home workshop or retail establishment.

In the original process, water gilding, genuine gold leaf is applied to a colored ground of gilding clay mixed with animal glue. The clay has a high iron-oxide content, which gives it a barn-red color. The glue is the binder for the coating, and can be burnished to a high gloss and reactivated with moisture to hold the leaf to the clay. Because leaf is an uninterrupted sheet of reflective metal—not ground-up particles in a dulling binder—it has a luster that paint cannot match. Renaissance frames were probably left very bright, to look like solid gold. But during generations of being dusted and cleaned, the gold wore off the high places, dirt accumulated in the low spots, and the frame acquired a soft patina that pleases us more today. Contemporary gilders simulate this patina by sanding or scratching the leaf to expose the color underneath, applying imitation flyspecks (meant to be the work of generations of flies), and using a thin wash of paint instead of waiting centuries for dust to build up.

I buy unfinished molding instead of milling it myself. A splendid array of shapes and sizes, in a variety of woods (mostly bass, poplar and virola), can be bought wholesale from distributors, or one-frame's-worth at a time from frame shops. Old frames can be salvaged and refinished, too. While you can work on a frame after it has been assembled, it is easier to gild the lengths separately because you won't have to fold the leaf into tight corners. Cut the sides of the frame a little longer than necessary—you will make fresh miters after the leafing and antiquing have been completed.

Whether you are gilding a frame, a box or a piece of furniture, begin by priming the wood with orange shellac (4-lb.-cut, diluted with about five parts alcohol) to seal it and set up the fibers for sanding off with 150-grit paper. Remove the fuzz, then paint on two or more coats of acrylic paint. This base coat softens the molding shape and provides tone, just as clay originally did. Commercial molding companies often use a brilliant crimson under the leaf. A muted red, like burnt sienna, looks more like the real thing. For silver leaf, a blue clay was frequently used. When I gild with aluminum leaf, to simulate old silver, I prefer a black ground.

You can get acrylic paint in tubes from an art supply store. Mix it roughly half-and-half with acrylic medium, thin enough to brush smoothly but with enough body to fill small irregularities. Acrylic paint is a polymer, but if you catch it before it cures, you can clean up with soap and water. Two coats can be applied in an hour or so, and the ground will be ready for sanding after it has dried overnight.

Sand the ground coat smooth, then apply one or two coats of undiluted 4-lb.-cut orange shellac, sanding lightly between coats. This step is important. If the surface isn't completely sealed, the adhesive that holds the leaf will dry too quickly in patches, and the leaf won't stick there.

Since we don't have animal glue in our ground, we must apply a layer of gold size (adhesive) to hold the leaf. The size is an oil-based varnish specially developed for gilding. It comes in two varieties—slow and quick. Quick size dries in about an hour or so, but I've found it too irregular for good results. I use the slow size, which reaches the proper tack in about 12 hours and is workable for 12 hours after that. Whichever you use, the object is to have as thin a coating as possible, with just enough tack to hold the leaf. If size is applied too heavily, or accumulates in low places, it will skin over but remain liquid underneath. This will turn to goo and spoil the job when you rub the leaf down. Gold-leaf size will polymerize if there is any air in the can, so when I open a new liter I immediately put it into 2-oz. medicine bottles and seal them tightly. In my shop, where I leaf 20 ft. to 30 ft. of molding a week, an ounce of size lasts a month or more.

I apply the size using a velveteen pad about 2 in. square. On frames without carving this pad gives me better control than a brush would, and when I'm finished I can just throw the pad away. Slow size comes either clear or with yellow pigment added for visibility. I use the yellow, and apply just enough to be able to see a faint yellow color over the ground. Apply size in the late afternoon. By the following morning it will be ready to gild, and it will keep its tack through most of the day—you don't have to rush. A properly prepared frame will seem to have dried too much—the size will not feel tacky, but smooth and hard, with a squeaky clean kind of feeling. A fingerprint may prevent the leaf's adhesion, so try to do your

Erwin Oskar Deimel, a retired aerospace engineer, owns Oskar's Picture Framing in New Hartford, N.Y.

Photos: L.P. Pacilio

To apply the metal leaf, first prepare the wood surface with shellac and acrylic paint. Then apply a special oil-based varnish. When the varnish is tacky, transfer the leaf to the molding using a paintbrush. Cover the high spots first to avoid tearing the leaf, which won't stretch into the valleys.

Buffing the leaf with cotton forces it to conform to the base coat's polished surface. Excess leaf is dusted off.

testing, if you must, on some inconspicuous part of the frame.

Leaf is available in several forms: most commonly in books of 25 sheets, about 5½ in. square, separated by paper sheets, or in bulk packs of 50 sheets stacked together, 10 packs to a box, about 7 in. square. I use bulk leaf, picking it up from the box with a 1½-in. paintbrush, and laying it on a flat surface so it can be cut. With scissors, cut strips of the desired width. Slip one strip of leaf, with the help of the paintbrush, onto a piece of cardboard a little longer than the leaf, and slide it onto the sized surface of the frame. Aim for the right place. Once the leaf touches the size, you will only tear it if you try to move it. But if you have placed it a little crooked, no matter. Lay it down as it lands and overlap the next piece to fill the gap. The leaf will stick only to the size, not to itself, and the extra will be dusted away later.

Leaf doesn't stretch. On many moldings, it will stick to the high spots and tear raggedly when you try to force it into the low spots. The solution is to gild the high sections first with narrow strips of leaf, coming back to coves and valleys later.

After the entire length is covered with leaf, take two or three cotton balls and rub the surface smoothly but firmly to ensure that all the leaf contacts the size. Rub in the direction that will press the overlaps down, not tear them up. Give an extra rub parallel to each joint. If there is a holiday (bare spot) in the job, place a piece of leaf over the spot and press it into place with cotton, then rub the patch smooth. The hairline joints between leaves are called spiderwebbing and will become part of the antiquing.

If your size was too heavy or not dry enough, wrinkles in the leaf will set into the finish when you rub it down. Puddles of undried size can smear over the surface, irreparably dulling

it. In this case, it is best to let the size dry thoroughly, then sand the leaf smooth and gild again. Usually, though, the problem is poor or spotty adhesion. If the problem is extensive, sand and reprime. Small blemishes, however, can be corrected by adhering fresh leaf with shellac. Dab on a thin layer with your fingertip, feathering the edges so a ridge doesn't form. Within a few seconds, the shellac will have the correct tack for the leaf to be applied.

Unlike real gold, schlagmetal is subject to corrosion, so to prevent it from tarnishing, seal the surface with the same dilute alcohol-shellac mixture used to prime the wood. This will reduce the glare of the leaf slightly, but the molding is quite garish at this stage, looking like a chocolate candy wrapped in gold foil. It will need even more antiquing to tone it down.

To obtain a typical finish, first apply the thin sealer coat, then give the molding a coat of undiluted orange shellac to make the gold a little deeper in color, a little redder or warmer. In fact, even aluminum leaf can usually do with some warming up. Next paint the molding with an antiquing coat of acrylic paint, a mixture of burnt umber with a little black added, then wipe it off lightly with a paper towel to leave some color in the low areas and a light, streaky finish in the high spots. When this is dry, use a toothbrush and some dark paint to imitate flyspecks. Point the toothbrush at the frame, then stroke the bristles toward you. Tiny drops of paint will spatter the frame. New flyspecks are raw umber, ancient ones are black. They are put on not so much to immortalize the housefly, but to give depth to the finish. From a few feet away, they will not be noticeable. Remember what we are aiming for: years of considerate care that have nevertheless left their mark, not what looks like half-a-day's vandalism.

To age your molding, scrub off some gold. Sandpaper rubbed with the grain imitates the effect wood movement has on clay. Fine steel wool can rub the gold from the high spots to expose the ground color. You can stipple the wash coat instead of wiping it, and you can increase contrast by wiping the wash coat away from the high spots with a damp paper towel. Instead of the dark wash coat, you can try raw umber and white, which makes a warm gray. After the frame has been mitered and joined, you can touch up the joints with a little antiquing color to cover up any hairline of raw wood. Experimentation will show you a boundless variety of finishes. I once tinted the shellac with aniline dyes to yield a molding of warm brown-gold with a stripe of brilliant green—the colors of a Japanese beetle.

A final coat of clear acrylic medium will yield a remarkably durable, low-luster finish. In ten years, I have never had a job come back because the finish failed. I have scrap pieces that have been kicking around my outdoor kindling shed for years, exposed to heat, humidity and drifting snow. They still look as good as gold. □

EDITOR'S NOTE: Gilding supplies are available in small quantities from Dick Blick Co., Box 1267, Galesburg, Ill. 61401. H. Behlen Bros. sells supplies for both oil and water gilding through a network of distributors; for more information, write to them at Rt. 30 N., Amsterdam, N.Y. 12010, or phone (518) 843-1380. Other sources worth checking out are Art Essentials, Drawer 260, Monsey, N.Y. 10952, and The Durham Co., Box 1548 GMF, Boston, Mass. 02205.

For further reading, get a copy of *Gold Leaf Techniques,* by Raymond J. LeBlanc, revised by Arthur O. Sarti, 1980, available from ST Publications, 407 Gilbert Avenue, Cincinnati, Ohio 45202.

Gilding: On the trail of Cennino

by Henry E. Sostman

Clocks tell time, but time also tells on clocks. The clock at right is one of two that were built in Holland in 1722, with hand-cut clockworks by Jonathan Marsh. Clockmakers in the early 18th century made only the movements, and Marsh's were put into twin cases by some unknown woodworking shop. My wife's ancestors bought this one new.

It is only recently that my wife, Theodora, and I have lived in a house whose ceiling can accommodate the clock's 9½-ft. height. We had the works restored, and the movement keeps excellent time now. All the delightful figures—the boy who pulls a fish out of the river once a minute, and the windmill that turns when the hour and half-hour strike—work again. I restored the case myself, because I wanted to have a hand in its future.

Moisture and age had reduced the crowning figures to bare wood. The angels had lost their trumpets and wings. Atlas, in the center, looked like he was losing his battle to hold up the world. A photograph of the twin clock provided a design for the missing parts and confirmed that the figures had been covered with gold. I was anxious to learn about the techniques used by the original maker, but information was scanty. Medieval painters, excellent gilders, kept their methods secret. During the Renaissance, however, one artist broke security. He was Cennino d'Andrea Cennini, and his book tells almost all we know about tempera painting and its integral component, gold. In a translation by Daniel Thompson, *The Craftsman's Handbook*, I found the source for a process that has remained virtually unchanged for at least 500 years. Although I substituted modern materials, I tried to recondition my angels in the spirit in which they had been made.

One chapter of Cennino's book takes the reader through the gilding process. In the 15th century, the first step was to choose a gold coin and deliver it to the local gold beater, who methodically pounded it between sheets of leather until it became flattened into many leaves. Cennino even tells us that the beater "ought not to get more than a hundred leaves out of a ducat."

The wood was prepared with many coats of gesso and clay, smoothed and polished with stones. Cennino used powdered chalk for gesso, and Armenian bole for clay, both mixed with a

An angel restored and gold-leafed.

binder made by boiling animal skins. Fine carving could be incised into the surface before the gold was put on, and the surface burnished to look like solid, polished gold. Cennino used a dog's tooth to burnish the gold. Today, gilders use a tooth-shaped agate.

I used plaster and gelatine for the gesso, and Hastings clay instead of Armenian bole. To adhere the leaf, I substituted slow-drying size for Cennino's boiled parchment glue. I used as much care and time to prepare the surface as Cennino said was necessary. After so much work, it seemed a foolish economy to substitute brass leaf. Brass would have to be sealed with a lacquer or shellac that would deteriorate in a few decades, while pure gold would never tarnish, and its thinness would allow it to follow every detail of the carving without hairline wrinkles. It seemed to have every advantage, so I took Cennino's advice, and for gold I used gold. □

Henry E. Sostman is vice president of the Yellow Springs Instrument Co., Inc., in Yellow Springs, Ohio. He is a registered Professional Engineer whose activities include temperature physics and Federal regulatory law. Photos by the author. Cennino's book, translated by Daniel Thompson and published by Yale University Press in 1933 as The Craftsman's Handbook, *is available from Dover Books, 180 Varick St., New York, N.Y. 10014.*

The stately clock with its golden crown.

Water-Gilding

How to match the golden age's incomparable shine

by Nancy Russo

This girandole from about 1820, designed by H.H. Richardson, holds candles that reflect light into the room and bathe its own water-gilt profusion with dancing beams.

Period furnituremakers who don't work with gold are missing out on some of the most passionate furniture ever made. It's true that gold leaf, misused, can be garish. But at its best, burnished gold has visual qualities that pull a design together, bringing order to elements that, finished in another way, would be incomprehensible. A woodworker, furniture designer or frame maker today can incorporate bright or antiqued gold into his work in much the same way that he might use inlaying, marquetry or carving.

There are two fundamentally different ways to apply gold leaf, and each has its place. Water-gilding was once the principal method for ornamenting objects of real value—panel paintings, clocks, furniture, architectural members, and picture and mirror frames. It was used as far back as ancient Egypt and has remained virtually unchanged since the Middle Ages. Water-gilding is crucial to many period styles, but it has become obscure in the last eighty years or so. Few people outside the trade recognize a water-gilt surface, much less understand how it's done.

Nowadays, oil-gilding (see pages 77-79) is much more common. It is an ancient and durable method of attaching leaf to wood, glass, metal or just about any surface that can be made nonporous with a sealer. The leaf, either real gold or imitation, is pressed onto a coat of high-quality varnish that has been allowed to dry to a particular tack. Today, oil-gilding with 23-karat gold leaf is used primarily for outdoor work, from signs to state capitol domes. Because gold does not tarnish, the surface can be left unsealed, and the shine will last as long as the support and varnish remain intact. Most picture-frame moldings are oil-gilded these days, too, but with aluminum leaf or gold-colored "metal leaf" which is then distressed and antiqued with glazes. Oil-gilding is quick, and if you use imitation leaf, it's relatively cheap.

Water-gilding, in contrast, is rare to-

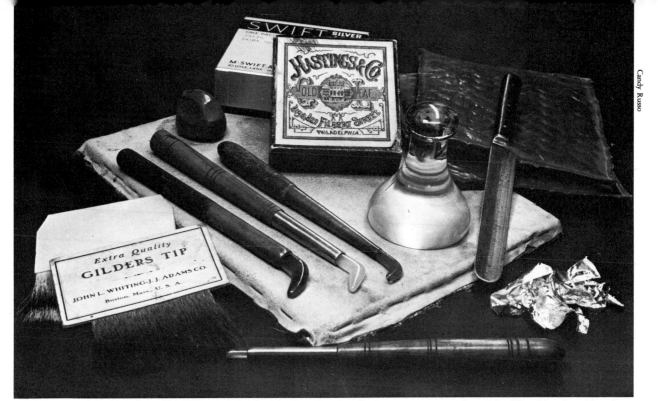

Leaf can be cut on a leather pad with a smooth-edged knife, whose handle here rests on some sheets of rabbit-skin glue. Also shown are agate burnishers, boxes of leaf, and a pestle for grinding lump clay, a piece of which sits at the back of the pad.

day, partly due to the cost of gold but also because of the time and labor involved. The leaf is laid on a many-layered ground of gesso and clay, both with hide glue as a binder. Then the surface—actually the ground itself, under the gold—can be polished by rubbing it with an agate burnisher. The tops of moldings and carvings can be burnished to a mirror-like reflection, and the hollows left with a matte, metallic luster, creating an incomparable richness of surface.

Antique water-gilt items slowly dull with age, mostly from environmental pollution, which eventually becomes difficult if not impossible to remove. These pieces were rarely protected with a finish and can be ruined by water, a fate many have suffered from careless cleaning. In many cases, although the gold is gone, the surface beneath may be reactivated and gilded again. But gesso that's been exposed to dampness for any length of time decomposes, softens irreparably, and must be replaced.

Small repairs are best done by patching. My feeling about complete re-gilding of antiques is, don't if you don't have to, but if you do, stick to the original gilding technique and burnishing patterns, and don't artificially age or "antique." The gold will mellow in its own time, whereas the various finishes used in antiquing are apt to change rapidly, drastically altering the effect.

Materials and tools—Today, most gold leaf is machine-beaten to a thinness of 0.00003 in., thinner than any piece of paper. If laid on a dry surface, a sheet of gold will sail off with the slightest puff of air. If crumbled in the hand, it disintegrates and all but disappears. Machine-beaten leaf is four times thinner than its medieval counterpart, and so thin that it is virtually transparent, which allows any color beneath it to shine through, especially when the gold has been partly worn through. Oil-gilded surfaces, toned to imitate this effect, never have the brilliance and depth of a burnished surface.

Pure gold is called 24K (karat). Gold leaf, which is 23K, is alloyed with 1K silver or copper, or a combination of the two. These other metals color the gold slightly cooler or warmer.

The standard leaf today is $3\frac{3}{8}$ in. square and comes in "books" containing 25 leaves. There are 20 books to a pack, the wholesale unit, enough for an experienced gilder to cover 30 sq. ft. One manufacturer, M. Swift and Sons, 10 Love La., Hartford, Conn. 06141, currently charges about $275 per pack.

The two main types of gold leaf are loose leaf and patent leaf. Loose leaf is sold in two commercial grades: surface gold and glass gold. Surface gold may have small holes or imperfections, but these will be backed up in the book by a smaller piece of leaf for patching the

gaps. Glass gold has no irregularities, because patches would show through when gilding on glass. Patent, or transfer, gold is leaf slightly adhered to a piece of tissue in the book. The tissue extends beyond the edges of the gold, so you can pick up each leaf by hand, which is especially helpful when gilding outside on a windy day.

Silver leaf is about three times thicker than gold leaf. Many Victorian picture frames were leafed with silver, then sealed with an alcohol-based, transparent, amber-colored lacquer to make them look like gold. In most cases, the silver has begun to tarnish—black spots can be seen beneath the gold lacquer. Some Victorian frames were deliberately tarnished in decorative patterns before being gold-lacquered.

"Dutch metal" refers to what is now called gold "metal leaf." It is made of copper and zinc, and is larger than gold leaf and thick enough to handle. The same is true of aluminum leaf, which came into use in the 19th century.

Because of the increasing thinness of gold leaf, by the 17th century a tool was needed to handle loose leaf, and the gilders' tip came into use. It's a wide, flat brush of badger or squirrel hair, 2 in. long, with a cardboard handle. The tip transfers the gold from the book to a pad or directly to the work. The gilder rubs the tip over her hair or face to collect a minute amount of oil (not to

Candy Russo

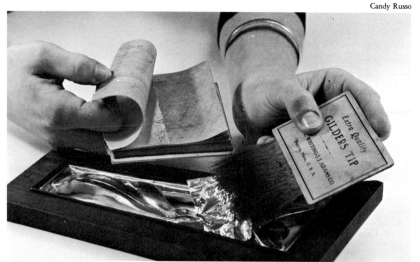

Candy Russo

The gilders' tip picks up and transfers the gold from its padded book. A beginner may instead opt to use 'patent gold' (where each leaf comes lightly adhered to a sheet of paper), or to press waxed paper over the leaf for easier handling. The piece here, part of a table by Sam Bush, is shown as it would look being patched after burnishing.

create static, as is sometimes thought), and the oil provides just enough stick for the gold leaf to adhere to the tip for transferring.

If a full sheet of gold is not needed, it can be cut to size with a gilders' knife. The knife is not sharp and has no rough edges to catch and tear the gold. Gold leaf can be cut and transferred directly from the book with the aid of a piece of cardboard for stiffening and a piece of leather padding inserted between the last two pages, as shown in the photo above.

After the gold has been laid and the proper amount of time has elapsed, the gold can be burnished. The burnishers used today are made of polished agate fitted into a ferrule with a paintbrush-type handle. The common agate has a slightly crooked shape and a smooth, rounded point. This shape is in imitation of a dog's tooth, such as those used by Renaissance gilders, and remains the most practical for all-around use.

Procedure—The wood to be water-gilded is first sanded to remove sharp edges and corners, and then many coats of gesso are applied, forming a "bed" for the gold. Gesso is a mixture of whiting (calcium carbonate, ground very fine and washed) and rabbit-skin glue, with the consistency of heavy cream. It is kept hot to maintain brushability, because rabbit-skin glue congeals just like other hot hide glues when cooled to room temperature. Usually six or seven coats of gesso are sufficient, especially if the wood is a fine-textured one such as poplar or basswood. The gesso and its

application are extremely important for a good gild and burnish.

You can either use a pre-mixed, packaged gesso, or make it from scratch. The packaged type, Grumbacher's Dry Ground Gesso, is a mixture of whiting and glue pellets. For large jobs, it's cheaper to make your own gesso: Mix 1 oz. by weight of rabbit-skin glue to 4 fl. oz. of water. Allow the glue to completely swell and soften at room temperature, which can take from 15 minutes to several hours, depending on its particle size. Sift 3 to 4 cups of whiting through a wire strainer. Measure 4 fl. oz. of water into a metal container, and slowly add the sifted whiting until the mixture mounds on the spoon and begins to look just slightly less smooth and glossy. To make sure that the whiting is completely absorbed, I shake it into the can from a spoon, slowly, until the water won't absorb any more, then I add more, stirring out any lumps, until the mixture mounds. Heat the glue mixture in a double boiler over low heat until it melts. Add 3 fl. oz. of the melted glue all at once to the whiting mixture. Using a good brush with no loose hairs, slowly stir from the bottom in one direction until the gesso is well mixed.

Both kinds of gesso will keep for a few weeks if refrigerated, but will gradually break down. If the gesso begins to look a little watery on top, it may be too soft to use. Don't take chances with gesso. If in doubt, make a new batch.

For use, heat the gesso in a double

boiler, adding a few drops of water each time you heat it to compensate for evaporation. Overheating, either too often or too hot, can break down the glue and can also cause pinholes, the bane of a gilder's existence. If pinholes develop in the first full-strength coat of gesso, they will telegraph through the successive coats, and even the top coat of clay will have pinholes. To avoid them, work in a warm, dry room and keep the gesso from cooling in the pot as you work. If small bubbles develop while you're making the gesso, and some always do, agitate the container, letting them rise to the surface. Then when the gesso cools and skins over, just peel off the skin. You can also add a wetting agent, such as oxgall (available from an art supply store), which will help the bubbles rise to the surface. If in the end your final dry coat of gesso shows pinholes, try wetting your finger and rubbing over the gesso until the sludge fills the holes.

After the gesso is heated, apply it first as a primer coat. Dilute the gesso to half strength with water, brush it on and let it dry. The first full-strength coat is scrubbed on quickly for good adhesion, especially important if the wood is open-textured. A good-quality, ¾-in. wide, square-end sable brush is the right choice for all stages of gilding. Wet the brush with water and squeeze it dry, then apply the gesso, working quickly and with the brush fairly well loaded. Avoid over-brushing, or the surface will become lumpy. Each coat can be applied as soon as the previous coat has dulled, until you've built up the thickness to as much as 1/16 in.

When the gesso is dry, surface it absolutely smooth with sandpaper, either wet or dry, or scrapers. I usually start with 320-grit aluminum oxide paper and work down to as fine a paper as necessary to eliminate all sandpaper marks without actually putting a polish on the gessoed surface, because if this happens, the clay will resist bonding to the gesso. It's important not to sand the gesso into sharp edges or corners which could be knocked off or chipped. Shallow, ornamental carving can be done with regular carving tools after final-sanding. Gesso carves crisply and cleanly.

Next comes the gilders' clay. This is the red coating sometimes seen peeking through worn gold leaf. It's a very fine-textured, unctuous material that takes a polish when rubbed with the agate burnisher. Red clay looks best under gold leaf when rub-through antiquing effects are used. Blue-gray, white, black and yellow clays are also common, the color of the clay affecting the tone—warm or cool—of the final gold finish. Dark clays are used under silver leaf, while yellow clay helps to hide breaks in the gold in the matte areas. Commonly, the whole object will be given several coats of ochre clay over the gesso, then the areas to be burnished will be given a few additional coats of red clay or dark gray clay.

Clay is sold in solid lump form from Europe, or as a thick pre-ground paste packed in small jars. Gilders' clay formulas are a closely guarded secret of the makers. Modern gilders' clay probably contains some additives such as glycerin, whiting and dyes, which are meant to extend and improve the clay.

The clay must be ground in water to a smooth-as-silk consistency, rabbit-skin glue (or gelatin) and water added, and several coats of the mixture brushed over the surfaced gesso. The recipe I use makes about ¼ cup. I like to make only as much as I need for a given job. If you are working with lump clay, first grind it to a powder. I have a piece of fine steel screen, which I bought at a hardware store, stapled over a deep wooden box. Holding the clay as if I were grating cheese, I rub it over the screen to pulverize it. Grate about two rounded tablespoons' worth, put it into a clean metal container, such as a tuna can, then add water to form a paste. Now strain the clay to remove any grit. I force it through an extremely fine piece of brass mesh soldered onto a copper cylinder; some people use several layers of fine nylon stocking. Jarred clays, which you might expect to be grit-free, are sometimes not. At best, gritty clay will make the gold less bright. At worst, grit can ruin your burnisher and cause it to scratch the gold on future jobs. After straining, add water, stirring with a pointed sable brush until the clay mixture is thin enough to drop off the brush one drop at a time. Before the mixture reaches this point, it will be necessary to add the water very slowly, drop by drop, or the clay will be too thin.

Now make up the rabbit-skin glue, using the same proportions as for gesso. Melt the glue in a double boiler and add it to the clay/water mixture by dribbling it down the side of the can in a thin, steady stream, stirring all the

time. Almost immediately, the clay will begin to clabber, or curdle. Sometimes it suddenly gets quite thick, almost stiff, and other times a slight thickening is barely discernible. Keep adding the glue steadily. Just after the clabbering stage, the clay will begin to thin out again. You want to bring it back to the point where it drops off the brush one drop at a time. As the glue is added, the clay goes through these stages very quickly, from thin to clabber to thin again, so go slowly and carefully.

To be on the safe side, I always test each batch of clay on a gessoed sample piece. Apply a little clay, leaf over it, and test how it burnishes. After testing the clay, brush it on the surfaced gesso. Several coats are needed before the clay looks opaque and covers the gesso completely. Keep the clay warm while you work, as you did for the gesso, and try not to let it pool in the hollows, or pinholes may develop.

The clay mixture has very little body, and even five or six coats will not hide defects in the gesso. The clay should not need to be surfaced, but if you notice any grittiness when it has dried, you can smooth it with a worn piece of 400-grit or 600-grit sandpaper and polish out with a piece of linen or a white Scotch-Brite scrubbing pad. Avoid steel wool—it leaves particles behind, and some brands are protected from rusting with oil, which can ruin the clay surface.

Now the gold leaf can be applied. The clay surface where the first pieces of gold leaf are to be laid is first flooded with a solution of water and alcohol. This activates the glue in the clay, creating adhesion. The proportion of alcohol doesn't matter too much. I use about 1 part methyl alcohol to 3 parts water. When gilding with silver leaf, which is heavier than gold, or if the leaf didn't adhere perfectly on the test piece, I add a tiny pea-sized piece of rabbit-skin glue to the solution. Be careful, though—too much glue will dull the burnish.

Really flood the surface, because the layers of gesso and clay will absorb the water like a sponge. If the clay looks dull instead of wet and shiny, the gold will not stick. Using the gilders' tip, quickly pick up the gold and with a smooth motion transfer it to the work. I rub a dab of Chapstick on my wrist and pass the tip over it occasionally so that the gold will adhere. You'll find that using the gilders' tip takes a little practice. The larger the pieces of gold need-

ed, the more practice it takes to lift and transfer the leaf smoothly, without the gold folding up before it reaches the surface. Don't be intimidated by the fact that it is gold and is so fragile. A few wasted pieces amount to only a few cents, and you will waste some. After most of the water has been absorbed and the gold flattens out, tamp it down lightly with cotton and lay the next few pieces, overlapping the edges slightly.

When the whole piece has been gilded in this manner, the matte areas are burnished with cotton to ensure good contact and to bring up a rich luster. The "skewings," loose pieces of gold at the overlaps, come off at the same time. With a clean piece of cotton, lightly rub over the gold in a circular motion, applying more pressure as the skewings are removed. The gold will look like solid, polished metal. This is a matte gild.

Highlights can now be burnished mirror-bright. The areas to be burnished should not be bone-dry, but they shouldn't be too damp, or the burnisher will tear through the gold. Glide the burnisher back and forth over the gold, and if everything is just the way it should be, you'll find you can apply quite a bit of pressure. Burnishing is one of the craftsman's real rewards for preparation of the ground. The Latin word *brunir,* from which "burnish" is derived, means brown, and aptly describes the gold as it changes from a pale color to dark, metallic reflections. The burnisher presses folds and overlaps into each other; these double-thick areas appear as more solid areas in worn, antique pieces.

The whole job can now be left as is, antiqued, or given a protective finish. Any finish will dull the gold, and for this reason many old pieces were never sealed at all. Nitrocellulose lacquer, sprayed or brushed, dulls the gold less than other finishes. Orange shellac is often used instead, to warm the color. Don't worry if the finish coat blooms (whitens slightly) as you apply it. It will dry bright and clear. ☐

Nancy Russo has been gilding and restoring since 1971, and now has her own shop, Gold Leaf Restorations, in Portland, Ore. Gilding materials can be obtained from H. Behlen & Bros. (call 518-843-1380 for a local distributor); from Art Essentials, Box 260, Monsey, N.Y. 10952; and from sign painters' suppliers and good local art-supply stores.

Lacquer Finishing
How to spray a mirror finish

by George Morris

High-gloss lacquer finishing is time-consuming and rigorous. It requires meticulous surface preparation, special equipment if you're going to do much of it, and a carefully followed schedule of application with constant inspection and correction along the way. The reward is a stunning, jewel-like surface that offers a high degree of protection. A good lacquer finish has the quality of a mirror, and if improperly prepared, it will unforgivingly reveal every irregularity in the surface. By the time a surface defect manifests itself in the lacquer film, it's usually too late to correct it. Thus it's especially important to learn how to judge the quality of the wood surface before you apply any finish.

Preparing the surface—Looking straight into a surface you can pick out obvious flaws like scratches, nicks and holes, but if that is all you do, you miss most of what will become painfully obvious later. To find less pronounced defects you will need to position a light source and your eye so that shadows are created and observable. Imagine a landscape at the moment the sun is setting. Even the subtlest of features casts a shadow. The surface you are preparing is analogous to the landscape; a light bulb is the sun, and your eye is opposite the bulb. You are now in a position to observe the topography, but what is it you are looking for? The answer is found in recalling what you did to the surface and in anticipating the effects.

If you hand-planed the surface, there may be long, sharply defined ridges recording the path of the edge of the plane iron. A machine planer will yield a scalloped surface, the radius of the cutterhead arc repeated. Sanding and scraping may produce more varied effects, especially as the density of the wood varies. Sanding removes softer areas more quickly than harder areas. If the piece is composed of more than one kind of wood, or if the wood grain is uneven, as in fir or oak, you can expect the surface to be uneven although you have taken care to work consistently. Relatively dense areas in the wood will stand proud of the surface and, from our sunset perspective, will be revealed as shadows following the figure.

When sanding, back up the abrasive paper with some hard material—wood, hard felt or rubber blocks. For contoured surfaces, back up the paper with posterboard or a bit of flexible plastic, or at least fold the paper in half and glue it to itself with rubber cement. Your paper must not be able to conform to the irregularities you are trying to remove. Take care also to sand in line with the figure, and to release pressure from the paper at the end of each stroke, to avoid swirl marks.

Avoiding the pitfalls of scraping requires more skill. Scrapers work most efficiently on dense wood; softer materials compress under the cutting edge instead of standing up stiffly to be cut down. Thus the scraper's effect on the landscape is opposite that of sandpaper. The softer areas spring back after the scraper has passed, leaving them higher than the denser areas and producing a ribbed surface that on some woods looks like a neatly plowed cornfield at dusk. The fix is a quick follow-up sanding with a hard backup block.

Another effect of poor scraper technique is chatter, analogous in our landscape metaphor to a washboard section in a dirt road. Along a dirt road a car bounces rhythmically in response to some small irregularity in the surface, its tires digging out a little more dirt with each bounce. The next car amplifies the washboard effect. Scraper chatter is produced in the same way, by holding the scraper at a constant skew angle and by passing it a few times over

Low-angle view of this lacquered guitar surface reveals a perfect mirror finish, the result of careful planing, scraping, sanding, spraying and more spraying.

This rosewood surface appeared smooth when viewed head-on, but low-angle light reveals the washboard pattern of scraper chatter. Lacquer will make such flaws painfully obvious, when it's too late to correct them without removing the entire finish. Take a good look at the surface in the correct light before you start to spray.

the same spot. To avoid chatter you must repeatedly change the angle of approach or the skew of the blade, or both.

Other trouble areas surround the designed-in features of a surface: round holes, slots, inside corners and the like. Scrapers and sandpaper tend to fall into slots and holes, producing general depressions around them or, in the case of scrapers, troughs radiating out from them. Only hard sanding blocks can save you. Inside corners require planning and perhaps a specialized tool. If the surfaces adjacent to the corner have their grain running parallel to the crease, it's not hard to sand the corner smooth. But if the grain of one or both surfaces runs perpendicular to the crease, you can clean up using a tool I call a chisel-scraper, simply a chisel sharpened as usual but with a burr added by drawing the edge over a flat steel surface. An ordinary scraper has some thickness, which keeps the cutting edge from reaching into the corner. But a chisel-scraper's edge is thin. An inexpensive ½-in. chisel with its corners removed (for safety) is ideal. However, the best precaution when finishing inside corners is to surface them completely before gluing, and to remove all squeeze-out before it dries. The hidden danger of working around any problem area is that it encourages special attention, resulting in a local surface that's inconsistent with the rest of the object.

Lacquer is a low-wetting finish, which means it does not appreciably penetrate the wood, but lies on it as a film. The surface tension of this film will draw it away from any sharp edge, leaving precious little there and making it easy to sand through later when leveling between coats. Therefore, as part of your pre-finishing surface preparation, soften, if not actually round, all edges of the work to be sure they will remain adequately coated. The slight falling off of a surface as it nears the perimeter has another advantage. It compensates for the tendency in leveling between coats to do extra work near the edges, which makes it more likely you will sand through the film there. This relieving the surface near the edge prevents time-consuming spot repairs later.

Having removed all surface irregularities and prepared all the edges, you can begin final sanding with fine papers backed by hard-felt or rubber sanding blocks. Hardwood blocks with coarse abrasives are good for dimensional leveling, but fine papers on hardwood blocks tend to glaze and will streak the surface with burnish marks. There's little value in finish-

sanding beyond 320 grit. You will see some improvement of the surface past this point, but once lacquered the surface will return to what it looked like at 320 grit. Also, grits finer than 320 do little more than burnish the wood, making it more difficult for the lacquer to stick without blistering.

Equipment—Lacquers can be applied by brush, pad or spray, and in most cases the quality of the finished product will be the same. But because some of the exotic hardwoods, rosewood for instance, contain resins that are dissolved by lacquer thinner, the finish can get muddy and can stain adjacent lighter woods when it's dragged around with a brush or pad. Otherwise, small objects such as jewelry boxes can be finished without investing in any more than some good brushes. The steps in the finishing process are the same for brushing or spraying, the only differences being in the speed of application and the time involved in leveling the finish.

The decision to spray may depend upon where you live. All cities and most towns have restrictive codes regulating the design and use of spray facilities, because of the extremely volatile, poisonous and potentially explosive nature of the material. Some codes are stricter than others and require explosion-proof rooms, water curtains, sprinkler systems and asbestos blankets, not to mention outrageously expensive insurance. Spraying is usually illegal in an urban environment, unless you make a substantial investment in equipment. Short of setting up a clandestine operation, you could rent access to a spray booth from a school or body shop. Nitrocellulose lacquer, the type most commonly used for wood finishing, is composed of nitrocellulose (an ingredient in gun powder), various ketones, acetates, toluol, plus other nasty stuff. Codes or no codes, you owe it to yourself and anyone close to you to take adequate precaution against the dangers. You should wear a good-quality chemically filtered respirator, even if you spray outside—an inexpensive alternative to further investment if the environment and weather permit.

If building a booth is possible, the simplest one would need an enclosed space, entry and exit filters, explosion-proof lights, and an exhaust fan with an explosion-proof motor. The fan, mounted in an exterior wall, would necessitate some kind of weather shield—louvers, for instance. Such an assembly can be bought ready to install from most auto-body-shop

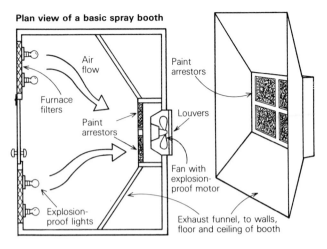

Plan view of a basic spray booth

Air flow

Furnace filters

Paint arrestors

Explosion-proof lights

Paint arrestors

Louvers

Fan with explosion-proof motor

Exhaust funnel, to walls, floor and ceiling of booth

suppliers. In front of the exhaust fan you need a filter wall perhaps 3 ft. square. The filters themselves are called paint arrestors and are also an auto-body-shop supply. For best vapor evacuation, a funnel should be built from the filter wall to the complete height and width of the booth, which should be as small as is comfortable to work in. Clean conditions require that the entry air be filtered, and here furnace-type filters covering an area a few times larger than the exhaust area, directly opposite the fan, will work. The door should provide a tight seal and should open outward, to maximize the usable space inside. The light source should be located behind you, so you can see reflections on the surface of the work as you spray.

Spray outfits are of various types, the simplest being the self-contained "airless" type for which you don't need a compressor. These guns are electromagnetic piston-drive mechanisms that run off standard house current. A small amount of fluid is siphoned up and propelled out the nozzle at 60 cycles a second. Although that might seem pretty quick, it doesn't compare with the force of an air-powered gun. Airless guns also clog easily and have a bad habit of spitting at the work. Nevertheless, they will get the job done faster and more evenly than brushes or pads, and may be all you need.

If time is important, or if you already have a compressor, an air gun is a better choice for its faster rate of application and finer atomization. The size of the gun should match the scale of the work. Most lacquering is done on relatively small objects, so a modest gun with perhaps a pint capacity is sufficient. Whatever the size, don't buy a cheap gun; you will curse that decision from day one.

To power your air gun you need a steady supply of compressed air at between 30 PSI and 40 PSI, the steadier the better. For steady flow and complete control of the pressure, a compressor with a holding tank and an air regulator is superior to cheaper direct-feed, continuous-drive systems.

Application—Lacquering consists of three stages: filling, leveling and polishing. Throughout, you should be inspecting the surface for defects and correcting them, as explained in the box on p. 88. There are probably as many ways of getting the job done as there are people doing it, so what follows

EDITOR'S NOTE: You can buy most lacquer-spraying equipment and supplies from auto-body-shop suppliers and from Sears. Major manufacturers of spray units include DeVilbiss Co., Box 913, Toledo, Ohio 43692 and Binks, 9201 West Belmont Ave., Franklin Park, Ill. 60131.

should be seen simply as one good method among many.

The question most frequently asked by the novice is "How many coats of lacquer do I put on?" This question can't be answered as it can for painting; painting is accomplished when the surface is opaquely covered. Lacquering is not simply a covering job, for lacquer is not clear paint. On bad lacquer jobs you can actually see two surfaces, a thick layer of clear plastic and under that the surface of the wood. Done properly, however, you see one surface of polished wood. It is gotten that way not by the mere addition of clear stuff, but by a cyclic process of adding material and sanding it off until the surface being treated is truly flat, at least to the degree that the eye no longer distinguishes any texture. Only enough material must be left on the surface to enable you to polish it without breaking through to the wood. So the answer to the question "How many coats?" must be left at "Enough," that is, however many coats it takes to complete the job of leveling and polishing.

Effective spray technique is largely a matter of speed and consistency, graceful motion and thoroughness. You are trying as quickly as possible to coat a surface evenly and completely, with no unblended areas. In effect, you want to have the entire object wet at once. To do this the gun must be supplying its maximum amount of fluid, and you must move quickly from surface to surface in a preconceived pattern that will ensure thoroughness, with tightly spaced strokes that overlap each other and the object's edges.

The process begins with the application of a sanding sealer diluted with an equal amount of lacquer thinner. Sanding sealer is a kind of lacquer specially formulated to raise the grain of the wood, to provide a base for better adhesion and to be easily sandable. It gives you a preview of the finished surface, allowing you to locate and repair any imperfections.

After perhaps an hour's drying time a wood filler can be used on open-pored woods. Most wood fillers consist of chalk, plus a touch of clay and pigment, carried in a mineral spirit or naphtha vehicle. The pigmented chalk is left in the pores of open-grained woods, where it fills most of the space. Buy neutral filler and color it yourself with dry poster paint, toning it down with lampblack to suit whatever wood you are filling. This will save your having to buy endlessly different colors. Thin the filler about 25% with naphtha and apply it with a rag, working the surface constantly while the filler is drying. It will soon begin to collect on the rag. Now wipe the surface across the grain to clean off all excess filler. For large-pored woods, like oak, a second application may be necessary after three hours' drying time. Eight to twelve hours later, sand the surface clean with 320-grit paper to remove filler residue and raised grain. You will sand through the sealer coat in places, making an awful mess, but the next coat of sealer, applied just like the first, will blend perfectly.

The surface will now appear improved but not yet truly flat, and it will take the remaining sealer coats, applied heavily but sanded almost completely off, along with subsequent lacquer coats, to complete the leveling process. These will be spread out over a period of days, with no more than four coats applied per day. On the first day I stay with the sealer, applying three wet coats one to two hours apart. A wet coat means that the solution is applied so heavily that it floods the surface, leveling itself to a mirror gloss just one taste short of drooling. This welds the material to the previous coat and ensures adequate film thickness. As the lacquer coats build, a

Drawing: Lynn McVicker

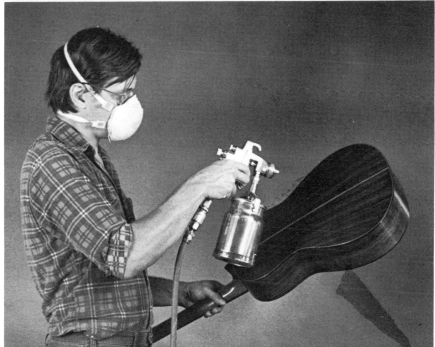

Morris demonstrates the proper relative distance from and angle to the surface being sprayed. Hand-holding the guitar allows more sensitive positioning in relation to the light. He's using a full-size DeVilbiss type JGA gun, siphon-fed from a quart cup, which is suitable for spraying large objects without the need for frequent refills. DeVilbiss type EGA gun, top right, is right for objects the size of a guitar and smaller. Its cup can be replaced with a small mayonnaise jar, permitting quick color changes. The Binks model 18 gun, right, has a pressure-fed hose instead of a cup. The hose supplies lacquer under 10 PSI from a 2-gal. holding tank. Such a system is light, versatile (it can even be used upside down) and good for production work. At top, an edge-grain section of a piece of lacquered rosewood at X28 magnification shows its enormous pores and the filler (white at upper right) under the finish. The lacquer film tapers in thickness toward the corner because the film shrinks as it dries.

thoroughly wet application is necessary or a layered structure will result, which is prone to blistering and ghosting. Also, because of the low solids content of lacquer you need the thick coat just to have anything left after the thinner has evaporated. Straight from the can, the solids content is about 20%, and when mixed with equal amounts of thinner it is 10%. Compared to varnish, which is about 50% solids, this is like mixing one quart of varnish with one gallon of thinner.

Perhaps the most important thing to understand about this low solids content is the fact that while the thinner is evaporating, the lacquer film is shrinking. Only one-tenth of what you spray will remain as a film on the wood. The rate of evaporation and shrinkage is extremely fast at first, so the surface can be touched within minutes of being drenched. But the

evaporation rate decreases rapidly, and enough thinner is trapped within the film so that shrinkage is still perceptible after a week of drying. It is bad practice to apply more than three, at most four, coats of lacquer without allowing an overnight dry to let most of the trapped thinner escape. Otherwise, the thinner will be buried under so much lacquer that it will take weeks to evaporate completely.

After the first three coats of sealer dry overnight, sand the surface thoroughly with 320-grit paper on a block. This dulls the shiny surface, but the low spots will still shine. The goal is a uniformly matte surface with no shiny spots, but you may sand through to the wood in places. When this happens spray more sealer and sand again, until there are no shiny spots anywhere. Now spray one last coat of sealer to coat any wood that's been sanded bare, and begin spraying the first lacquer coats. Lacquer is usually diluted with an equal volume of thinner, and it's sprayed at the same rate as sealer, a coat every hour or two, no more than three coats per day. Let dry overnight and sand with 320-grit paper the next day. Repeat this cycle until you can level-sand the entire surface without sanding through to the wood anywhere. Then apply the final three coats and allow the surface to stabilize and harden for about five days, before final leveling and polishing.

Final sanding can be done with either 500-grit stearated paper dry (available from auto-body-equipment suppliers), or with 600-grit paper wet—there's no difference in the final result. As water can mar the wood if you sand through, I recommend the dry 500-grit paper, used with a felt sanding block behind it and with a reciprocating, in-line motion to prevent build-up of dry lacquer dust on the paper. The surface and paper must be constantly wiped clean, for this white powder clogs the paper and mars the surface.

When free of all telltale shiny spots, wipe the surface clean and continue this abrasive action with the first of two polishing compounds, coarse and fine, which will produce the mirror finish. I use Meguiar's brand compounds, Mirror Glaze I for the coarse and Mirror Glaze III for the fine. (For the name of your local distributor, write Meguiar's, 1 Newport Pl., 1301 Dove St., Newport Beach, Calif. 92660.) Both can be used on a lamb's-wool pad, rubbed by hand or with a buffer. They are best kept in covered plastic squeeze bottles; apply to the pad, not to the surface, to guard against dirt scratching the finish. Use buffing compound sparingly and wet it frequently with water to create a slurry that helps to float the surface clean and keep the abrasive cutting. I usually buff in line with the figure when using the coarse compound, and in a circular pattern when using the fine.

The quality of the finished surface depends completely upon the success of each step, from the preparation of the wood to its final polish. Critical inspection will reveal when a flaw is created. Once you start spraying, it is too late to repair the earlier stages, but if you need to respray once you've begun polishing, first wash the surface with alcohol and water, 50/50, to remove polishing residue. The surface may be rebuffed at any time in the future with the fine compound to restore its original luster. □

George Morris makes guitars in Post Mills, Vt.

Troubleshooting the spray schedule

Drools and sags: The gun is too close to the surface, or you are moving it too slowly, or you have passed over a spot too many times. If caught right away, simply hold the surface horizontal and give no direction for the excess fluid to run, or smear the drool flat with your hand. A flat smear will dry and be sanded out much more quickly than a thick drool. But do not break a drool that has scabbed over.

Overspray: Lacquer not absorbed by the surface because it is dry upon contact. Either the spray gun is being held too far from the surface, or air pressure is too high.

Ghosts: Cloudy, amorphous apparitions, the result of having trapped overspray within the finish. Ghosts are usually discovered while polishing, since the interlayer phenomenon is porous and does not polish. It must be remelted either by some careful work with the polishing wheel, to warm and soften the surface, or by the use of a pulling rubber. Pulling redissolves the surface using a diluted thinner (cut 50% with alcohol). The fluid is applied sparingly to chamois leather wrapped around an egg-sized cotton wad. Stroke the puller quickly and firmly across the surface a few times until the ghost dissolves.

Bubbles: Air trapped by spray turbulence, most common when spraying straight into a corner. To minimize, direct spray in line with the corner.

Blisters: A local adhesion problem encouraged by the surface's being banged. Blisters are more likely if the wooden surface was burnished or coated with something incompatible with the lacquer. Before taking the finish off completely and repreparing the surface, try puncturing the blister with a blade and adding a drop of thinner to act as a glue between film and surface.

Fish-eye: Small circular features, sometimes iridescent, from either oil or silicone on the surface. Remove oil with naphtha, and remove silicone with a lacquer additive designed to eliminate the effect.

Checking: Random fissures in the hardened film caused by uneven shrinkage across the thickness of the film itself. It could be the result of extreme temperature change whereby the film cracks as does glass when quickly passed from boiling to freezing temperatures. Shrinkage can also be uneven if the surface of the film dries before the thinner within the film has a chance to escape. The hardened surface will pull itself apart when the thinner trapped beneath it eventually evaporates, as does a mud pond drying in the sun. The effect is minimized by keeping the film thickness as thin as possible. Trapped thinner is the result of insufficient drying time between coats, or more than a few coats applied in one day.

Crazing: Subtle, small cracks in the film, caused by spraying fresh lacquer over old finish. A close cousin to checking, it is avoided by sanding the old finish very thin before respraying.

Pits: Unfilled pores or gaps in joints. If these are found before spraying begins, it's simply a patching problem to be fixed with wood splints, a sawdust-and-glue mixture or shellac stick melted into the pit and sanded smooth. If pits are found during the spray schedule (they'll appear white when filled with powdered lacquer) lacquer putty will do the trick. Lacquer putty is undiluted lacquer that has been left to evaporate until it's the consistency of thick honey. It must be applied between coats with a small, flat stick, allowed to dry overnight and sanded level the next day before spraying is continued.

Sand-through: If you sand through the lacquer to the wood in the middle of a surface, either respray the entire surface to the edges, masking everything else with newspaper to avoid overspray, or respray through a cardboard mask with a small hole cut in it to minimize overspray. Beware of ghosts. I have had success respraying minor repairs using acrylic lacquer on top of the nitrocellulose finish to prevent these visitations.

Dull spots: If, regardless of how thoroughly a surface is polished, it still does not gloss, you are probably polishing sealer, which will never gloss. The cure is to spray on more lacquer.   —G.M.

Q & A

Curing lacquer orange peel

How do you cure orange peel in lacquer finishing—the crinkling disfigurement of the lacquer film as it dries?
— *Michel Chevanelle, Acton Vale, Quebec*

GEORGE MORRIS REPLIES: Orange peel is caused by the lacquer's drying or turning to gel on the surface it is sprayed on before it has a chance to flow and level. If thinning the lacquer doesn't help, try raising the temperature of your spray area or of the surface being sprayed. Spraying conditions that are too cool cause the lacquer to gel before it can flow and level itself—it then dries in a rough orange-peel surface. Heating the lacquer slightly may also help, but use only a non-flame heat source. I usually put the lacquer cup in front of a heat register for a few minutes before spraying. If the air pressure to the spray gun is too low, the lacquer will not atomize properly, resulting in the poor flow and leveling that cause orange peel. Airless-type spray guns can be particularly troublesome in this regard. Holding the gun at just the right distance from the surface is also important and you should move it just steadily enough to apply as much lacquer as possible without causing drips and runs. If nothing else seems to work, lacquer manufacturers make additives that can be mixed into their finishes to retard orange peel. Finally, you can correct an orange peel surface by wet-sanding back to the previous coat and respraying the surface with fresh lacquer.

Dashboard restoration

I'm doing some restoration work on 1940s Jaguars and Bentleys. What did manufacturers use to glue and finish the veneered dashboards? This finish has to be glass-smooth, withstand extreme fluctuations in temperature and humidity, and protect the wood against ultraviolet light. — *Richard W. Morton, Redwood City, Calif.*

DONALD STEINERT REPLIES: In the 1940s, hot hide glue was used to attach the veneers. A modern alternative is hot-melt glue sheets (available from Bob Morgan Woodworking Supplies, 1123 Bardstown Rd., Louisville, Ky. 40204), which are heated with a household iron. Don't use contact cements.

The dashboard veneer was finished with either varnish or lacquer, neither of which is immune to the effects of temperature, humidity and ultraviolet rays. Even today, there is no clear finish that will stand up to the extremes a dashboard can experience. I refinish the woodwork in many $120,000 Rolls-Royces that are less than three years old!

In my restoration work, I spray on a catalyzed polyester resin, but this is pretty toxic stuff, and tricky to work with because of its 20- to 40-min. pot life. You can use a varnish product such as McCloskey's Bar Top Varnish, or a bartop lacquer. Both require many light coats, followed by wet-sanding with very fine grit wet-or-dry paper. Finish up with rubbing compound. If you follow the procedure in George Morris's article (see pages 84-88), you'll get good results.

Staining maple to reveal grain

How can hard maple be stained to bring out the delicate grain? Commercial maple furniture is opaque red to orange. I'm doing a floor that needs the protection of a good finish and a nice light- to medium-brown color, with no loss of grain pattern. — *James M. Harris, Chantilly, Va.*

DON NEWELL REPLIES: Commercial furniture is usually finished with red to orange semi-opaque or opaque wash coats to achieve a standard maple tone. To accentuate the grain of maple, you must use a completely transparent stain. I would use an alcohol-based aniline stain, probably a "golden oak" color. Aniline stain is more likely to be absorbed selectively into the maple's structure, thus highlighting it.

You didn't ask about a finishing material for your floor, so I assume you know what you want. But in case you haven't considered it, Waterlox Gym Floor Finish is good and durable. Another good finish is shellac. It is surprisingly durable, unless some of your friends spill straight whiskey on it.

My interest in staining maple began with Kentucky rifles, which are known for their curly maple and rich, 200-year-old patinas. Trying to find a commercial stain was fruitless, while the many traditional staining techniques (potassium permanganate, chromium trioxide, nitric acid with dissolved iron) were either dangerous, hard to control or had undesirable side effects. By chance I found a supplier of pure-color liquid aniline dyes, which, after some experimentation, produced brilliant colors of great and subtle variety with all of the grain brought out.

Begin with concentrated liquid aniline solution (available from the Wallbrunn Paint Co., 1177 Wilmette Ave., Wilmette, Ill. 60091). It comes in red, yellow, brown, orange, green, blue, blue-black and jet black. The dyes are soluble in water, alcohol or in a special stain solvent. I dilute them with 5 or 6 parts water to 1 part stain.

I have two approaches to finding the color I want. The first is to begin mixing various quantities of the stains, testing them on a piece of wood or paper, until I get a pleasing color. The second is to have in hand a color to match. I start experimenting with small quantities in a tiny 50-ml beaker. Guessing at a formula I think will match the original color, I measure out a small amount with an eyedropper. After the colors are all mixed, I add enough water, again with an eyedropper, to dilute the colors by 5 or 6 to 1. The procedure makes very small quantities and so dilute that 4 to 6 applications are needed to build up the color. I test it on a piece of waterproof paper, first writing the formula at the top. Then, using a Q-tip, I put 6 or 8 stripes of stain across the paper. After these dry, I stain all the stripes again, except the top 2. After all 6 or 8 applications, you can compare the test stripes to the original.

You usually find that your conception of how the original color was put together is wrong. So back to the formula for an adjustment and a mix of a new test stain. This may seem tedious but can be relatively fast. In the stain mentioned above, which I recently mixed, the total time needed was a few hours stretched over a four-day period with about twenty different stains mixed. Yet despite the fact that I made two false starts before finding the right formula, the final stain matches the original color. I was convinced the original had a touch of red in it, but indeed it did not. Once the stain is matched on the paper strip, I switch to a test piece of wood and finish it exactly like the project itself. With these procedures I have found many beautiful, unique stains, all exceptionally clear and grain-accentuating.

Final formulas may seem strange or overly complex. My recent stain has 8 parts orange, 2 yellow, 2 jet black and 1 brown; it produces an exquisite honey-brown color. I study my final test-stain blocks in many lights: incandescent, fluorescent, direct sunlight, north light and subdued evening light to get the tones right. A two-stain process often heightens the figure in gunstock woods like curly maple. I apply a weak brown or black stain during the whiskering stage. A final sanding removes the stain from the hard curl and leaves it on the soft curl. Staining a second time adds the desired color to the hard curl and darkens the soft curl even more. — *Lynn Fichter, Harrisonburg, Va.*

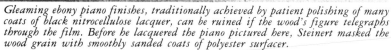

Gleaming ebony piano finishes, traditionally achieved by patient polishing of many coats of black nitrocellulose lacquer, can be ruined if the wood's figure telegraphs through the film. Before he lacquered the piano pictured here, Steinert masked the wood grain with smoothly sanded coats of polyester surfacer.

That Piano Finish
Modern method makes opaque lacquer gleam

by Donald M. Steinert

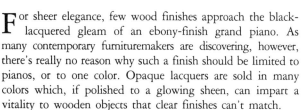

For sheer elegance, few wood finishes approach the black-lacquered gleam of an ebony-finish grand piano. As many contemporary furnituremakers are discovering, however, there's really no reason why such a finish should be limited to pianos, or to one color. Opaque lacquers are sold in many colors which, if polished to a glowing sheen, can impart a vitality to wooden objects that clear finishes can't match.

Traditional piano finishes consist of many coats of nitrocellulose lacquer painstakingly built up over a carefully filled and sanded wood surface. Brought to a high gloss by hours of polishing, such a finish is more time-consuming than difficult to achieve. In the interest of expediency, some modern piano-makers, particularly in Europe and Japan, have turned to clear and colored polyester finishes. This material dries and builds faster than lacquer, so fewer coats are needed. It also forms a harder, stabler surface that masks wood figure, keeping it from telegraphing through the top coats.

Polyester finishing requires equipment that is impractical for the small shop, so I've experimented with a polyester/nitrocellulose finish. My method combines the stability and surface-smoothing qualities of polyester with the workability of nitrocellulose lacquer. While not easy, especially for the beginner, this technique can be mastered by anyone willing to take the time to experiment.

From *Fine Woodworking* magazine (January 1984) 44:58-61

Preparing the surface—The success of any lacquer finish, opaque or clear, depends on the smoothness and stability of the surface to which it is applied. Mahogany is traditionally the favored wood of pianomakers because it is fine-textured and relatively stable, so the lacquer film is less likely to stretch and crack as the wood swells and shrinks with the seasons. Maple, poplar and most cabinet plywoods are also excellent for lacquering. Oak, fir and pine are poor choices.

Even a mild-figured wood such as mahogany has open-pored grain which must be filled before lacquering. Paste wood-fillers and/or sanding sealers are usually used for this purpose, but I've had better luck with my polyester system. Paste filler, a fine silica powder suspended in an oil vehicle, is messy to apply. Unless you allow plenty of drying time, at least several days, the oil may react with the lacquer, possibly dimpling the lacquer film later. Though easier to work with, lacquer sanding sealers are formulated to be readily sandable, which makes them brittle and prone to cracking.

The polyester filler I use is Prestec 2090 gray sanding surfacer, and it's available in quantities as small as one quart from Simtec, 1188 North Grove, Bldgs. K&L, Anaheim, Calif. 92806. Prestec also comes in white and black. Like the fiberglass compounds to which it is related, Prestec is a two-part system: a viscous resin, and a methyl ethyl ketone peroxide (MEKP) hardening catalyst which you buy separately from a body-shop supply house. The hardener may be sold under different brand names, so just ask for MEKP polyester catalyst. Prestec is about 97% solids, so one coat of polyester is about equal in thickness to six or seven coats of lacquer. It adheres well to wood, cures in one to 24 hours, and is fairly elastic, thus it serves as an effective intermediary between the wood and the nitrocellulose lacquer that goes over it.

Prestec 2090 must be sprayed, and it's only fair to point out that this material is demanding and somewhat hazardous to handle. MEKP is toxic and extremely flammable. A single drop of it accidentally splashed into an eye can blind you, so be sure to wear proper eye protection at all times. Work in a well-ventilated shop, or work outdoors if the weather is warm and dry. Wear an organic vapor mask when you're mixing and spraying, and a dust nuisance mask when you're sanding the dry film.

The biggest disadvantage of polyester is its limited pot life. The resin will set up in 20 to 40 minutes, and if it hardens before you've emptied and cleaned your spray gun, the gun will be ruined. Mix only as much resin as you will be able to spray within the pot life.

To prepare a surface for polyester, sand it to at least 100-grit or finer. Knots, gouges and other defects should be filled with automotive body compound, then sanded flush. I don't use plastic wood fillers because they usually shrink. Unless you're ready to clean up a major mess, don't spray polyester over an old finish. The old finish will soften and you'll have a hard film floating on jelly. Strip off the old coating, sand well, and dust the surface with a lacquer-thinner-dampened rag, allowing 24 hours for drying.

Prestec should be mixed according to the directions on the can. For safety, I add the catalyst with a laboratory pipette (photo, above right). Thinned to the appropriate viscosity with acetone, polyester is actually easier to spray than lacquer. With the compressor's air regulator at about 40 PSI, I hold the gun 8 in. to 16 in. from the work, applying a mist coat first, followed by a heavier hiding coat 3 to 5 minutes later.

Polyester catalyst is toxic and extremely flammable. To avoid splashing it, Steinert adds it to the resin with a glass pipette, available from laboratory supply houses.

You don't have to wait until one coat cures before applying the next. Keep building the film until it's as thick as you want. Open-pored woods will require a thicker coat than will closed-grain ones.

Polyester takes longer to surface-dry than lacquer does, and it will collect dust. But that doesn't matter because it will be thoroughly sanded before the top coats go on. Depending on how much catalyst you add and on the temperature and humidity, Prestec will dry in about 45 minutes. I usually allow 8 hours of air-curing before sanding. Small objects can be force-dried in an oven set at 110°F to 150°F. If you try this, let the polyester air-dry for a while first to avoid blistering.

Spraying the top coats—Sand the hardened polyester with open-coat garnet paper, starting with 100-grit and finishing with 220, without skipping any grits. Sand by hand or with a straight-line power sander. But don't use an orbital sander—the swirls will telegraph. Don't rush sanding, either; the smoother you get the polyester, the smoother the lacquer coats will be. If you decide to sand finer than 220-grit, switch to silicon carbide paper. I vacuum the dust between grits, then wipe the surface with a naphtha-dampened rag.

Of all the materials suitable for opaque finishes—lacquer, enamel, polyurethane and even colored polyester—I think nitrocellulose lacquer is the most practical because it's a solvent-release finish, which means its volatile solvents evaporate to leave behind a film of coalesced nitrocellulose particles. Each successive coat softens the previous one, so, in effect, multiple coats of lacquer blend into one integrated coat, with none of the intercoat adhesion problems often encountered with polymerizing finishes (such as polyurethane or epoxy), which dry irreversibly by molecular cross-linking. Lacquer films remain dissolvable indefinitely, so scratches and sand-throughs are easily repaired, and refinishing can be done at any time, even if the cured lacquer needs to be stripped off.

Opaque lacquers are sold in hundreds of types, colors and

Photos: Patricia F. Steinert

gloss ranges. In ten years of experimenting, I've found that the nitrocellulose lacquers developed for the automotive industry are tougher and polish out better than those formulated for wood, though both types have essentially the same working properties. Also, colored automotive lacquer is easier to buy because it's sold or can be ordered by any local autobody supply house, as can most of the materials and tools I've mentioned. If you can't buy opaque lacquer locally, try my supplier: Bay City Paint Company, 2279 Market St., San Francisco, Calif. 94114. Bay City will custom-mix colors to match your sample, in quantities as small as one quart. You can fine-tune the color by adding universal colorants.

Though some craftspeople prefer the acrylic lacquers that industry is increasingly using (see box, below), I don't much care for them. Acrylic lacquer builds faster by virtue of its higher solids content, but I've had trouble getting it to adhere to wood and it's not compatible with polyester. It neither flows out as well as nitrocellulose nor polishes as nicely when dry.

I start top-coating with four double coats of lacquer, sprayed on at 40 PSI to 50 PSI with the gun 8 in. to 12 in. from the work. A double coat is just that—two coats sprayed one right after the other without allowing the initial concentration of solvent to evaporate or "flash," which it will do in 5 to 10 minutes in moderate weather. Lacquer has flashed when you can run the back of your hand over it lightly without sticking. Between double coats, I do wait for the flash, during which time some dust always gets into the film, creating nibs which must be sanded out later.

You may be tempted to spray the lacquer at a thicker viscosity, hoping to build the film faster. But solvents are trapped by a thick, wet coat, causing the film to shrink unevenly into a crazed or checked surface. On the other hand, the lacquer will run on vertical surfaces if it's too thin. Experiment to find the right viscosity. To avoid fisheyes—small, circular flaws where the lacquer won't adhere due to minute surface contamination—I add Du Pont fisheye eliminator to the lacquer. By the way, polyester filler can also fisheye. Prevent it with Simtec's eliminator, which is called B-32.

After spraying four double coats, forget about the project for at least 24 hours. Fooling around with the finish at this point will compound any problems, or cause new ones. If the first four coats dry trouble-free, dry-sand with 400-grit silicon carbide paper to knock off the dust nibs. Major imperfections, such as drools, runs and sags, should be wet-sanded out by hand with naphtha or mineral spirits as the lubricant. Clean the surface with a fresh naphtha-soaked rag, let it dry, and then spray four more double coats, exactly as before.

Let the lacquer dry for at least two weeks at 65°F to 70°F before polishing it. A month would be even better.

Final-sanding and polishing—Wet-sand the cured lacquer with 400-grit silicon carbide using either naphtha or a half-and-half mixture of paraffin oil and mineral spirits as the lubricant. Don't lubricate with water, though. If you accidentally sand through to bare wood, water will raise the grain. On small pieces, hand-sand, backing your paper with a felt or cork block. Sand a larger piece, such as a piano, with a pneumatic straight-line power sander. *Never* wet-sand with an electric power sander—the risk of shock or fire is too great. I used to be miserly with costly silicon carbide paper. I've since learned that using dull paper is slow, and it will never leave the uniformly smooth surface that fresh, sharp paper will.

Sanding through the top coats at the arrises—the line where two surfaces meet at an exterior angle—may be unavoidable. I minimize this problem by "banding" or spraying a heavier build along the edges. Where sand-throughs do occur, repair the damage by thinning a teaspoon of lacquer to brushing consistency, then laying a thin bead of the lacquer on the bare

---

Colorful finishes with acrylic lacquer
by George Morris

Fast and richly colored opaque finishes are easily achieved by spraying clear nitrocellulose lacquer over acrylic-lacquer color base coats. I combine these two very different materials for two reasons. First, colored acrylic lacquers are readily available in any quantity at automotive supply stores in my area, while opaque nitrocellulose lacquers are much harder to find. Second, acrylic lacquer dries to a hard film much more slowly than does nitrocellulose, remaining tender and imprintable for as long as two to three weeks after spraying. A clear top coat of fast-drying nitrocellulose solves this problem.

Since opaque color is the desired end, you can skip the otherwise necessary step of using paste wood-filler by choosing a dense, nonporous wood or plywood for the lacquered object. I prepare wood for colored lacquer just as I would for clear lacquer, smoothing surface irregularities with a scraper, followed by sanding with a felt or wood block wrapped in 120-grit, then 220-grit.

Using an alcohol-based aniline dye, I stain the wood to match the color of the acrylic lacquer I'll be using. Dyeing the wood has two advantages: it makes strong colors more achievable with only two or three color coats, and the inevitable dings and dents are less noticeable. Avoid water-based dyes because they raise the grain. I let the dye dry for 5 minutes, and then with a soft cloth I clean off the powdery residue left behind before proceeding with the color coats.

I spray on two coats of acrylic, waiting 10 minutes between coats. Before each coat flashes, I check for flaws by examining the wet film in oblique light, and I correct them right away, knocking down runs and sags with a finger or a brush before the film sets any further.

Sanding them out later is as messy as sanding slightly wet paint.

I wait an hour, and then spray on three coats of clear nitrocellulose lacquer, allowing an hour between coats. After the initial three clear coats have dried overnight, I sand with 320-grit stearated paper to level the surface. Then I clean the surface with a tack rag, and spray three or four more coats of clear lacquer to complete the job. It's best to wait a few days before wet-sanding, using water as a lubricant, with 600-grit wet-or-dry paper. I follow this with a final buff with McGuire's Machine Glaze Nos. 1 and 3 or equivalent polishing compounds for high gloss, or 0000 steel wool for a satin finish. □

George Morris teaches guitarmaking at The Vermont Instrument Workshop in Post Mills, Vt. His article on lacquering is on pages 84-88.

Sand-throughs at the arrises may be unavoidable. Fix them by painting a bead of lacquer over the exposed area. As the bead dries, it will shrink into an invisible repair.

Steinert polishes built-up lacquer by hand or with an automotive lamb's-wool bonnet. He starts with medium-grade compound, finishing with a fine-grit called swirl-mark eliminator.

spots with the edge, not the tip, of a ¼-in. wide sable artists' brush (photo, above left). As the lacquer dries, the bead will shrink flat, making the fix virtually invisible. If you accidentally sand through to the polyester on a flat surface, scuff the area with 600-grit paper and spray on several thin coats of lacquer. Let the repaired surface dry thoroughly and pick up where you left off. You can accelerate drying with a heat lamp, but be careful; the lacquer will blister if you get it too hot.

Once the entire piece has been wet-sanded, clean it up with a soft, naphtha-dampened rag. Check for flaws, then wet-sand again, this time with 600-grit paper. When you complete this step, the lacquer should be dull but absolutely smooth and delightful to touch.

I let the lacquer dry for 24 hours before beginning to polish it with any one of a range of auto polishing compounds made by Du Pont, Ditzler or 3M. Small objects are best polished by hand, but for large surfaces I use a Bosch rotary buffer with a lamb's-wool bonnet, cleaning it often with a tool sold for this purpose. Any buffer will do, except high-speed body grinders, whose friction is likely to heat and soften the lacquer. For hand-polishing, I use old diapers.

For both power- and hand-polishing, three grades of compound will be adequate: a medium-duty rubbing compound and two finer compounds. Start with the medium compound. If you're hand-polishing, smear a ribbon of compound on the surface and rub in a straight-line motion, with the grain. Bear down hard when you begin, and try to overcome the natural tendency to polish in an arc. As the compound dries and the shine begins to show, reduce pressure to a light buffing. Repeat this procedure with the fine compound.

Follow the same steps if you machine-buff. Be careful, though; if you park the buffer in one place or push down too hard, the lacquer will heat up and wrinkle or "orange peel" slightly. If this happens, stop polishing, let the surface cool, then resume with a gentler action. A bad burn will have to be

wet-sanded and/or sprayed again.

Hand-polishing leaves streaks in the surface; the power buffer leaves minute swirls. Both kinds of marks can be removed with a very fine compound commonly called swirl-mark eliminator (photo, above right), which can be hand- or power-buffed.

By now, you should have a brilliant, mirror-smooth surface. All that remains is to blow off the compound residue with compressed air and give the piece a light dusting with a tack cloth. I use a toothpick to get compound out of the nooks and crevices. To enhance the depth of the sheen, some piano finishers spray on a clear lacquer top coat after polishing. But I've found that this is just another opportunity for dust to collect, and a clear finish over a colored one is harder to repair.

Fresh lacquer needs more babying than do other finishes. I caution my customers not to place heavy objects such as lamps or vases on a new lacquer finish for at least two to three months, to avoid imprinting. For periodic polishing and dusting, I use swirl-mark eliminator or automotive waxes and polishes. Furniture care products that contain silicon, Johnson's Pledge for example, will likely turn hazy a day or two after application. Never dust a lacquer finish with a dry cloth, regardless of how soft it is.

I've found that producing a polished lacquer finish is a very physical, almost athletic activity which demands patient practice, not to mention the ability to survive a fair number of setbacks, to get right. Try it first on scrap plywood or on an unimportant piece. Once you've developed a feel for the materials and tools—particularly the spray gun—I'm sure you'll be amazed with the classy, colorful surfaces you'll be able to produce. □

Donald Steinert, of Grants Pass, Oregon, has left teaching to work full-time restoring and refinishing pianos, furniture, and Rolls-Royce woodwork.

Q & A

Refinishing old leather top

I am refinishing an antique end table with an inlaid leather top, with gold leafing around the borders of the leather. —Paul Hoke, St. Clair Shores, Mich.

SANDY COHEN REPLIES: You should not use paint or varnish remover; either could damage the leather or lift the gold. First, determine what the old finish consists of by trying to remove patches with various solvents in an inconspicuous place. Most likely the finish is shellac. If it is, soak a pad of soft, lint-free cloth with denatured alcohol and gently wipe the surface of the leather with a circular, French-polisher's motion. Turn the cloth often, adding plenty of alcohol until the finish is removed. Allow it to dry and repeat. Be gentle over the gold to avoid rubbing it off. If the finish is varnish or lacquer, use a 50/50 mixture of alcohol and lacquer thinner. Should the leather be dirty, clean it with saddle soap and water, and if the leather has grain, use the soap sparingly.

If the gold is real, no preserver is needed. To preserve and polish leather that's in good shape, all you need to do is slop on a generous amount of a mixture of 40% lanolin and 60% neat's-foot oil and let it soak in for three days. Then rub in the residue with your fingertips and remove the excess with an absorbent cloth. Polish lightly with a piece of flannel. For flaking leather, instead of using neat's-foot oil and lanolin, apply a coat of white shellac with a cotton ball and a deft touch. Use a circular motion and don't go back over a place that has already begun to dry. Use shellac as a last resort, when the leather is flaking and needs to be consolidated.

Restoring leather-top table

I've been asked to restore an old black walnut table that has considerable local historic value, since it was brought to South Pass, Wyo., in the 1860s by wagon over the Oregon Trail. I should have no difficulty, except—how was the top made? It now has a face 71 in. by 35 in., with a 3½-in. frame around a panel ⅛ in. deep. What was in the depression—veneer, leather or possibly green felt? —Raymond Gayle, Pinedale, Wyo.

ANDY MARLOW REPLIES: The only reason for veneering the depressed area would be to use burl walnut, which in an area that size and depth is out of the question. Also, if the recess approaches ⅛ in. in depth, felt can be eliminated. That leaves leather. I would suggest using a strong magnifying glass to see if a few fibers might still be adhering to the surface.

The table described by Raymond Gayle sounds similar to one that has been in my mother's family for several generations. When the table was restored, it was found to be black walnut. The leather inset was removed, and my mother chose a leatherette of soft forest green to be laid in, with a narrow flat metallic gold braid bordering it. An elderly cousin viewed the restored table, and was astonished at my mother's choice of green leatherette and gold braid. It turned out that the original leather inset was a soft forest green color, and the original braid trim metallic gold. Years later, I came across a similar table in an antique shop in Oregon. It, too, was of black walnut, with a green leather inset bordered by a narrow flat metallic gold braid. I don't know if the green leather/gold braid combination was the only one used for these tables, but the combination is certainly attractive with the black walnut. —Marika Urso, Danville, Calif.

Repairing piano finish

We have a fine old grand piano with typical crazed varnish finish. An old piano tuner told me to feed the old finish with boiled linseed oil thinned with paint thinner. This went well the first two applications. After the third, it would not dry to the feel of a finish that could be sanded. It's been four months and it is soft but not tacky. —Ralph Z. Neff, North Canton, Ohio

GEORGE FRANK REPLIES: There are only three ways to cope with an old finish: remove it completely and refinish; clean it and apply a sealer so the new finish is never actually in contact with the old; and the way you chose, the riskiest of all, to add a finish that would melt into the old one. This can only be done if you know what the old finish is, and even then it is hazardous because you don't know what it has been cleaned with, or what traces remain on the wood.

At this point I would try some experiments. First, wash the finish with gasoline. Be careful, ventilate and allow no chance of fire. Soak an area well, wipe it dry a few minutes later, and by next morning the softness may be gone. Second, try a wet Brillo pad, wash and rub an area with elbow grease and wait overnight. If neither trick works, you'll have to strip it off and start over.

Lubricating clocks and pianos

After making the gears, I assembled my clock and it worked beautifully. Then I finished it with Watco and the clock stopped running. The finish felt smooth, but apparently the surface friction between the gears increased greatly. I rubbed graphite on the gears and the gears started to run again, but it required more than twice the weight it did before. I am making another clock and I wish to apply a finish that will not increase surface friction between gears. —Rod F. Gimpel, Idaho Falls, Idaho

ANDY MARLOW REPLIES: Your problem could have a number of causes. Did you notice if one gear and pinion would stop at a given spot each time? If so, not enough tolerance was allowed in that area. If, on the other hand, the clock ran evenly for an hour or more with the addition of weight, insufficient tolerance overall is indicated, which will cause you trouble seasonally with or without finish. I doubt the finish itself caused enough friction to stop the movement. Unless you must finish your new clockworks, I suggest using WD-40, a lubricant available from auto-supply stores. If color is necessary, try a water stain, let dry thoroughly, spray lightly with sanding sealer, sand with 240-grit paper, spray no more than two coats of lacquer cut 50% with thinner, and finish with a shot of WD-40.

Pianos also have precision wooden actions, often requiring lubricants to reduce friction to the absolute minimum. I use two lubricants in my grand-piano restoration shop that I would like to recommend. McLube 1725 is a colorless, dry film lubricant, available in aerosol or liquid form. It dries almost instantly to a transparent haze almost invisible on wood, and has an extremely low coefficient of friction. McLube 1708 (aerosol only) contains the same fluorinated hydrocarbon lubricant as 1725, plus molybdenum disulfide. This is an amazing, ultra-low-friction coating; 1708's only limitation is its color, a matte gray-black. Sometimes this can be turned to advantage by careful masking, leaving an attractive band of charcoal "finish" that will not smear off. The advantage of both these lubricants is that they contain no oils, greases or waxes and are perfectly dry. Therefore, they don't get gummy or fouled with dust and dirt. WD-40 is great but is not my choice for wooden surfaces. McLube products are made by McGee Industries, 9 Crozerville Rd., Aston, Pa. 19014; (215) 459-1890. —Thomas McNeil, Lansing, Mich.

Leather on Wood
How to inlay it and tool it with gold

by Sandy Cohen

Inlaid and gold-tooled box top.

I love the feel and texture of fine leather. It is pliable, strong, and, with the proper care, enduring. In fact, I have written this article on an inlaid desk surface of fine-grained olive-green morocco, richly tooled in gold and black, matched to fine English oak, a joy and a delight.

Creating such a surface is not that difficult, but it takes practice to get the feel. First the leather is cut and pasted into a recess as deep as the leather is thick. After the leather is inlaid, a design is stamped or rolled in with a heated brass tool. Gold tooling involves the further steps of sizing the impression with glair (an egg white/vinegar mordant to which gold adheres) and restamping the design over gold leaf. Some of the tools needed are quite specialized and a few are expensive, but they can be improvised with good results.

Combining wood, leather and gold is an ancient and honorable practice. This technique was introduced into Europe in the late 15th century by the Moors. Craftsmen who practiced this art were among the very first to come to America, and many of our founding fathers were directly involved in it. Benjamin Franklin, for example, sold leather to craftsmen. All over the world, palaces and cottages alike are richer because of the marriage of wood and leather on books, chairs, desk tops, tabletops and boxes. The 17th-century Dutch, among others, used gold-tooled leather wallpaper.

The first thing to do is to obtain the leather, because it must fit into a recess routed or paneled to a depth equal to its thickness. And because goats and cows, like woodworkers, come with hides of varying thickness, it's best to have the leather in your hand before doing any routing or grooving. Don't go by the supplier's sample cards because your hide will most likely be thicker or thinner. Goats and cows are the two best and most popular hides, but you can use anything from moose to shark. I would not recommend sealskin because it is too oily, or sheepskin (often called "roan") because it does not wear well. Avoid "skiver," which is sheep hide split very thin. While ideal for labels on books and covers for cameras, it is far too thin for the top of a desk or a card table.

Cowhide is a good choice. When it comes off the cow it is fairly smooth, a perfect surface for writing. Some manufacturers, however, roll it under big steel drums that emboss the leather with a grain that simulates the more expensive goatskins called "morocco." With cowhide, though, take care that no ferrous metal touches the leather when it is damp, or a dark and very permanent stain will result.

Goat is tougher than cow and easier to handle when wet, but considerably more expensive. The best goat is morocco; the best morocco, Niger. Since goats are small animals, you

Sandy Cohen is assistant professor of English at Albany (Georgia) State College. An avid amateur woodworker and leatherworker, he has demonstrated leather bookbinding for an educational television series.

will probably have to use cowhide if the area to be covered is more than two or three feet square.

Hides are usually sold by the whole skin or, in the case of large cows, by the side. Buy a side to avoid the spine, which is darker in color, rougher in texture and somewhat unsightly. Spines are good for book spines, but not secretary tops. When ordering your leather, send the dimensions of the area to be inlaid, and perhaps a rough diagram, to ensure that you get a large enough hide. You will need some extra for cutting and paring and will probably want the scraps to practice tooling before going on to the real thing.

If you want your handiwork to last, buy leather that is stamped "guaranteed to withstand the PIRA (Printers Industry Research Association) test." Technicians at the British Museum found that leather subjected to the modern tanning process decays because it creates sulfuric acid out of the sulfur spewed into the air by automobile exhaust, smoke, and so on, or absorbs free sulfuric acid already in the air from the same sources. They also found that treating leather with a potassium lactate solution interferes with acid absorption and hence prevents decay. Such PIRA-treated leather is considerably more expensive, not only because it has been treated but also because only the better grades are deemed worthy.

You can treat your own leather simply and inexpensively, both before and after tooling. Wipe the leather with a clean, dry flannel rag, then apply a generous amount of potassium lactate solution, available from leather suppliers, with a cotton ball. The next day, apply an even more generous amount of leather dressing and let it dry for three days, then wipe off the excess and polish gently with a flannel rag. The best leather dressing I know is Formula No. 6, a 2:3 mixture of anhydrous lanolin and neat's-foot oil. Buy it ready-made or mix your own. Potassium lactate prevents decay; dressing keeps the leather moist and supple. You should apply the potassium lactate solution and dressing to any valuable pieces of leather you have. PIRA-treated leather needs treatment only after tooling.

You will also need some paste to attach the leather to the wood. I recommend paste rather than glue because paste penetrates the pores better and makes for a longer-lasting bond. I know of leather pieces many hundreds of years old that are still sticking tightly, though they were pasted "only" with starch. My favorite formula is as follows: In a clean wide-mouthed jar, place 3 tablespoons of a gloss laundry starch such as Argo, ¼ teaspoon of powdered alum, ¾ tablespoon of powdered white chalk such as that used for chalk lines, 2 drops of oil of wintergreen, and enough cold water to stir into a mixture the thickness of cream. *Slowly* add boiling water, stirring constantly until it suddenly thickens. Then stop adding water, but stir until the mixture is smooth.

You will also need some newspaper for pasting up the leather. Get unprinted news (from art-supply stores) if the

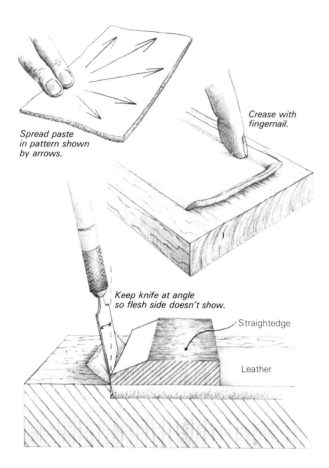

Spread paste
in pattern shown
by arrows.

Crease with
fingernail.

Keep knife at angle
so flesh side doesn't show.

Straightedge

Leather

leather is very light-colored, or "fair," that is, undyed.

Once the leather has arrived and you have routed or paneled the recess to receive it, cut a pattern out of light cardboard or heavy wrapping paper. This pattern should fit the recess exactly. Then place the pattern on the leather, flesh side up (the "fuzzy," undyed or "bad" side that will be pasted) and mark the leather. Before cutting, turn the leather over to be sure you are satisfied with the grain and texture on the good side. If not, reposition your pattern on the back. When the leather is marked, cut it slightly larger than pattern size with a sharp, small-bladed knife and straightedge.

Now place your leather, good side up, on a piece of newsprint and lightly sponge with water—only enough to dampen the leather. Use a cotton ball for all sponging, wiping and gold lifting. This dampening causes the leather to stretch out slightly and dry tight and flat. Now turn the leather over and

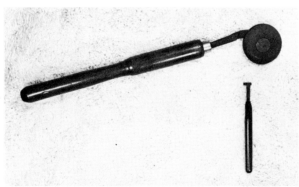

Gold can be tooled with either roll (top) or stamp.

apply the paste, spreading it with a round brush or with the fingers in the pattern shown. Spreading it this way ensures that the leather stretches evenly. Then fold the pasted side of the leather over on itself to "set" for a minute or so and spread paste on the wooden surface. Don't use too much paste—you don't want it to squeeze through the pores of the leather. Next, unfold the leather and spread it smooth in the recess, stretching it out with your fingertips in the same way you spread the paste. When it begins to stick, run your fingernail along the borders to crease the leather enough to see where to trim, then cut along the crease line with a knife and straightedge. Hold the knife with the handle angled away from the leather to ensure that no "white," or flesh, shows on the surface. If your leather is cowhide and your straightedge ferrous metal, put a piece of waxed paper between them to prevent unsightly staining.

With your fingertips, push the trimmed leather toward the borders for a good tight fit. The leather should be sticking by now. To be sure that it won't buckle or pull away from the borders, you might want to turn over the whole pasted-up piece and rest the leather on a few sheets of newspaper or unprinted news. The surface beneath the paper must be smooth; any imperfections will be transferred to the leather. Apply some light pressure with books and allow it to dry overnight. Do not apply too much pressure or the paste will seep through and give the leather a grey cast impossible to remove. The inlay should be perfect in the morning. But if any edge or corner has not stuck, dampen it with a small brush, lift slightly, repaste and work it into place.

There are two basic kinds of tools for tooling leather: rolls and stamps. Rolls are brass wheels with a continuous design engraved on their edges. One simply heats the tool on a stove and runs it along the leather. Rolls are quite expensive, and used ones are very hard to find. Even more expensive are the rolls with their own heating elements. The main advantage of rolls is that they save time, especially on long borders. But stamps, which have one design engraved into brass and are fitted with a wooden handle, can do an equally good job. They are much less expensive and can even be cut from brass scrap or bronze brazing rods.

Make sure the gold you buy is genuine. There are a lot of imitations on the market, many of them cleverly packaged. Genuine gold must by law say "genuine gold leaf" and give the gold content in carats. Real gold comes in books of 25 leaves, each 3¼ in. sq. Be wary of labels that read "gold metal leaf foil," or some such. Most phony gold leaf that I have tested tarnished completely within six months after application, some within two.

To cut your gold leaf you need a gold cushion and knife. The cushion is a piece of wood at least 6 in. sq., padded lightly with cotton, then covered with a soft leather, flesh side out. A new piece of chamois from your local auto supplier is perfect. This leather is sprinkled with rottenstone or very fine pumice to keep the gold leaf from sticking to it. You can use any thin-bladed, sharp, flexible knife, or buy one made specially for cutting gold.

Gold also comes in tooling rolls of Mylar atomized on one side with gold and presized. This is the easiest form of gold to use and gives excellent results. With Mylar rolls you don't need a gold cushion or glair. And they come in other metals and color pigments besides genuine gold.

If you are going to use gold leaf, you will need glair, the

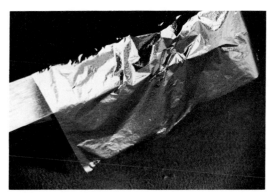

Special gold knife, lightly dusted with fine pumice, lifts sheet of genuine gold leaf. Beware of imitation gold, which tarnishes within months.

Lightly greased cotton ball transfers bit of gold leaf from gold cushion (in background) to glair-treated section of leather.

Heated stamp presses gold from Mylar roll into glair-coated impression.

mordant that makes the gold stick to the leather. Traditional glair is a preparation of egg white and vinegar. If you don't think eggs will make the gold stick as well as something more modern might, let me tell you that it has been used for well over 400 years. I have seen a number of books that were tooled with egg glair in the 16th century; the gold is still intact and bright. To make glair, beat up one egg white with ¼ teaspoon of vinegar until it froths. Let it sit overnight in a covered dish, then strain it into a jar with a funnel and a filter of clean cotton linen—a piece of an old bedsheet is fine. Keep the jar tightly covered. After a while the glair will smell horrible, but will still be usable.

If you don't want to make your own glair, you might want to try B. S. glair, a varnish formula based on French glairs first developed in the 18th century. It is much less troublesome to use, requires less heat, allows more time before it is ineffective and gives cleaner results.

If you are going to use gold leaf and traditional glair you must prepare the leather. Wash it over with a cotton ball slightly dampened with water, or water and vinegar. Some people like to put a little paste into the wash water, but I find that it dulls the leather. Old-time finishers often add some clear urine. I have never tried it. Now, with a good artist's brush, brush the glair only over the area to be tooled. Egg glair discolors the leather slightly, so neatness counts. When the glair is dry (when it looks dry and isn't sticky), apply a second coat, not as generously as the first. While it dries, prepare your gold leaf on the cushion. Open the book of gold to expose the first leaf. Slip your knife, which is free of grease and lightly dusted with rottenstone or fine pumice, under the gold, lift it, and transfer it to the cushion. If it does not lie flat, blow on it gently from directly above. Then cut the gold into appropriate strips with a very light back-and-forth motion. Cut only the gold, not the cushion.

As soon as the glair is dry, smear some light grease, such as petroleum jelly, onto the back of your hand, then rub a cotton ball in the grease to transfer a minute amount to the cotton. Rub the cotton gently on the leather wherever you intend to lay gold. This tiny amount of grease will hold the gold in place until it is tooled. Now lift a strip of gold with the lightly greased cotton ball and place the gold on the greased leather.

With the gold strip in place, heat the brass roll until it just sizzles when touched to a damp cotton ball or sponge. The etched surface of the tool should be shiny; if it isn't, buff it

on a piece of leather rubbed with red, or jeweler's, rouge. An etched surface that does not shine will mean a gold surface that does not shine.

The correct pressure and heat to apply are a matter of practice, since every piece of leather is different. But that is what your scrap leather is for. Cowhide needs less heat than goat, and for goat the tool should just sizzle.

Once the leather has been sized with egg glair, it must be tooled as soon as possible, certainly within two hours. With B. S. glair, once the second coat is dry (which takes an hour) the surface can be tooled anytime within two months, or longer. The tools can be cooler, with less chance of burning the leather, and you don't need to add moisture by sponging the leather with water, paste, urine or anything else.

If you don't have a roll, you can obtain excellent results with a stamp. Amateurs may get better results because one works with a paper pattern the exact size of the leather inlay. Using any paper, make the pattern; then draw light pencil lines on it with a straightedge where you intend your border to be. Using your brass tool and an ink stamp pad, mark the border on the pattern. When it is to your liking, place tracing paper over the pattern and restamp the tracing paper in the same way you stamped the pattern. Tape the tracing paper to the wooden borders of the leather, clean the ink from your tool, heat it slightly (to the point where it is uncomfortable to touch) and impress through the tracing paper onto the leather. If needed, go over the impressions with the tool directly on the leather. Rock the tool in slightly in all directions to make sure the whole tool touches the leather, but be careful not to make a double or smeared impression. The impressions on the leather should be clear but not too deep. Then they are painted in with glair, greased and inlaid with gold leaf. The gold will stick only on the glair, where the heated tool touches it. The impressions should show through the gold; if they don't, pat the gold down with the cotton ball until they do.

If the gold cracks or tears, put another piece of leaf right over the first. In fact, it is probably a good idea to lay down double thicknesses of gold all over. When the gold is in place, re-impress the heated tool into the impression. The tool should barely sizzle when laid on the wet sponge. Hold it on the sponge until it just stops sizzling, then impress it on the leather. With B. S. glair, the tool can be a bit cooler.

With presized gold on Mylar rolls, simply tape the roll in place, shiny side up, then impress the heated tool. There

Full-sized paper pattern, right, has been traced, then imprinted in leather, before tooling border with presized Mylar roll.

Fumed Oak Finish
Old-time process still has advantages

by Sam Allen

If you've ever tried to match the finish on a piece of antique oak furniture, it may have been a frustrating experience. That's because many oak pieces (Mission furniture, for example) were finished by fuming, a process difficult to duplicate using modern stains. The color of fumed oak ranges from a light honey to a medium dark brown. Exposing the wood to ammonia fumes darkens the wood by changing it chemically. Ammonia reacts with tannic acid in oak to produce the color change. Mahogany, chestnut and walnut can also be fumed. As long as the tannic acid content of the wood is the same, the color will be uniform from piece to piece.

Even if you don't restore antiques, you may want to try fuming on your oak projects. Fuming has many advantages. Since it works a chemical change in the wood, it doesn't hide the figure characteristics. No brushing is involved, so irregularities such as streaks, lap marks, stain buildup in corners or on carvings and intricate moldings are completely eliminated. And because the ammonia vapors penetrate the surface of the wood, the color change goes deeper than a thin coating.

The main disadvantage of the process is that ammonia fumes irritate the eyes and nose and cause coughing and choking. For this reason, fuming should be done outside or in a well-ventilated room. The process also requires an airtight container to enclose the piece being finished, which may pose a problem for large furniture.

When you are building a project to be fumed, try to use boards with uniform color. If you can, choose all your lumber from the same tree; it will then fume to the same color. But this is usually impossible. You can sort the boards by numbering them and fuming a small piece of each, keeping track of the results. Then you can select the pieces that most closely match. If you must use dissimilar pieces of oak, the lighter ones can be darkened by sponging on a weak solution of tannic acid before fuming. This will raise the grain, so sand the wood as you would for water stain. Experiment on a sample piece to get the correct amount of tannic acid. About 5% acid to 95% water is usually a good starting solution.

Fuming—Fuming an entire object is not hard to do. Start by finding an airtight container. For a small object, a Tupperware-type box with snap-on lid will work well. For larger pieces, you can construct a plastic tent. Build a framework of 2x4s or 2x2s and cover it with the type of black plastic sheeting used in the garden to keep down weeds. Seal the seams with heating-duct tape. Don't use clear or translucent plastic because sunlight hitting one area of the project and not another will affect the reaction time and make the color uneven.

Next, add ammonia to the container. The best ammonia to use is 26% ammonia, or aromatic spirits of ammonia. Aromatic spirits—the kind used to revive people who have fainted—is available at drugstores in small bottles. If you need only a small amount, this is the easiest to find. If you'll

---

is no glair, wash-up or fuss. You cannot do intricate patterns with a Mylar roll, but for borders it is perfect—the roll itself is a guide to straightness.

Once the gold is impressed, clean off the excess by wiping with a piece of flannel, then applying naphtha or benzine (not benzene, which is dangerous and will remove all the gold if you have used a Mylar roll). If the gold has not stuck properly, either the glair was too weak or dry, or the tools were too cool, or the tool failed to touch all corners. If the gold is dull, or "bleeds" over the impression, the tool was too hot or the glair too wet. Places that do not stick can sometimes be reworked if you are very careful.

Tooling in "blind," that is, without gold, is tricky, but correctly done, it leaves a rich, dark impression. Use a warm tool and slightly damp leather. If the tool is too hot, it will burn the leather, something much easier to do when the leather is moist. The tools should be just hot enough to be uncomfortable to hold for more than a second. Sponge over the section of the leather to be tooled just before the tool touches it. On light-colored leathers, sponge the entire piece, so as not to leave water marks. Touch the tool repeatedly to the same place until the desired darkness is achieved. Each time the tool touches the damp leather the leather is made drier, and the tool cooler, and each time, you must hold the tool in place longer. Some workers advocate holding the tool in a candle until it is sooty with lampblack, then impressing this soot to the leather. I don't recommend this method because the soot can smear. It is far less permanent and looks not as rich—like staining pine to make it look like oak.

A final treatment of potassium lactate solution and leather dressing completes the job. □

AUTHOR'S NOTE: Specialty shops carry leather and tooling supplies. Basic Crafts, 1201 Broadway, New York, N.Y. 10001 sells leather, stamps, adhesives and gold (catalog). Talas, 213 W. 35th St., New York, N.Y. 10001-1996, has leather, stamps, gold, adhesives, potassium lactate, Formula No. 6 and B.S. glair (catalog). Amend Drugs, Box 797, Hillside, N.J. 07205, and Newberry Library Bookshop, 60 W. Walton St., Chicago, Ill. 60610, both sell potassium lactate and Formula No. 6. A good general supplier is Tandy, 330 Fifth Ave., New York, N.Y. 10001 (catalog), though the leather I've tried was quite below par. For gold and custom-made engraving rolls, try Ernest Schaefer, 731 Lehigh Ave., Union, N.J. 07083.

From *Fine Woodworking* magazine (May 1981) 28:70-71

need large quantities, the 26% ammonia sold by chemical supply houses will be cheaper (check the Yellow Pages). Ordinary household ammonia can be used, but the process will be slower. If you use household ammonia, be sure to get the type without detergent, coloring or perfume.

Place the ammonia in several saucers and space them around the inside of the tent. Small objects that need to be fumed on both sides can be propped up on wooden pyramids that come to a sharp point. The small contact area of the pyramid point won't leave a visible mark. Never use metal to support the work. Steel in contact with the wood during the fuming process will sometimes cause a blue-black mark on the wood. Keep this in mind when you are preparing a project—don't install any metal hardware before fuming. Exposed nailheads will create a mark, but nails set below the surface are usually no problem.

The subject of nails brings up another consideration. Ordinary wood putty won't be colored by the fuming process, so don't fill holes until after the fuming is done. Then color the putty to match the finish.

As fuming proceeds, peek occasionally at the wood. Remove the project when the color is slightly lighter than the color you want. After coming out of the tent, the wood will darken slightly since the reaction continues for a while. It usually takes about 24 hours to get a medium dark brown.

When you are restoring an antique, though, you may want to fume only a few small areas, not the entire piece. One way to do this is to glue some cotton in the bottom of a glass jar and add a few drops of ammonia to the cotton. Don't add too much or the ammonia will drip onto the work. Put the mouth of the jar on top of the spot to be refinished. Keep a close watch on the color and stop the ammonia treatment just before the spot reaches the same color as the surrounding finish. Let the wood air out thoroughly and check the color. If it's still too light, put the jar on the spot again for a little while.

Another touch-up technique is not really fuming—the ammonia is applied directly to the wood with a brush. This process will raise the grain if you use water-based ammonia. To avoid raising the grain, use aromatic spirits of ammonia, which is alcohol based. It will behave like a spirit stain. Wet the wood first and sand as you would for a water stain. Let the ammonia stay on the wood until the color is close to the surrounding finish, then wipe it off with a damp cloth. Ammonia evaporates quickly, so you'll have to apply it repeatedly to keep the area wet. Covering the spot with a jar lid or something similar will retard evaporation. Check the color when the wood is thoroughly dry and repeat the application if necessary.

Finishing—You can apply shellac, varnish or lacquer over fumed oak, but if you want to duplicate an original antique finish, the surface coating should be wax. Old-timers frequently made their own wax by shredding beeswax into turpentine. The mixture

was set aside until the wax was thoroughly dissolved, then turpentine or wax was added until the consistency was like thick cream.

If you don't want to make your own wax, you can use a commercial paste wax such as Trewax. The wax will fill the pores of the wood. The natural tan color of the wax will usually harmonize well with the color of the wood. If you find that the wax is too light or if it goes white after drying, you can add a little burnt umber pigment in the same manner as described below for making black wax.

Black wax on fumed oak used to be a very popular finish. With this finish the pores stand out prominently because they are filled with black wax. This type of finish was generally used on quartersawn oak. To make black wax, liquefy paste wax by warming its container in a pan of hot water. Heat the water first, then remove it from the stove before placing the can of wax in it. When the wax is liquefied, add lampblack or some other color. To be compatible with the wax, tinting colors should be of the universal type (see the article on pages 37-39). Let the wax harden again and apply it to the work. The wax will accumulate in the pores as you rub it in, but the coating on the other areas will be so thin that the pigment won't cover the color underneath. You can get the same effect if you are using a finish other than wax by rubbing in Silex wood filler colored with lampblack.

Ebonizing—Ebonizing is another way to finish that uses the tannin content of oak. Ebonized oak is black with white

Ammonia reacts with tannins to darken oak; old-time finishes bring out the figure. Oak samples, top to bottom, are unfinished, fumed with natural wax, fumed with black wax, and ebonized.

pores. First, put some distilled vinegar in a glass jar; drop in a handful of steel nails and let the mixture sit about a week. The vinegar is ready when it is grey and cloudy looking. Prepare the wood as you would for a water stain, then brush on the vinegar, which will turn the oak bluish black. Apply several coats of the vinegar, letting it dry between coats.

When the oak is dark enough, brush on some liquid ammonia. This will neutralize the acid left on the wood by the vinegar. At this point the wood should be deep black with a slight purple tinge. Next apply a thin coat of sealer. The purple tinge will disappear and the oak will be a beautiful black. All of the characteristics of the wood will still be visible in the blackened surface. That is why this process is superior to simply painting or staining the wood black.

Now apply white wood filler to make the pores stand out white, and finish as you choose. Because of the contrast of white pores against a black surface, the pores become dominant visually, so select boards that have interesting pore patterns. To emphasize them even more, you may want to brush the boards with a wire brush before applying the vinegar solution. Since oak is so hard, lightly brushing it will not scratch the surface; it will only clear out the pores. □

Sam Allen designs and builds furniture in Provo, Utah.

Q & A

Finishing church doors

We have six church doors, veneered in oak, and have stained and finished them with several coats of good spar varnish. The trouble is that the finish doesn't last a year before the weather causes it to peel and flake off. Can you help? —George Seibel, Stratford, Conn.

DON NEWELL REPLIES: Spar varnish, marine varnish and other similar exterior finishes almost always degrade within a year and require refinishing. The major cause is ultraviolet light, which attacks the molecular bonds in the varnish. Many modern products contain ultraviolet absorbing compounds, but they don't help all that much.

I suggest using a penetrating finish, which deposits protective materials inside the wood rather than building up on its surface. Penetrating finishes will also degrade in time, but since there's no surface film to worry about, refinishing is merely a matter of applying another coat or two of the same product. You may have to sand or steel-wool lightly to remove surface dirt before refinishing, but that's all the preparatory work required. Since your doors have been varnished, you'll have to remove this old finish and expose the bare wood before using a new penetrating finish.

Watco Exterior Wood finish should serve well, or try Waterlox Marine Finish, thinned a bit with mineral spirits to ensure good penetration. Brush on a first coat, keeping the surface fairly wet. When the wood has soaked up all the finish it will take, wipe it dry and let it harden overnight. Apply a second coat the next day, again wiping off the excess.

If you want to stay with surface film products, try ZAR Imperial Polyurethane or McCloskey Marine Varnish. Another preparation worth trying is called Deks Olje, put out by the Flood Co., Hudson, Ohio 44236. It's a gloss finish for salt-water boat woodwork.

I think it is not only the material you use that gives you trouble, but also the way you are finishing the doors. The most important parts of the door (to the finisher) are the top and bottom edges. These have to be well sealed to make them weatherproof. I always carry a small mirror with me to check the bottom edges, and in 99% of all cases this is where the trouble starts.

I suggest you remove the doors to your shop (cover the open doorway with plywood). Strip the doors with a good remover, wash them with lacquer thinner, sand (no steel wool), stain and varnish. We use Sherwin-Williams Marvethane for a sealer and second coat, sanding between with 240-grit finishing paper. Let the finish harden for a week before re-installing the doors. Be sure to give the end-grain edges top and bottom double passes when spraying. Using this method, the finish on your doors should last five to eight years. —Jan Hieminga, Westwood, N.J.

Neutralizing lye-bath stripping

Our front doors had been stripped by immersing them in a lye bath. I was told by the dealer that I must apply straight vinegar to them to neutralize the lye. The doors were hung, the better side to the interior and the other side to be stained on the outside. The painters applied an Olympic barn red stain to the exterior before I applied the vinegar. Afterward I noticed brown streaks on the unfinished interior sides, sticky and wet to touch. I applied liberal doses of vinegar to the interior side of both doors. After a time, the exterior of the doors began to bleed; the stain ran. The painter suggested varnishing on top of the stain, and we did. The doors are now a complete mess. —Patricia M. Brooks, Manakin-Sabot, Va.

DON NEWELL REPLIES: Undoubtedly, the lye remaining in the wood after stripping is partially responsible for the mess on the exterior of your doors. It will degrade your stain over a period of time. It probably will also attack the varnish that you put over the stain. Your only recourse is to take off all the varnish and stain you can, using any of the paint removers carried by your local hardware store. Then wash both sides of the doors with vinegar in order to neutralize the lye deposits in the wood. Then wash well with clear water, let dry and sand or steel-wool off any grain that may have raised. Now you can begin again with the stain and/or varnish.

But back to the sticky streaks. I suspect that you have pitchy wood, with the pitch or gum coming to the surface either under the influence of time and heat or the lye treatment, or both. Sometimes by washing the streaked areas several times with a solvent such as mineral spirits, you can eliminate the condition, especially if the gum or pine resin is mostly on the surface. But if it is deep down in the wood, it usually is a non-repairable condition. I've had pitchy wood streaks in pine "bleed" for years, in severe cases.

Consistent color in cherry

I recently constructed a headboard of veneer plywood with solid cherry trim. The finish is Deft. The problem is the veneer seems to have soaked up more finish than the trim, resulting in a darker shade. How can I get a consistent hue? —Don Carbhoff, Plainfield, Ill.

As professional refinishers we have had great success overcoming the problem of a veneer absorbing more stain than the solid stock it's next to. We use sealer made of 70% thinner and 30% lacquer, lacquer-shellac or varnish (we usually use lacquer). We spray this watered-down sealer lightly on the veneer, just enough to seal the porous surface. When the surface has dried we use "tired" sandpaper (worn-down 220-grit silicone carbide) on the veneer until the surface is cleaned of lacquer. When we apply our stain, there is still some porosity in the veneer, and you can control the stain variation almost to the match. —Lewis Stein, Chatham, N.J.

Consistent stain for sapwood

I've just purchased a cherry coffee-table kit from a "reputable" manufacturer, and the tabletop has several large areas of sapwood. How should I stain adjacent pieces of sapwood and heartwood? —Ben Blackwell, Albuquerque, N. Mex.

DON NEWELL REPLIES: I would use two or three thin coats of a penetrating oil/pigment stain, such as those put out by Minwax, to blend areas of cherry sapwood into heartwood. Pick the color closest to the tone of the heartwood (or buy two cans and mix your own). Apply the stain with a wad of cloth or a narrow brush, going only to the edge of the sapwood. If you run over onto the heartwood, rub or brush the color out quickly so you don't get a hard edge showing where the stain stopped. Handle the stain delicately, particularly at the edges of the sapwood, so the touched-up areas don't show. Keep in mind that when the stain dries (in about 24 hours) it will be lighter than it is when wet.

When the wood is properly colored and the stain is dry, steel-wool the surface lightly to remove any pigment residue. Then apply your finish. Minwax is an excellent material, but if you are planning to use lacquer, let the stain dry for a week before applying it. Use a thin first coat to help seal in the stain before applying full, wet coats. With varnish or oils, you need no waiting period.

Smoke Finishing
Rubbed-in soot colors pine

by Robert B. Chambers

An acetylene torch, starved of oxygen, produces a large, yellow flame instead of a tight, blue cone. The yellow part of the flame is incandescent carbon, much of which is deposited on the wood.

When the surface is evenly wiped, some carbon particles remain as a coloring agent, and will be sealed in by top coats of polyurethane. Under the finish, the wood continues to age naturally.

Here's a smoked finish that can give provincial furniture a mellow patina. An acetylene torch, starved of oxygen, lays a coat of pure carbon on the wood. When you wipe the carbon away, the surface retains enough to give the piece a translucent glaze that allows the wood to age and develop natural color beneath it. Unlike the burning process popular for plywood in the early 1950s (see page 102), smoking does not raise the grain pattern or char the wood. I learned the technique from a graduate student in one of my woodworking classes when we were trying to create a driftwood effect for a stage design that had to bear close scrutiny.

I have used smoke finishing on pine, birch, basswood and little bits of Philippine mahogany. It works best on white and sugar pine, but does not work well if the wood has a high pitch content: the process brings the pitch to the surface, the carbon sticks to it, and you end up with black streaks. Small specks of pitch can look interesting, but for a uniform effect, the clearer and drier the wood the better.

Generally, smoking will give you the same highlights and dark, low areas as a stain, but it doesn't interfere with the wood's natural color the way stain does.

As with any finishing, begin preparing the surface by thoroughly sanding or scraping. All traces of glue must be scraped or sanded away, or you will have light spots. After sanding, blow off the dust. It can build up in corners and crevices and keep the carbon from reaching the wood. If you don't have compressed air, a damp rag will work, but do not use a rag dampened with anything flammable. Be sure the wood is completely dry and dust-free before you begin smoking, or the coat won't be even.

The smoking itself is done with a standard oxygen and acetylene welding rig equipped with a heating tip. Do not use a standard brazing tip—the flame spread is too small and will result in burn lines. If you don't have an acetylene rig, you can get similar results by barely browning the wood with propane—don't blacken it—and then rubbing lampblack into the wood. This will give you an idea of what the finish looks like, but the acetylene will give broad coverage and work much better on an actual piece of furniture.

Set the oxygen pressure at 8 lb. and the acetylene pressure at 8 lb. Light the acetylene first and turn it up to a "mild roar." At this point little bits of black soot will be descending all around you. Add oxygen gently until most of the smoke is gone, but don't add so much that you get a secondary blue cone in the middle of the flame. It takes very little oxygen.

Now use the torch with long, even, slightly overlapping strokes to "spray" the wood black. Keep the torch head about 8 in. to 10 in. from the wood, depending on your particular rig. Follow through on each pass so that you begin the spray before you get to the work and continue it off the work in one steady motion. If you stop or backtrack you will get buildups, just as you would in spray painting. Continue until the piece is uniformly black. You will have a deposit of soot on the work—but no charring of the wood itself.

Wipe the piece down thoroughly with clean rags, changing them frequently, until it takes a lot of elbow grease to get more carbon off the wood. Wrap the cloth around slivers, wedges or pointed dowels to wipe corners and crevices.

Now you are ready to seal the finish. My old standby is Sears satin polyurethane. I have found that it will harden the soft pine I like to work with, and make the wood stand up to the destructive spills, stains and teenagers of a normal household. It's best to spray on the first coat. If you do use a brush, though, just flow on the first coat with the grain. Brushing it will pick up the carbon, causing streaks. Experiment on a scrap to get a feel for it. Fine steel wool and a tack rag between coats will give you a good finish after about three or four coats. After that I usually finish up with a coat of Goddard's paste wax applied with 0000 steel wool and buffed with a soft cloth.

The first time I used this technique I was delighted with the immediate results, but I'm even more pleased by the way the wood continues to age and warm under the finish. □

Robert B. Chambers teaches in the theater department of Southern Methodist University and runs Design Imagineering in Richardson, Tex. Photos by the author.

The Charred Bedroom Suite

By George Frank

The result of Frank's experimentation: before scorching, edge; after scorching, top.

When Maurice Lafaille invited me to lunch, I knew that he wanted something. When he took me to one of the finest restaurants in Paris I knew that he had something big on his mind. And it was.

In 1928 Lafaille was a young, handsome, talented and poor interior decorator, dedicated to beauty and innovation. When the main dish was served, he produced a small package, about 6 inches square. At his request, I opened it and unveiled a finely detailed statuette of Buddha. He asked me what I thought of it, and I answered that it seemed to be exquisitely carved, a work of art without any doubt, but that I was far from being a competent judge of its value. "George, take a closer look at the hair," he said, and I did. The hair was made of fine lines, each about the thickness of a human hair, but the color of the lines alternated, light and dark, light and dark. Lafaille then produced a powerful magnifying glass. I saw that the dark lines were produced by fire, or burning, and the light ones were the natural color of the wood. How the wood was scorched in such narrow bands is still a mystery to me.

"And what do you think of it now?" inquired Lafaille. "Simple," I replied. "If I did not have this thing in my hand, I would say that such a job is impossible." Lafaille then dropped the bombshell: "George, I am designing a bedroom suite for the Baron Rotschild, and this is the finish you are going to do for me."

I called him an idiot, a dreamer, an imbecile, and told him that even if I could do the finish, it would take me at least 2,000 years. "George, you do it," said Lafaille. He paid for lunch and we zoomed back to my shop.

Lafaille was right; he knew me well. The problem did not let me sleep. The next day I borrowed my girlfriend's electric iron, my elderly neighbor's charcoal iron, several soldering irons—and got nowhere. I cursed Lafaille, but I kept looking for the solution. I spilled alcohol on the wood and set it afire, then tried slower-burning turpentine with the same results: zero.

There must be a special God helping woodfinishers. A lead pipe, carrying water to my kitchen, sprung a leak. I called a plumber, who fixed the leak with a blowtorch.

The next day I had my own blowtorch and as I scorched the surface of my sample fir board, I knew I was on the right track. With a stiff brush I could easily take off the completely charred soft part of the wood grain (the earlywood layer of each year's growth), uncovering light, uncharred wood beneath. The hard veins (the latewood) remained dark, scorched, intact. With each experiment I came closer to the solution, and the next day Lafaille took my samples to the Baron. He was thrilled. He sent his Rolls-Royce to fetch us, and that day I learned the true meaning of haute cuisine.

About two months later the Baron's bedroom suite was ready to be scorch-finished. Both the Baron and Lafaille came to the shop to watch me char the surface of the wood. If there is a God helping woodfinishers, there must be gremlins making innovators' lives miserable. The intense heat of the blowtorch made the wood shrink, crack, split, and bend before our very eyes. In less than half an hour the bedroom suite was ruined, or at least the parts I burned with my blowtorch were. Tears ran from my eyes, not only from the smoke, but from the realization that I had failed.

Without any doubt the scorched finish was something new, original and beautiful and neither of us was ready to throw in the towel. Lafaille and I decided that the bedroom suite had to be rebuilt, but that the wood must be burned before furniture was made of it. Moreover, we adopted a frame-and-panel construction to allow further shrinkage. The Baron agreed, and assured us that he would assume the cost, regardless of how many times I had to rebuild his furniture. Two or three months later, we delivered the first bedroom suite made of scorched pine to the Baron Rotschild's country home at Chantilly. It may well still be there.

About a month later, when Maurice Lafaille invited me for lunch, I knew that he wanted something. He did. And by the time the main dish was served he produced from his pocket a handful of virgin hemp, but that is another story . . .   □

George Frank, retired master woodfinisher, now lives in Florida.

Q & A

Aromatic cedar chest
Regarding finishing an aromatic cedar chest: it seems that a compromise is necessary between sealing the wood and still allowing for the cedar smell. Some people have suggested sealing only the exterior, but isn't half a sealing the same as none? If it is impossible to properly seal the cedar, how much warpage can I expect for a ⅞-in. thick, solid cedar, 2-ft. by 2-ft. by 5-ft. chest?
Paul A. Palo, Port Hueneme, Calif.
ANDY MARLOW REPLIES: You won't have warpage trouble if the grain on all four sides runs laterally. The inside doesn't have to be finished.

From *Fine Woodworking* magazine (November 1979) 18:36-37

About our answermen

SANDY COHEN is an avid amateur woodworker and leatherworker. He has demonstrated leather bookbinding for an educational television series.

JIM CUMMINS, associate editor of *Fine Woodworking* magazine, has restored and framed pictures for over 15 years in Woodstock, N.Y.

GEORGE FRANK, a retired European master wood finisher and author of *88 Rue de Charonne: Adventures in Wood Finishing* (The Taunton Press), lives in South Venice, Fla.

TAGE FRID, recently retired as professor emeritus of woodworking at Rhode Island School of Design, is author of the series *Tage Frid Teaches Woodworking*. All three volumes, *Joinery: Tools and Techniques; Shaping, Veneering, Finishing;* and *Furniture-making,* are available from The Taunton Press.

OTTO H. HEUER is a chemist and consultant specializing in wood finishes.

R. BRUCE HOADLEY, professor of wood technology at the University of Massachusetts at Amherst, is the author of *Understanding Wood: A Craftsman's Guide to Wood Technology* (The Taunton Press).

IAN J. KIRBY is a designer, cabinetmaker and educator at his studio in Cumming, Ga.

OSCAR MACQUIDDY teaches antique restoration and refinishing in Los Angeles, Calif.

ANDY MARLOW was a professional wood craftsman, a designer of traditional furniture, and author of several books on reproducing antiques, including *Classic Furniture Projects.*

MICHAEL MCCANN is a consumer activist with the Center for Occupational Hazards, New York, N.Y.

GEORGE MORRIS makes and finishes guitars in Post Mills, Vt., where he also teaches at The Vermont Instrument Workshop.

DON NEWELL, author of *Gunstock Finishing and Care,* is a former paint and varnish chemist who lives in Farmington, Mich.

MORRIS SHEPPARD designs and makes furniture and cabinets in Los Angeles, Calif.

DONALD STEINERT restores Rolls-Royce automobile woodwork in Grants Pass, Ore.

LELON TRAYLOR teaches tool and manufacturing technology at Southern Illinois University, Carbondale. He has been reproducing museum pieces for more than three decades.

HERB YATOVITZ is a chemist for National Chemical and Plastics Co., a manufacturer of wood lacquers and finishes.

Index

FINE WOODWORKING
Editorial Staff, 1975-1985

Paul Bertorelli
Mary Blaylock
Dick Burrows
Jim Cummins
Katie de Koster
Ruth Dobsevage
Tage Frid
Roger Holmes
Cindy Howard
John Kelsey
Linda Kirk
Nancy-Lou Knapp
John Lively
Rick Mastelli
Nina Perry
Jim Richey
Paul Roman
David Sloan
Nancy Stabile
Laura Tringali
Linda D. Whipkey

FINE WOODWORKING
Art Staff, 1975-1985

Roger Barnes
Kathleen Creston
Deborah Fillion
Lee Hov
Betsy Levine
Lisa Long
E. Marino III
Karen Pease
Roland Wolf

FINE WOODWORKING
Production Staff, 1975-1985

Claudia Applegate
Barbara Bahr
Pat Byers
Deborah Cooper
Kathleen Davis
David DeFeo
Michelle Fryman
Mary Galpin
Dinah George
Barbara Hannah
Annette Hilty
Jenny Long
Johnette Luxeder
Gary Mancini
Laura Martin
Mary Eileen McCarthy
JoAnn Muir
Cynthia Lee Nyitray
Kathryn Olsen
Mary Ann Snieckus
Barbara Snyder

If you enjoyed this book, you're going to love our magazine.

A year's subscription to *Fine Woodworking* brings you the kind of practical, hands-on information you found in this book and much more. In issue after issue, you'll find projects that teach new skills, demonstrations of useful tools and techniques, new design ideas, old-world traditions, shop tests, coverage of current woodworking events, and breathtaking examples of the woodworker's art for inspiration.

To subscribe, just fill out one of the attached subscription cards, or call us toll-free at 1-800-888-8286. As always, we guarantee your satisfaction.

Subscribe Today!

6 issues for just $25
Offer valid through 9/1/92

Fine WoodWorking®

Use this card to subscribe or to request additional information.

1 year (6 issues) for just $25—over 24% off the newsstand price
Outside the U.S. $30/year (U.S. funds, please) Canadian residents add 7% GST

Name _____

Address _____

City _____ State _____ Zip _____

☐ My payment is enclosed. ☐ Please bill me.
☐ Please send me your *Fine Woodworking* book and video catalog.

B2AJ

Fine WoodWorking®

Use this card to subscribe or to request additional information.

1 year (6 issues) for just $25—over 24% off the newsstand price
Outside the U.S. $30/year (U.S. funds, please) Canadian residents add 7% GST

Name _____

Address _____

City _____ State _____ Zip _____

☐ My payment is enclosed. ☐ Please bill me.
☐ Please send me your *Fine Woodworking* book and video catalog.

B2AJ

Fine WoodWorking®

Use this card to subscribe or to request additional information.

1 year (6 issues) for just $25—over 24% off the newsstand price
Outside the U.S. $30/year (U.S. funds, please) Canadian residents add 7% GST

Name _____

Address _____

City _____ State _____ Zip _____

☐ My payment is enclosed. ☐ Please bill me.
☐ Please send me your *Fine Woodworking* book and video catalog.

NO POSTAGE
NECESSARY
IF MAILED
IN THE
UNITED STATES

BUSINESS REPLY MAIL
FIRST CLASS MAIL PERMIT No. 19 NEWTOWN, CT

POSTAGE WILL BE PAID BY ADDRESSEE

The Taunton Press
63 South Main Street
P.O. Box 5506
Newtown CT 06470-9971

NO POSTAGE
NECESSARY
IF MAILED
IN THE
UNITED STATES

BUSINESS REPLY MAIL
FIRST CLASS MAIL PERMIT No. 19 NEWTOWN, CT

POSTAGE WILL BE PAID BY ADDRESSEE

The Taunton Press
63 South Main Street
P.O. Box 5506
Newtown CT 06470-9971

NO POSTAGE
NECESSARY
IF MAILED
IN THE
UNITED STATES

BUSINESS REPLY MAIL
FIRST CLASS MAIL PERMIT No. 19 NEWTOWN, CT

POSTAGE WILL BE PAID BY ADDRESSEE

The Taunton Press
63 South Main Street
P.O. Box 5506
Newtown CT 06470-9971